The most brilliant professor I knew in medical school often could not explain how he arrived at a diagnosis. His intuitive ability was simply dazzling, but he stumbled with explanations. In *Intuition in Psychotherapy*, psychotherapists Marilyn Stickle and Margaret Arnd-Caddigan explore this gift of intuition. They show that beneath logic and reason are ways of knowing that are nonlocal, ways that are not limited to specific points in space and time. This unifying expression of consciousness amplifies and extends one's mental power exponentially, enabling us to know things we are not "supposed" to know when we limit ourselves to reason, logic, and the here and now. And because this way of knowing connects us nonlocally with others, it facilitates empathy, compassion, love, and caring. Recognized throughout human history, this view of consciousness is surfacing in many disciplines. This fascinating book shows why, and suggests that it is only a matter of time until the abundant evidence for these intuitive, nonlocal ways of knowing are openly acknowledged in every major discipline.

—**Larry Dossey, MD**, Author of *One Mind: How Our Individual Mind Is Part of a Greater Consciousness and Why It Matters*

I was delighted to see this wonderful new book that brings together the worlds of science and spirituality, for the latter is only a realm of science not yet thoroughly explored. An effective psychotherapist is able to settle down in deeper consciousness so that s/he can resonate with the patient. What is fascinating about *Intuition in Psychotherapy* is the way the authors succeed in presenting the material both scientifically and appealingly. This book will have broad appeal both within and outside of the therapeutic community. I highly recommend it.

—**Richard Dietrich Maddox**, Certified Teacher of Transcendental Meditation and Author of four amazon #1-bestselling novels

In reading the book I was delighted to see that many of the chapters discuss characteristics and features that enable the positive use of intuition and build upon the essentiality and importance of developing a positive professional relationship in therapy. I appreciate both the authors' contention that intuition can be seen as a form of interactive communication stemming from a deep connection between people and the fact that intuition can complement practice models such as cognitive-behavioral and solution focused. The book fills a gap in scholarly literature on the important role that intuition can have in effective counselling, and would be emphasis of how intuition fits with or complements models such as these of value to students and practitioners interested in learning more about intuition.

—**John Coates, PhD**, Professor Emeritus, St. Thomas University, Fredericton, Canada

This excellent work makes an invaluable contribution to social work, counselling, and, more broadly, our understanding of the human experience and condition. Based on their important qualitative study and considerable combined expertise, Marilyn Stickle and Margaret Arnd-Caddigan's work explores clinical intuition using an interdisciplinary perspective yielding rich findings, not the least of which include attuned listening and deep inner awareness. Strong in both theoretical exploration and development and applications to clinical practice (the therapeutic alliance in particular), this groundbreaking book is a must read for those who are interested in counselling or who are simply seeking more robust human communication and engagement.

—**Arielle Dylan, PhD**

Building on the "art and science" of social work practice, Margaret Arnd-Caddigan and Marilyn Stickle shed light on the use of intuition in clinical practice. Thoroughly grounded in theory, research, and practice, this important study highlights how self-awareness, instinctive understandings, and trust can be powerful tools in counselling practice. Applicable to a variety of counselling professions, including social work, this valuable book provides a foundation for understanding the nuances of the therapeutic relationship, as well as increasing self-awareness and trust among therapists and service users. This excellent work will be an important addition for anyone interested in the helping profession who wants to broaden their understanding of communication, therapeutic relationships, and use of self.

—**Jenni Cammaert, PhD, MSW**, Assistant Professor, School of Social Work at St. Thomas University

This book is an exhaustive exploration of the thinking and research on intuition from a broad theoretical and practical spectrum. The authors skillfully compare the practices and insights of a diverse group of research participants to findings from other relevant research. The results are an informative, thought provoking combination of data, theory, and practical instructions . . . The findings from previous research and the authors' conclusions substantiate the existence of human connectiveness and that communication occurs in a variety of nonverbal and verbal forms. The effective use of intuition in clinical practice requires self-awareness and the ability to be focused and in the moment with the client. The reminder of the value of knowledge, skills, self-awareness, ethics, and transparency in the therapeutic process is refreshing. Although intuition is the focus of the book, the "how to" content offers valuable information for any clinician in the process of honing their skills.

—**Charlotte L. McConnell, ACSW**, retired CEO of Family and Child Services of Washington, DC, Inc., and former faculty at Howard University School of Social Work

Intuition in Psychotherapy weaves theoretical, scientific and holistic models into a tapestry of self-inquiry, self-development, and mindfulness. This book enables us to reflect on the ins and outs of intuition. The authors challenge clinicians to allow intuition to lie dormant or enliven it with openness and wonderment. Moreover, the researchers have nudged clinicians either new to the field or experienced in the field of psychotherapy to respect the gifts of intuition, and so doing, we honor the client.

—**Patricia A. Ruiz, PhD, LCSW**, Child and Adolescent Psychotherapist

The authors have written an important book for all therapists, regardless of clinical orientation. In addition to its use by therapists, this would prove useful to all those seeking deeper human connections.

—**Gretchen McKnew LCSW, ACSW**, Private Practice

Intuition in Psychotherapy captures the inner essence of therapeutic practice. From a "brain" perspective intuition lives in the limbic-heart and the visceral-gut systems, our emotional brains. These two systems connect us with spirituality, human relatedness, nature, and much more. Therapists track our client's journey in our emotional brains while also holding ourselves apart, utilizing the fiber of our thinking brain to assess our words and treatments. The authors have cleverly outlined the "tuned-in" psychotherapist's journey of intuition with their clients using research and analysis. This is a beginning, I believe, to a new knowledge of practice.

—**Lynn Turner, PhD, LCSW**, Reiki Master and Certified Chakra Energy Healer

Intuition in Psychotherapy

Intuition in Psychotherapy provides an unprecedented look at the phenomenon of clinical intuition, outlining its role in psychotherapy and providing a framework to develop intuitive skills that will positively impact practice.

Based on qualitative research and extensive first-hand interviews, the text illuminates how an awareness of intuitive processes can benefit therapists' diagnostic and treatment outcomes. Chapters provide a context for the use of intuition within current thinking in psychotherapy and highlight different forms of intuition that can be purposefully incorporated into clinical practice. Suitable for trainee and practicing psychotherapists, the text explores common intuitive processes and offers guidance for how practitioners might develop a unique therapeutic style.

As understanding of intuition becomes mainstream in psychotherapy practice, *Intuition in Psychotherapy* will serve as a key point of reference for years to come.

Marilyn Stickle, MEd, MSW, LCSW, has worked for decades developing a model of practice that includes clinical intuition. She is currently in private practice in Arlington, Virginia, where she treats adults in individual and couples psychotherapy.

Margaret Arnd-Caddigan, MA, MSW, PhD, LCSW, teaches and researches psychotherapy practice at East Carolina University. She is the director of the Greenville Psychoanalytic Study Group and has a private practice in which she conducts psychotherapy, clinical supervision, and consultation.

Intuition in Psychotherapy

From Research to Practice

MARILYN STICKLE AND MARGARET ARND-CADDIGAN

Routledge
Taylor & Francis Group
NEW YORK AND LONDON

First published 2019
by Routledge
52 Vanderbilt Avenue, New York, NY 10017

and by Routledge
2 Park Square, Milton Park, Abingdon, Oxon, OX14 4RN

Routledge is an imprint of the Taylor & Francis Group, an informa business

Library of Congress Cataloging-in-Publication Data
A catalog record for this book has been requested

ISBN: 978-1-138-35105-9 (hbk)
ISBN: 978-1-138-35106-6 (pbk)
ISBN: 978-0-429-43552-2 (ebk)

Typeset in Dante and Avenir
by Apex CoVanatge, LLC

Contents

Preface

We (Marilyn and Margaret) met at a psychoanalytic conference in 2015 where we were both giving presentations on intuition in psychotherapy. We attended each other's sessions and agreed to have lunch. At some point we decided that we would like to explore the possibility of conducting research together.

Marilyn approaches the material from a clinical perspective, having spent most of her career in private practice following earlier work in a state psychiatric facility and a community mental health center. She began developing her own model of intuitive practice at a time when the subject was a difficult one to discuss among her colleagues. She brought decades of personal experiential learning in the nuances of blending intuition into psychotherapy practice, familiarity with psi research, and the practices and published works of gifted intuitives. She also brought a strong desire to do research on how other clinicians think about and use intuition.

Margaret is an academic who teaches clinical practice and researches clinical process. She also has a private practice. While conducting a study on how therapists make decisions around boundary dilemmas, she was surprised by how many participants relayed that they used their intuition or a "gut feeling" as part of the decision-making process. Not surprisingly, several academic journals declined to publish these findings. This led Margaret down the road to learn more about intuition from an academic perspective: she read the work of research psychologists and neuroscientists, as well as theoretical treatments of the subject of intuition from a variety of schools of psychotherapy.

Since the first meeting, we have found our differences to be enlivening and challenging but ultimately have come to appreciate that the differences bring a richness and complexity to the subject. What we shared far outweighed those differences—an unlikely combination, or a *coincidentia oppositorum*.

We both came to that first meeting with a conviction that many therapists use intuition as a valuable part of their practice process. We wanted to know more about how they think about and use intuition and felt passionate about the potential for our profession in sharing this knowledge. Our research reflects current thinking among practicing psychotherapists that will validate, empower, and inform many clinicians so that they can speak openly about their use of and interest in this aspect of practice. In turn, we hope that it will enable them to bring their full complement of gifts and talents into the consulting room. As research on clinical intuition builds, our hope is that highly intuitive practitioners will step forward to talk openly about and teach what they understand and have learned through their private processes.

There are many people who have made this project possible. We owe a profound debt of gratitude to the participants who shared their stories. In many cases, these therapists were reluctant to discuss their experiences and perspectives. As will be elaborated, they have felt the sting of disapproval for their unconventional beliefs and approach to therapy. Yet many of them felt that the time has come to be candid. Their commitment to helping other therapists access an important source of helpful information finally outweighed their reticence to disclose their truths. We thank them for their generosity.

We would like to give hearty thanks to Jessica Hazel, our auditor. She patiently and carefully read multiple iterations of coding, stacks of email exchanges between us, and the notes we created that reflected our individual and joint processes. She was as invested in the legitimacy and usability of our work as we were.

Marilyn would like to thank her patients, from whom she has learned the value of clinical intuition, and the organizations that have supported her training workshops and presentations. She is also grateful to Carol Fitzpatrick, who has taught her about direct experience, and Michael Smith, who helped in manuscript preparation. She also thanks her family, especially Warren, who supported her in the early stages of her intuitive explorations, and Chelsea for the love and bonds we share.

Margaret would like to thank the Greenville Psychoanalytic Study Group: Lindsay Price, Amber Perry, Dayna Farrington, and former member Frank Moore (as well as Jessica Hazel). They agreed to read much of the literature that appears in this volume and engaged in thoughtful discussions about the strengths and weaknesses of numerous treatments of clinical intuition in relation to their own practices. These discussions undoubtedly implicitly influenced the final product. Thank you also David, Eamon, Leah, and Liam.

Introduction

The field of psychotherapy has evolved over time, deepening our understanding of the role of relationship and interconnection in the clinical process. Initially the role of the therapist was to work as a neutral observer, diagnosing and defining for the patient both the nature of illness and the means to its resolution; the relationship was the vehicle for establishing the authority to do so. The roles of therapist and patient reflected the prevailing Newtonian scientific model: there are laws that govern the therapy relationship that are both hierarchical and linear. The model Freud constructed was focused on a theory of the mind; the therapist was to act with the precision of a surgeon, setting all emotion aside.

Evolving thought has changed our views of how psychotherapy works. Over the past century, as psychoanalytic theory has evolved, quantum science has played a major role in developing our understanding of the nature of relationship, interconnection, and consequently how we practice psychotherapy. We now understand that we cannot be neutral observers, that what we think affects the therapeutic process whether spoken or not, and that connection plays a fundamental role in all of human experience. These insights from quantum science change earlier analytic understanding, making what seemed to be impossible possible. Further, intuitive experiences described in the early days of psychoanalysis as "telepathic communications" find a new language in emerging fields of scientific inquiry into intuition. Our research attempts to bridge the gap and elaborate on what those communications are and how they are used in clinical practice. Fundamental changes to our working model of psychotherapy are now underway. Earlier reports of intuition can be found in Rumi, who elevated it in his poetry in the late Middle Ages, more currently in Einstein's writings, who privileged it over rational thought, and by Malcolm Gladwell[1] who described analytic versus intuitive decision making as the most important new field in psychology. Virginia Satir, writing in the late 1980s, described the importance of understanding that we communicate our feelings no matter how well we think we are disguising them.[2] She was describing levels of communication that take place at the intuitive level beyond words and feelings.

The rich diversity of information on intuition available through the broad literature, enhanced by the writings of gifted intuitives, further informs our general understanding. There is growing interest in what intuition is, where it comes from, and its reliability. An expanding corpus of research lends support to what many psychotherapists from diverse theoretical orientations have experienced: intuition is an important part of the treatment process. And while theoretical material on clinical intuition is expanding, there are very few studies on intuition specific to the therapeutic process and to the practical application of clinical intuition.

So what is clinical intuition? We purposely did not define the term at the outset of our research, preferring to allow the experiences and insights of those who use it to tell us what it is. After combing over the conversations we had with therapists who use intuition to help them navigate the process of psychotherapy, we arrived at this definition: Clinical intuition is the acquisition of information about or relevant to the client and/or course of therapy, attained by means other than overt communication. Clinical intuition also informs the application of this information, contributing to the process of psychotherapy, and ultimately enhances the well-being of clients.

This book is the product of decades of experience with the exploration and use of clinical intuition and a two-year qualitative research project conducted by the authors to determine how clinicians use intuition in their work. Twenty-three therapists were interviewed on their definition and use of intuition in their practices, with the ultimate aim of using the information collected to help other therapists who wish to engage in intuition-informed therapy. Our purpose in writing the book is to develop a foundational understanding of intuition that opens the conversation across theoretical perspectives and practice settings.

The major findings of our research support the importance of intuition in all treatment stages including building, maintaining, and ending the clinical relationship. Being fully present with the client in the moment allows the therapist to form a collaborative working relationship, integrating intuitive awareness that informs experience on both macro and micro levels. On the macro level, information from the field of interconnection is variously referred to as universal connectedness, the field, the higher self, God, the divine, and the unknown, depending on individual thought systems. On the micro level, the role of intuition informs the therapist on how to facilitate connection within the individual, in the therapy relationship, and in the life of the client outside of treatment. Facilitating connection is managed intuitively, in the case of psychotherapy, through the forms that intuition takes. Everything that we need to know to navigate the clinical relationship is available by learning to trust the subtle impressions we receive as we connect to a particular patient. Like a GPS system, intuition is direct knowing of what is important in the moment, filling in logic and rational processes that rest in the background. Recalculating along the way intuition assists us moment to moment, giving us direction on how to recognize and deal with what arises. As we learn to trust our inner GPS system, intuition strengthens giving us remarkable guidance in finding our way through the complexities of the therapy relationship and our client's lives.

Our knowledge of intuition is also facilitated by decades long research in psi that supports four pillars of intuitive understanding: clairvoyance, clairsentience, clairaudience, and claircognizance; the capacities to see, feel, hear, and know clearly. The theme of interconnection as it is reflected in these forms of intuitive awareness is the thread that runs through the book. We examine the psychotherapeutic process from the perspective of identifying how intuition can operate subtly in the background of the therapeutic encounter; indeed, one of the findings of the research is that many therapists use intuition outside of their own awareness. Other therapists are keenly aware of their use of intuition, having learned how to incorporate it with great expertise in the therapeutic process, suggesting a bell curve between unawareness and advanced skill in employing intuitive process. The variation of intuitive ability reflected in our research provides a framework for suggestions on how to develop intuitive skill along with the mindset and understanding that supports intuitive development.

Chapters in this book are laid out to give the reader perspectives on how intuition works as a process in the clinical setting, organized in a way that shows how the process unfolds. They are based on an analysis of the information provided by the therapists who were interviewed for our research study. The voices of the therapists we interviewed make up the fabric of our chapters; we wove them throughout to add both personal depth to our explorations of intuition and to help concretize difficult concepts. We hope, too, that readers sense the self-exploration and empathy in their accounts and are inspired to think more about intuition's rightful place in therapy.

In the spirit of self-exploration and professional development, we've included Implications and Applications sections at the end of our main chapters (2–9) to help readers practically apply our research findings. In this way, we encourage practitioners to think of this not only as our (the authors' and participants') exploration of intuition and therapy but as a shared dialogue across the community of psychotherapists.

Chapter 1 gives the context for how intuition fits within current thinking in psychotherapy. Chapters 2–5 highlight the therapeutic use of intuition in practice settings. Chapters 6–7 discuss therapist characteristics and values, experiences, and practices. Chapter 8 describes concerns about the intuitive process. Chapter 9 discusses clients' intuition as a treatment objective. Chapter 10 synthesizes the most important aspects of intuitive development and includes intuition as a fundamental pillar of practice.

The Appendix contains our research design, data analysis, and quality assurance protocols along with descriptions of our participants. The overarching worldview that was foundational to the research design is included along with research procedures. Chapter Tables in the Appendix serve as quick references for our major findings along with the Questionnaire that served as the basis for our in-person recorded interviews. We have also added a list of resources in the Additional Resources section of the appendix. This adds dimension to our book by pointing to historically important work and current references that inform and elaborate on intuitive processes.

Chapter 1, Current Knowledge and Perspectives: gives a brief history of intuition in clinical practice, discusses current knowledge in general and gives an overview of different perspectives on the subject of intuition.

Chapter 2, Therapists' Understanding of Their Intuition: Therapists explain their views of what intuition is and where it comes from, including a transpersonal source, accumulated knowledge/experience and wisdom, a coming together of diverse factors, and simply unknown.

Despite a diverse range of views and beliefs regarding religion and spirituality, they hold very similar views regarding a transpersonal aspect of their intuition.

Chapter 3, How Therapists Use Intuition in Therapy: The therapists in the study described the ways that they incorporate their intuitively gained knowledge into the the treatment process. They demonstrated that intuition can be an important source of information that can aid every aspect and phase of treatment, from establishing a therapeutic alliance, through diagnosis, treatment planning, and evaluation.

Chapter 4, Focus of Therapists' Attention: Where one focuses attention is an important element in the intuitive process. The therapists noted that they focus on several discrete phenomena, from internal experience, the client, the connection between therapist and client, as well as a more open, expansive awareness.

Chapter 5, Forms of Clinical Intuition: Intutively derrived knowledge can arrive in several different forms. The ability to successfully use intuition requires that one be able to identify that information is incoming. The therapists in the study described the ways that they experienced their intuition. Their ability to identify these subjective experiences may alert the reader to tune in to similar experiences as they begin to use intuition in therapy.

Chapter 6, Experiences and Practices Associated with Clinical Intuition: Therapists shared information regarding experiences they have had and practices in which they engage, which may have some influence on their abilities to use or access intuition. The participants discussed this material at much greater length than any of the other topics that emerged in the data analysis. The thoroughness of their considerations demonstrates the broad range of experiences clinicians draw on in their understanding and use of intuition in clinical practice. This chapter includes experiences participants described having outside of the clinical setting that are reported widely in the psi literature. These additional experiences are important, as awareness of them provides additional examples of intuitive experience that therapists may hear from their clients who discuss similar experiences in treatment.

Chapter 7, Characteristics and Values of Intuitive Therapists: These are the clinicians' descriptions of themselves or others whom they identified as intuitive. This includes concepts such as personal traits, qualities, capacities, values, and worldviews. In many cases, the participants clearly associated certain of these qualities with being intuitive; in other cases, they were simply describing themselves or other intuitive people. Participants also identified characteristics or values that they believe undermine intuitiveness.

Chapter 8, Concerns Regarding Clinical Intuition: This chapter includes concerns regarding the use of clinical intuition as well as concerns regarding the failure to use this resource. It gets to the very heart of the challenge in defining the use of intuition in each clinician's practice. Knowing the difference between logic/reasoning and intuition requires self-knowledge and the ability to discern the source of information; discernment develops with practice. Empathy is a primary characteristic of effective use of intuition, acknowledging the complexity of human experience and respect for each individual and the choices they make moment to moment.

Chapter 9, Teaching Clients to Trust Their Intuition: This chapter reflects the understanding that therapists who value the role of their own intuition in clinical practice place greater emphasis on the role intuition plays in the lives of their clients. Intuition-informed practice reflects a process of learning to listen deeply to the self, the capacity for self-exploration, development of coping strategies, understanding of long-term behavioral patterns, and creating change. Clients' growing awareness and ability to access their own self-awareness through intuitive processes reflects a primary goal of psychotherapy and is viewed as a treatment objective.

Chapter 10, Overarching Themes in Clinical Intuition: Several themes were expressed in different ways across research categories, indicating their particular importance to practicing clinicians. These include clinical intuition as a common factor across psychotherapy models, the importance of an alterocentric stance, continued self-development, the ability to sense connectedness, energy as a form that intuitive experiences take, and an understanding of what intuition is and where it comes from.

We hope these chapters culminate in a better understanding of clinical intuition and that they encourage practitioners to become more confident integrating it into practice. Part of this new understanding of intuition is the difficult work of developing a vocabulary. To do so, we take an interdisciplinary look at intuition—early psychoanalytic literature, current theories and models, neuroscience, psi literature, quantum science, popular literature—in developing a cohesive guide to applying intuition in clinical practice. It is our hope, finally, that this book is a catalyst for further research and debate; we stress throughout that this is our attempt to articulate previously unpolished thoughts on intuition, and it is in this spirit that we hope others will follow.

Notes

1. See, for example, Gladwell's book *Blink: The Power of Thinking Without Thinking.*
2. See Satir's *The New People Making.*

Current Knowledge and Perspectives 1

What we currently understand about intuition spans multiple disciplines with very different perspectives on the subject. These differing viewpoints share some common features as well as distinctions regarding how intuition is defined, how it operates, and the legitimacy of intuitively derived information.

The perspectives of business research, cognitive psychologists, psychoanalysts, nonanalytic psychotherapy theory, feminist scholarship, research centered on how intuition is used in psychotherapy and counseling, transpersonal psychology, the psi research, and finally a synthesis of the diverse threads of scholarship on intuition all contribute to a complex understanding of the phenomenon. This corpus with distinct differences in understanding highlights the need for additional research in general and a clear need for greater insight into the nature of intuition in the clinical context.

Business Research and Cognitive Psychology

Arguably, the interest among academic researchers in intuition may have been spurred by the recognition that very successful businessmen declared that they were using intuition to make important decisions. Ray and Myers (1989) recognized that "By the eighties, many business people acknowledged that intuition is an obvious cornerstone of business" (p. 247). He noted,

> Fairly solid evidence indicates that those who rely on intuition in their decision-making make more profitable decisions than do others. . . .

> eighty percent of those company leaders who had doubled their companies' profits in a five-year period had above-average precognitive powers (intuition).
>
> (p. 249)

At that point, researchers in the fields of business (management and entrepreneurship) and cognitive psychology turned their attention to studying what, exactly, intuition is, under what circumstances intuition is likely to be more or less reliable, and how one might enhance their intuitive capacities. Their work is collapsed here because of the degree to which they referenced each other's theories and findings.

Like all researchers, they brought their worldview to their work. Thus, without reflecting on this fact, most of the studies generated by these two disciplines begin with the assumption that intuition is a cognitive process that is the result of the operations of an isolated mind: that is, it happens within the mind-brain of the intuiter. This is a starkly different starting point than others who have studied the phenomenon, as will be explained in successive sections. Both business researchers and cognitive psychologists tend to understand intuition to be a cognitive capacity.

> System 1 thinking and reasoning [intuition] is hypothesized as evolutionarily the more ancient of the two systems . . . its core processes are rapid, parallel, and automatic, permitting judgment in the absence of conscious reasoning. . . . System 2 deliberative problem solving is more recent, its core processes are slower, serial, and effortful, permitting conscious abstract reasoning and hypothetical thinking.
>
> (Gore & Sadler-Smith, 2011, p. 304)

It must be noted that the notion that intuitive and deliberative judgment represent the results of two separate processes or systems has been challenged. Kruglanski and Gigerenzer (2011) are among a growing number of researchers who have hypothesized a unimodal model, in which "intuitive and deliberative judgments need not be based on different rules: The very same rules can underlie both" (p. 98).

Both models—the dual system or process model and the unimodal—posit that intuition is an individual phenomenon. For example, Kruglanski and Gigerenzer (2011) explicitly hypothesize that intuitive judgments, like deliberative ones, are accurate based on individual differences in processing capacity.

As a reflection of the assumption that intuition is a cognitive process within a single mind, the research protocols these researchers have employed focus on a person in an impersonal situation. For example, many of the studies focus on probabilistic inferences, such as requiring the research participants to quickly determine whether or not a city is the state capital (Glockner, 2008). Such judgments may have limited relevance to a clinical context. In the clinical context, there are two subjects. This may lead one to consider the possibility that intuition that involves two or more people may be different in important ways from intuition regarding impersonal objects or problems.

Another difficulty in potentially applying this research to the clinical context is the definition these researchers have used in their work. There is broad agreement that intuition is a response that is triggered with no apparent conscious effort (Hogarth, 2001). The term "response" becomes very important to this definition. In the cognitive psychology research, intuition is narrowly defined as the process of decision making that culminates in action (Betsch, 2008; Hogarth, 2010; Lieberman, 2000). It is differentiated from actions that are reflexes or instinctual (Hogarth, 2010). This definition excludes the experience of sudden insight or the acquisition of knowledge or information without a subsequent action. As will become clear, this contradicts the experiences of the therapists in this study.

While the cognitive research posits that intuition is a cognitive process, they agree that intuition has both physical and emotional components, although they disagree on the value of the emotional aspects of the phenomenon. For example, Deutsch and Strack (2008) have suggested that physical stimuli (such as a facial expression) automatically trigger a feeling state in the observers. These feelings are usually categorical, such as pleasant or unpleasant/approach or avoidance. The feelings may culminate in a bodily reaction, like a "gut feeling" (Damasio, 1999, cited in Gore & Sadler-Smith, 2011).

Departing momentarily from the cognitive research, Hans Welling (2005) has identified several feeling states that are regularly associated with the experience of intuition. The first feeling state he identified was a "feeling of confusion, alertness, or being disturbed or troubled" (p. 25). Another experience may be a pregestaltic experience, expressed in the negative in statements such as "there is something missing . . . something is wrong" (p. 26), or it may be expressed in the positive as "a sense of solution, [or] things are falling into place" (p. 26). One may find oneself with the feeling that something is somehow important "without knowing how they are related to one's feelings" (p. 26). One feeling that occurs with great regularity is the sense of certitude or feeling that the knowledge gained by the intuitive process is absolutely accurate (Petitmengin-Peugeot, 1999). There may also be a feeling of coherence or that the meaning of something is fully revealed (Charles, 2004; Petitmengin-Peugeot, 1999).

While the cognitive psychologists broadly agree that intuition is the non-conscious processing of information that includes an affective component, there are two very different views on the value of affect, as well as different explanations for how the intuitive process unfolds. One model is represented in the popular literature on intuition. This is the heuristic model, championed by Kahneman (2011). A heuristic is a simplifying shortcut to solve a problem and relies on trial and error. The heuristic model of intuition suggests that past knowledge and experience form cognitive patterns that are then applied to a current situation that shares some important features with those past experiences. The proponents of this model believe that the process is a highly biased operation, as it is the result of ease of retrieval (Kahneman). This, in turn, is an emotion-based process (Kahneman). This bias, according to Kahneman, renders intuition highly unreliable in most circumstances.

The learning theory models suggest a different process and outcome for intuition. These models share the understanding that intuition is the product of implicit learning (see, for example, Plessner, Betsch, & Betsch, 2008, for several such models). Rather than holding that emotions sully the decision-making process, the learning theory models suggest that "[I]mmediate feelings can reflect the sum of experiences made with an attitude object" (Betsch, 2008, p. 13). That is, emotions allow one to bypass slower cognitive processes. These researchers tend to credit intuition as more reliable than the heuristic model suggests.

Both the cognitive psychologists and business researchers have studied successful individuals who use intuition in business as well as other professions. Based on the business and cognitive psychology research, Agor (1989) developed a set of guidelines for developing intuition for successful decision making. He suggested that in order to develop intuition, you must first and foremost value the capacity, and develop the intention to use and trust it. This requires time. Agor suggested that you devote time to intuition and create a special space for developing it, tuning in to it on a daily basis. He indicated that you should engage in relaxation exercises to release physical and emotional tension on a daily basis. He likewise recommended a regular meditation practice to quiet the mind. With a quiet mind, Agor suggested you should adopt a stance of openness and receptivity, and enhance your sensitivity to internal and external stimuli. The research he reviewed indicated that honesty is a prerequisite for well-developed intuition. This means that you must develop the ability to observe and release forms of self-deception, develop the courage to face yourself, and ultimately trust yourself. He also recommended participating in nonverbal creative practices, such as art and music. The ability to see and accept things as they are is an important component to intuitive decision making, so blinkering what you want or fear is an important component in developing intuition. Agor also suggested love, acceptance, and nonattachment are important qualities to cultivate. He recommended keeping a journal to note when intuition is accurate and under what circumstance it proves to be inaccurate. Finally, he noted that finding a supportive group of people who accept and encourage the use of intuition will help you on the path to becoming more intuitive.

As will become clear over the course of this book, these suggestions are largely supported by the intuitive psychotherapists whom we interviewed.

The business and cognitive psychology models of intuition are centered on understanding intuition as a process within an individual mind. These processes must culminate in a decision to act in order for these researchers to label the experience intuition. This decision-making process is either tainted by or enhanced by emotional valuations within the operation, depending on which model one adopts. The result of differentially valuing the role of emotions leads to the theorists placing different assessments on the reliability of intuition.

Psychoanalysis: Intuition, Telepathy, and Unconscious Communication

Within psychoanalysis, there are three terms used that relate to the present study of participants' understanding and experience of intuition. These terms are intuition, telepathy, and unconscious communication.

Within the history of psychoanalytic thought, attitudes regarding intuition have evolved over time. Freud was outspoken in his aversion to intuition in relation to his scientific discovery. He affirmed this position in *The Question of a Weltanschauung* (1933/1989), wherein he stated that psychoanalysis is a science and therefore distinct from lower forms of religious thought. As a part of the *weltanschauung* of science, Freud stressed that psychoanalysis was based on empirical research, not knowledge "derived from revelation, intuition or divination" (p. 784). Even prior to this statement, Freud related intuition to occultism and other forms of extrasensory perception, which he roundly devalued (Reiner, 2004). For example, in *Beyond the Pleasure Principle* (1920/1989), he rejected the role of intuition in the clinical process.

While Freud overtly rejected intuition as an analytic tool, there is some evidence that he either did not see telepathy as a form of intuition, or else he changed his mind regarding the phenomenon. Radin (2006) has suggested that Freud had a personal experience that may have ushered in a change of heart. Ernest Jones (1957), a student of Freud, presented a compelling case that such a shift indeed occurred. For example, in 1921, Freud wrote in a letter to the psychic researcher Hereward Carrington, "If I had my life to live over again, I should devote myself to psychical research rather than psychoanalysis" (Jones, 1957, p. 392). In 1932, Freud stated in his *New Introductory Lectures* that "telepathy might be the kernel of truth that had become surrounded by fantastic occult beliefs" (Jones, 1975, p. 405). Freud may have moved from understanding telepathy as occultism to a legitimate phenomenon that could be explained scientifically once the occult trappings were excised.

Since Freud, the term "intuition" has met with mixed reaction among analysts. Piha (2005) has summarized some of the positions analysts have published on the topic of intuition. Rather than listing these in chronological order, he placed them on a continuum from disparaging to accepting. While Freud eschewed intuition in some of his work, Piha suggested that "he also implied in *On Beginning Treatment* (1913) that analysts should rely heavily on intuition" (p. 26).

Since Freud, more negative valuations of intuition tend to cluster around the notion that it is the product of narcissistic countertransference, and highly unreliable (Piha, 2005). Piha considered Kohut (1971) to be exemplary of this position. Equally pejorative, he noted that Tahka (1993) warned that the analyst's intuition is a countertransferential reaction that is born of the "insufficient capacity to tolerate puzzlement and delay" (p. 27).

More sympathetic to the concept, Moore and Fine (1990), based on the work of Arlow (1979), defined intuition as a preconscious synthesis of observations collected over time. In spite of this less demeaning understanding, they nonetheless warned that intuition is ultimately an inferior means of processing information (Piha, 2005).

According to Piha (2005), Arlow (1979) was an early proponent of the position that intuition is the result of metacommunication. That is, it is based on gesture, posture, rate of speech, etc. The importance of metacommunication in achieving an understanding of another's internal experience is highlighted later by Daniel Stern (1985), and following him, a host of Intersubjective analysts (see, for example, Beebe, Knoblauch, Rustin, & Sorter, 2005).

Piha (2005) argued that Reik (1948) focused closely on intuition, in spite of the fact that he rarely used the term explicitly. Much later, Brown (2009) referred to Reik's work on intuition in his own work on unconscious communication. According to Brown, Reik elevated intuition as an important analytic tool that arises in a shared dreamlike ego state that allows the analyst to have direct access to the analysand's emotions.

Other sympathetic accounts of intuition among analysts include Sharpe (1937), Noy (1982), and Waelder (1960). These writers stressed the role of the unconscious in intuitive experience, its value as a form of communication, and the fact that humans differ in their intuitive abilities (Piha, 2005).

Piha's (2005) treatment of intuition from an analytic perspective shared Spitz's (1965) position that those who scoff at intuition may do so as a defense to quell "uneasiness before which we cannot explain" (Spitz, 1965, p. 136, cited in Piha, 2005, p. 30). Piha asserted that intuition is a "rationally inconceivable ability to use archaic modes of comprehension as integrated functions of the ego" (p. 33).

Importantly, Piha (2005) did not include the Bionians in his overview of analytic thought regarding intuition. As Brown (2009) observed, Freud's suggestion to use one's unconscious as an instrument of analysis was inspirational to Bion's development of the importance of intuition in analysis. Bion (1970/1977) stated,

> The physician can see and touch and smell. The realizations with which a psycho-analyst deals cannot be seen or touched . . . For convenience, I propose to use the term "intuit" as a parallel in the psycho-analyst's domain to the physician's use of "see," "touch," "smell," and "hear."
>
> (p. 7)

Bion (1962/1977) noted that this capacity emerges in a state of "reverie or relaxed attention" (p. 87, cited in Williams, 2006, p. 87). Specifically, Bion discussed what he called, "F," or the psychoanalytic method of observing and recording a patient's state of mind; "Through F one can 'see,' 'hear,' and 'feel' the mental phenomena of whose reality no practicing [*sic*] psycho-analyst has any doubt though he cannot with any accuracy represent them by existing formulations" (pp. 57–58). This requires one to extinguish both memory and desire, to allow an unconscious process to unfold (Williams).

Following Bion, Jarreau (2012) has elaborated on the use of intuition in the psychoanalytic encounter. Like Bion, he equated the phenomenon with listening with the unconscious mind. He stressed that one must stop thinking, or at the very least not pursue more formal forms of theoretical cognition, in order to fully experience emotions that arise during time with a patient. In this state, free of memory and desire, one is able to apprehend the patient's emotional experience. For Jarreau, intuition may lead to insight into important aspects of the patient's unconscious, gained through unconscious communication.

While the term "intuition" has met with mixed approval among analysts, Freud appeared to be more comfortable with the term "telepathy." Campbell and Pile (2015) made explicit the identity between Freud's use of the term "telepathy" and unconscious communication. They demonstrated that Freud used the term "telepathy" to refer to the unconscious communication of nonrepressed material between two people. They stated,

> telepathy is intrinsic to the unconscious communication that takes place as transference in clinical or analytical settings. . . [it is] a sense of unconscious thought transference which is inseparable from the transference of affect . . . through transference and through his discussion of telepathy, Freud would continue to evoke the possibility of unconscious communication between individuals.
>
> (pp. 406–408)

Throughout the psychoanalytic discussions of intuition and telepathy, the term "unconscious communication" arises repeatedly. Farber (2017), following in the footsteps of Gooch (2007), has linked unconscious communication directly to telepathy and "other uncanny experiences" (Farber, 2017, p. 269). She stated that, "Telepathy can be understood as a type of unconscious affective communication or implicit relational knowing. . . " (p. 723). This form of communication is accomplished through the projective identification of dissociated material. According to Farber (2017), the projective identification, in turn, is accomplished via mirror neurons. This would, of course, require that the client and therapist be in proximity to each other during direct communication, able to see and/or hear the nonverbal and paralinguistic communication of the other.

Projective identification is a process recognized by a number of analysts. In this process, a person defensively blocks awareness of a characteristic, feeling, thought, etc. that they do not wish to acknowledge. They then project the unwanted experience onto another: in other words, they apprehend what they do not wish to accept in themselves as being present in another. The other identifies with the material or experiences as his or her own the feelings, characteristics, etc. that the first person has projected.

The analytic understanding of unconscious communication can also be traced to Freud's earliest work on psychoanalysis. As Fortuna (2015) observed, "Freud (1915) realized that the communication from the unconscious of one person to the unconscious of another can bypass our conscious awareness" (2015, p. 122).

Contemporary analysts have discussed unconscious communication in the context of intersubjectivity (see, for example, Alperovitz, 2013). Bass (2015) pointed to the work of Ferenczi as the beginning of a shift in the understanding of transference and hence the appreciation of unconscious communication in the analytic encounter. Bass credited Ferenczi with discovering the "unconscious dialogue central to human relations, development, communication, and symptoms formation" (Bass, 2015, p. 4). Bass stressed the bidirectional nature of this communication, in which both analyst and patient are equally open to receiving and transmitting material from each other's mind. This point is important: one must render oneself vulnerable to being "seen" by the other in order to "see" the other.

As an outgrowth of the intersubjective encounter, unconscious communication has taken a distinctly neurocognitive turn. Farber's (2017) work is entirely in keeping with the trend in Relational/Intersubjective analytic thought to use the findings in the fields of cognitive and affective neuroscience as well as developmental psychology to explain how people communicate nonverbally and unconsciously. This line of thinking is perhaps best unpacked in a 2009 special edition of *Psychoanalytic Dialogues*. In this issue, Trevarthen, Gallese, and Ammaniti and Trentini discussed the role of coordinated movements between two people, again, likely mediated by mirror neurons. According to these researchers, the coordination forms a "neuroanatomical basis for empathy and identification" (Seligman, 2009, p. 504).

There is one final term used by Donnell Stern (2013c) that, to the authors' minds, if not equivalent to intuition, at the very least overlaps with the concept to a large degree. Stern (2013c) discussed unbidden novel experience. He described the experience in this way:

> Novel conscious experience is unbidden . . . It arrives in our minds and bodies without an accompanying consciousness of effort or memory of process; the means by which we create it are not available to our inspection. We do not have access to what we would need in order to construct a phenomenological account of the genesis of the experience we create. . . . [T]hose contents generally appear spontaneously and suddenly, out of what feels like nowhere . . . the unbidden lies at the heart of therapeutic action, at once both the core of the process of change and the index we consult to assess it.
>
> (pp. 227–228)

Stern gave several examples of the analyst's unbidden experience in the clinical encounter. Each of them is an instance of the clinician knowing something about the analysand's thoughts or feelings.

> A patient looks up at me and I have the sudden perception that she is quite sad . . . Or a tone in her voice alerts me to a note of regret that I have missed until then . . . A flash of her eye awakens my awareness of her irritation at me . . . Something she says makes me understand that her worry that I will think she is self-indulgent is her mother talking. . . .
> (pp. 228–229)

Each of these examples is an instance of the clinician knowing something about the analysand's thoughts or feelings without explicit communication. We must note that in many of the examples noted above, Stern indicates a form of paralinguistic communication.

There are also several psychoanalytic schools that refer to field theory in the discussion of unconscious communication. It must be noted that among these writers, field theory is used as a metaphor (Stern, personal communication, 7/11/15). Stern (2013a) defined the analytic field as all of the ways analyst and analysand influence each other, all of the experiences they are capable of having with each other, as well as the outcomes of all of those influences and experiences. He chronicled the rise and shifting meaning of field theory within psychoanalysis, tracing the use of the term from Sullivan and the Interpersonalists through Bion and the Relational analysts, concluding that today the analytic field is a concept that "is at the heart of both interpersonal and relational psychoanalysis" (2013a, p. 390). For many analysts, the notion of a reciprocal exchange of information/influence, or an analytic field, is a key concept.

Recently, Rosenbaum (2011) synthesized the psi research with psychoanalytic theory (see below for a summary of the psi research). Many of the analytic practitioners reviewed above have continued to explore intuitive events while maintaining the integrity of analytic methods. These theorists acknowledge occasional but meaningful anomalous experiences. Others within the analytic aegis have attempted to reshape theory to parallel modern physics by developing a model based on field theory (Ullman, 1974, pp. 256–258).

Writing about telepathy and Freud's attempts to include it in analytic discourse, Rosenbaum (2011) wrote about her personal experience of perceiving a future event, and the emotions that were connected to the event. She suggested that the contributions of psi research render a compelling explanation for such experiences in a way that analytic theory thus far has not been able to do. She made a strong case for including understanding of psi phenomena in clinical work where "unconscious influencing and communication are the norm" (p. 84).

Rosenbaum (2011) noted that there is apparent resistance in the analytic literature to integrate the worldview generated by the psi research into analytic sensibilities. She demonstrated how important analytic considerations—including the confusion around boundaries, magical thinking, psychosis, the subtlety of psi effects—contribute to the belief that intuitions cannot be real. She suggested that this fact presents an obstacle to the acceptance of psi in psychoanalysis. In spite of these conceptual hurdles, she recommended that analytic thought will be enhanced by incorporating aspects of psi research into the continuing development within the discipline.

The overwhelming point in the analytic literature of diverse schools is that two human minds are capable of interpenetrating and reciprocally influencing each other. One person can "know" both some of the content as well as processes of another's mind without explicit verbal communication or deductive reasoning based on observable evidence (see, for example, Bass, 2015; Beebe et al., 2005; Campbell & Pile, 2015; Sands, 2010). That is, one person can come to know the subjective experience of another without explicit communication or even the overt intention to acquire that knowledge. They tend to remain agnostic about how, exactly, this is accomplished, although two current theories involve neurological activity or some form of field.

Nonanalytic Psychotherapeutic Treatments of Intuition

Therapists from a number of nonanalytic orientations have also been interested in intuition. In 2001, Rea engaged in a review of the literature on clinical intuition. He looked at early studies that supported the existence and advantages of the human capacity for nonconscious learning. Rea (2001) suggested that given the ubiquity of nonconscious processes in general, it would be naïve to believe that intuition is not used in the clinical arena and, indeed, a mistake to remove intuition from a therapist's cognitive toolkit.

Marks-Tarlow (2012) presented a theory of clinical intuition-based on the work of Allan Schore. She argued that clinical work that is not informed by intuition is ultimately unethical. This is because theory-driven work—what she referred to as "top down" (p. 8) processing—biases a clinician to see whatever the theory posits rather than the client's experience. She stated,

> In order to *be with* our patients rather than to *do to* and manipulate them according to preordained experience, we must stay close to ongoing subjective experience. . . [T]o cling to idea-driven strategies can actually

> interfere with the clinical process, rendering our responses rote, mechanical, or insensitive to nuance and detail.
>
> (p. 11, italics in original)

For Marks-Tarlow, staying close to ongoing subjective experience means opening up to the intuitive process.

Marks-Tarlow (2012) posited that clinical intuition is the result of right brain–to–right brain unconscious communication, as described in the work of Allan Schore. Schore (2005) has studied the right hemisphere of the brain for several decades. While his research was originally aimed at mother–infant interactions, he has stated that his work has direct relevance for therapist–client interactions. Through the use of positron emission tomography or PET scans and functional magnetic resonance imaging or fMRIs to study brain functions that occur in time frames beneath conscious awareness, Schore has documented,

> bidirectional implicit affective communications embedded in proto-dialogues. . . [C]oordinated visual eye-to-eye messages, tactile and body gestures, and auditory prosodic vocalizations [serve] as a channel of communicative signals that induce instant emotional effects . . . The dyadic implicit processing of these nonverbal . . . communications of facial expression, posture, and tone of voice are the product of the operations of the infant's right hemisphere interacting with the mother's right hemisphere.
>
> (p. 833)

Thus Schore, like other infant researchers, merges intuition with the nonconscious communication of microexpressions and other nonverbal behaviors (see, for example, the Boston Change Process Study Group, 2010).

Intuition is a cornerstone concept in Jungian psychology (Pilard, 2015). Pilard has noted that there is widespread popular recognition that Jung postulated that intuition is among the capacities that constitute psychological types. Jung's treatment of this conscious level of intuition represents, however, the tip of a proverbial iceberg.

> intuition in Jung's theory comes from the abysses of the deepest unconscious of psychology . . . intuition is present everywhere instead of just in types and functions. To try to untangle all the forms of intuition present in Jung's writing is to expose its central and pivotal position in his psychology.
>
> (Pilard, 2015, p. xiii)

Because of the centrality and complexity of Jung's treatment of intuition, a full explication of his theory is beyond the scope of this chapter. The interested reader is directed to Pilard's (2015) text. The important point here is that for Jung and Jungians, intuition is an important component of clinical method. Intuition underlies the techniques of active imagination and the constructive method. The constructive method is the clinician's process of grasping the client's developmental path by exploring seemingly inexplicable dream symbols that originated in the dreamer's unconscious (Pilard, 2015). Active imagination requires the individual to engage in activities that support the emergence of the collective unconscious. Among these are "dance, automatic writing, drawing, crystal gazing, and painting" (Pilard, 2015, p. xvi).

Carl Rogers (1980) also recognized the role of intuition in the clinical process, although he did not formulate an explicit theory of the phenomenon.

> When I am at my best, as a group facilitator or as a therapist, I discover another characteristic. I find that when I am closest to my inner, intuitive self, when I am somehow in touch with the unknown in me, when perhaps I am in a slightly altered state of consciousness, then whatever I do seems to be full of healing. Then, simply my presence is releasing and helpful to the other. There is nothing I can do to force this experience, but when I can relax and be close to the transcendent core of me, then I may behave in strange and impulsive ways in the relationship, ways which I cannot justify rationally, which have nothing to do with my thought processes. But these strange behaviours turn out to be right, in some odd way: it seems that my inner spirit has reached out and touched the inner spirit of the other. Our relationship transcends itself and becomes a part of something larger. Profound growth and healing and energy are present.
>
> (1980, p. 129)

Eric Berne (1949/1977, 1952/1977, cited in Schmid, 1991), the creator of Transactional Analysis, gave a prominent role to the concept of intuition. He defined the phenomenon as "knowledge based on experience and acquired through sensory contact with the subject, without the 'intuiter' being able to formulate to himself or others exactly how he came to his conclusion" (p. 4, cited in Chiesa, 2014, p. 130).

But Berne broadened the definition from knowing without knowing how one knows to knowing without necessarily having conscious awareness of the content of the knowledge.

> Not only is the individual unaware of how he knows something; he may not even know what it is that he knows, but behaves or reacts in a specific way as if his actions or reactions were based on something that he knew.
>
> (1949/1977, p. 5, cited in Schmid, 1991, p. 145)

This implicit knowledge leads one to perceive another based on patterns developed early in life. As Schmid (1991) observed, "Berne assumed that people react to their intuitive perceptions by alterations in their experience and behavior" (p. 145). By interacting with the other in a way that is consistent with this patterned perception, one elicits a response from the other that indeed repeats the pattern.

For Berne, the capacity to engage in the intuitive process is located in the Child ego state (Chiesa, 2014). It is a "function of the preverbal, prelogical, and emotional world, one released from both Adult thought processes and Parent value-related obligations" (Chiesa, 2014, p. 130). According to Chiesa, Berne believed that logic, judgment, and the process of verbalization interfere with intuition.

Schmid (1991) expanded Berne's (1949/1977) definition of intuition by viewing it through a Constructivist lens. He suggested that intuition is not simply the application of a predetermined template onto the current situation but an ability to apprehend what could be, what is possible or potential. Even though a therapist may not know what they know, they nonetheless communicate this unconscious knowledge in a way that spurs potential growth in the client. This process, he suggested, is key to the therapeutic alliance.

Transpersonal Psychology also embraces intuition as a legitimate means of knowing, in life in general as well as in the process of research. Key theorists in Transpersonal Psychology agree that the term is "not yet adequately defined" (Friedman & Hartelius, 2013, p. xxvi). Nonetheless, there are some clear parameters around the term. Friedman and Hartelius noted that there are three identifying linguistic components to the term: psychology, personal, and trans.

> As a psychology, it is focused on the scientific understanding of, and applications for working with, the individual, commonly seen as an isolated nexus of affect, cognition, and behavior . . . that which differentiates an individual from other individuals, as well as that which lends some degree of continuity to an individual over time and across space, is the usual defining *personal* aspects of the individual, or

> the personality. . . *trans*, most often seen as meaning *beyond* . . . when attached to the personal, implies somewhat of a disqualifier, referencing that the personal is incomplete.
>
> (p. xxv)

Thus, Transpersonal Psychology includes the systematic study of human experiences that go beyond the ego, or sense of self as a clearly bounded, separate entity. The field also explores and advocates for the psychological benefits of clients having a direct experience of a fluid, connected sense of self.

By stipulating that the focus of Transpersonal Psychology is "beyond-ego," the scholars who are developing this field wish to include the incorporation of exceptional human experiences into their research, theory, and practice. Exceptional human experiences include a number of mystical and paranormal phenomena.

Transpersonal Psychology is a multifaceted field that is centered on understanding human experiences that are "beyond-ego psychology, . . . an integrative/holistic psychology, and . . . a psychology of transformation" (Hartelius, Rothe, & Roy, 2013, p. 5). By stipulating that the focus of Transpersonal Psychology is "beyond-ego," the scholars who are developing this field wish to include the incorporation of exceptional human experiences into their research, theory, and practice.

Exceptional human experiences include a number of mystical and paranormal phenomena. Paranormal is defined as an experience that "cannot be understood in the context of conventional scientific standards" (p. 401). Among the paranormal experiences, Rock, Storm, Irwin, and Beischel (2013) identify extrasensory perception and further break this category down to include telepathy, which they define as "paranormal acquisition of information concerning the thoughts, feelings or activity of another conscious being" (p. 403, citing Thalbourne, 2003, p. 125); clairvoyance, or "paranormal acquisition of information concerning an object or contemporary physical event" (p. 303, citing Thalbourne, p. 18); and precognition, which is "a form of extrasensory perception in which the target is some future event that cannot be deduced from normally known data in the present" (p. 403, citing Thalbourne, p. 90). Rock and others have observed that "numerous parapsychologists . . . are also distinguished transpersonal psychologists" (p. 410). As the definition of intuition that was developed in the present work includes the experiences that Rock, Storm, Irwin, and Beischel (2013) have identified as extrasensory perception, the field of transpersonal psychology is relevant.

F.W. Vaughan, a noted transpersonal psychologist who focused particularly on transpersonal psychotherapy, published a book on intuition in 1979.

It must be noted that her intended audience was not restricted to therapists. She discussed the overall psychological benefits of accessing intuition, and thus one may infer that she held that this activity is appropriate for clients. Vaughan, working within the ontological commitment of transpersonal psychology, identified the source of intuitive knowing: she framed it as the ability to tap into the "infinite reservoir of the collective or universal unconscious, in which individual separateness and ego boundaries are transcended" (p. 4). The definition of intuition from which Vaughan worked is "mode of knowing and a psychological function which is potentially available to everyone. . . " (p. 57). She noted that her definition encompasses such experiences as

> mystical insights into the nature of reality . . . discovery and invention in science, inspiration in art, creative problem solving, perception of patterns and possibilities, extra-sensory perception, clairvoyance, telepathy, precognition, retrocognition, feelings of attraction and aversion, picking up "vibes," knowing or perceiving through the body rather than the rational mind, hunches, and premonitions.
>
> (p. 57)

She identified four levels of awareness that are associated with intuition: physical, emotional, mental, and spiritual. She identified the mental level with internal or imaginal images as well as aspects of intuition associated with thinking. It may take the form of sudden pattern recognition and, as the cognitive psychologists suggest, problem solving. She identified spiritual intuition as different from the preceding three forms of the phenomenon, due to the fact that it is not associated with physical or emotional feelings or mental activity. It is "a holistic perception of reality [that] transcends rational, dualistic ways of knowing and gives the individual a direct transpersonal experience of the underlying oneness of life" (p. 78). Vaughan stressed that one must enhance their self-awareness in order to be able to discern intuitive information that may arrive through these four ways.

Vaughan's book offers a set of instructions and exercises for awakening intuition. One must set an intention before beginning the process: because it is already "there," one must make a commitment to access the information that is available. The first step is preparatory: First, one must quiet the mind, which may be accomplished by meditation and physical relaxation techniques. Next, one must focus attention on "that aspect of reality that one chooses to contact. . . " (p. 34). The aspiring intuitive should cultivate a "receptive, nonjudgmental attitude that allows intuition to come into conscious awareness without interference" (p. 34), as well as sensitize oneself to the subtle forms that intuitive knowledge may take. This requires trust, openness, and acceptance. She also suggested that contact with others who can offer support and share experiences is helpful in the process of becoming more intuitive.

Vaughan noted that accessing intuition has beneficial effects. Along with the ultimate goal of helping people experience a sense of self that transcends the individual, bounded sense of self and experience self as part of the larger whole, there are effects that may be more in keeping with traditional psychotherapy objectives. For example, she stated that self-awareness is an important preparatory capacity to access intuition. She noted that "the development of non-judgmental self-awareness and its effect on intuition is often associated with improved self-esteem and a sense of inner direction" (p. 34).

This overview of the work of nonanalytic therapists regarding clinical intuition demonstrates that the phenomenon may be a common factor that spans therapeutic models. Analysts and psychodynamic therapists, Humanists, and theorists in Transactional Analysis have all suggested that psychotherapists may successfully use intuition in the conduct of therapy. As Vaughan's work suggests, helping clients access their own intuition may have beneficial effects for clients.

The Feminist Literature

While the feminist literature does not address clinical intuition specifically, it raises an extremely important point in relation to intuition and the current Western cultural devaluation of the phenomenon. Belenky, Clinchy, Goldberger, and Tarule (1986) adopted the general framework of personal epistemology (Hofer & Pintrich, 1997; Perry, 1970). Personal epistemology is a developmental theory that addresses the changing nature over time of what people believe about the nature of knowledge and how one comes to know (Hofer and Pintrich). Belenky et al. observed that the theory, like so many developmental theories, had been advanced from an exploration of men's experiences. The feminist researchers, perhaps not surprisingly, found a different arc among women. Belenky et al. found that there are five orientations to knowledge and truth that women experience. Women are initiated into a culture in which they are taught to embrace the truths espoused by authorities. While the "received knowers" (pp. 35–51) understood that authorities had "the truth," these women did not identify with that truth. Instead, they felt that the truths of the authorities did not include them.

It is the next level of personal epistemology that Belenky et al. (1986) identify with intuition. This is "subjective knowing" (pp. 52–86). Subjective knowers are "no longer subject to the dictates and whims of external authorities. . . [but attend] to her infallible gut instead of listening to external authorities . . ." (p. 53). For these women, "truth . . . is an intuitive reaction—something as experienced, not thought out, something felt rather than actively pursued or constructed" (p. 69).

It must be noted that for Belenky et al. (1986), subjective knowing and intuition are regarded as occupying the naïve end of the personal epistemology continuum. They charted a course in which women who attend institutions of higher learning are taught to suppress their intuition: "the subjective voice [of women] was largely ignored; feelings and intuitions were banished to the realm of the personal and private. It was the public, rational, analytical voice that received the institutions' tutelage, respect, and rewards" (p. 124).

Yet the women in this study demonstrated that continued development brought them into contact with their intuition once again. At the highest end of the personal epistemology continuum, Belenky et al.'s (1986) research suggests that women reclaim their intuition. They do so by integrating intuitive knowledge with knowledge that they have learned from others.

> They told us of weaving together strands of rational and emotive thought and of integrating objective and subjective knowing. Rather than extricating the self in the acquisition of knowledge, these women used themselves in rising to a new way of thinking.
>
> (pp. 134–135)

Carol Gilligan (2011), another noted feminist developmental psychologist, has also discussed intuition in the context of the marginalization of women's experiences. She discussed the process of patriarchy systematically invalidating women's experiences and has called for women to resist the drive toward dissociation of their subjectivity by trusting their intuition.

While the feminists do not directly contribute to the knowledge base of clinical intuition, their work makes a valuable point. Perhaps one of the reasons this important phenomenon has been overlooked in therapy and counseling is due to the cultured gendering of intuition. Given that intuition is viewed as a dominantly female characteristic, it is, by association, devalued.

Research on Clinical Intuition

There are only a few studies known to the authors at this time that focus specifically on therapists' and counselors' professional use of intuition.

Petitmengin-Peugeot (1999) is one such researcher. While psychotherapists did not comprise her entire research sample, they did make up a significant portion of the participants. One aspect of the research report was based on the psychotherapist subsample. In this subsample, the therapists discussed their concerted efforts to connect with their clients. They reported focusing on specific sites of their bodies and generating visual, kinesthetic, or auditory images of connections, such as a channel of light or energy vibration that created a bridge between the therapist and the client.

Charles (2004) conducted a focus group of psychotherapists who self-identified as relying on their intuition in their clinical practices. The study participants detailed what they experienced as the essential features of the intuitive process. They discussed the irrational nature of the experience, which included the recognition that it was difficult, if not impossible, to explain. Relevant cues (they did not detail how they knew which cues were relevant and which were not) are "picked up" (p. 69) either consciously or subliminally. The intuitive apprehends some connection or relationship between the disparate pieces of information, which seemingly come from nowhere. These pieces may come as symbols or images. The knowledge that emerges is a whole that is greater than the sum of the parts.

As in the Petitmengin-Peugeot (1999) study, the Charles (2004) self-reported intuitive clinicians also discussed the importance of the connection between themselves and the client. They suggested that there must be some "accord between the therapist and client" (p. 71) in order for the connections between the pieces of the clinical puzzle to emerge. The therapists discussed the degree to which their whole bodies were implicated in the process. Finally, the participants discussed the need to validate their clinical intuitions. As Charles stated, "subjective certainty does not guarantee veracity" (p. 71).

Jeffrey and Fish (2011) conducted a qualitative study of marriage and family therapists. The study described the therapists' understanding of what intuition is, its function in their clinical work, and how they experienced the phenomenon. Five categories emerged in the data analysis: the nature of clinical intuition in marriage and family treatment; intuition and the therapist–client relationship; spiritual dimensions of intuition; intuition and training; and finally, the felt resistance to recognizing the role of intuition from within the discipline.

In the first category, participants described the affective and sense-centered experience of knowing about their clients. The second category involves the relationship between the clinician and the client. The research participants observed that the client either facilitated or disrupted the intuitive process, emphasizing the fact that clinical intuition involves two active minds. The respondents also discussed the connection between the client and the therapist. They suggested that there is a force that connects everything. It is this connection that they believe makes intuition possible.

The third category was training. When clinical supervisors model the use of intuition, students are more comfortable using it professionally. Some of the respondents noted a sense of frustration that intuition was not taught in their regular coursework, given that it is such an important clinical tool.

Witteman, Spaanjaars, and Aarts (2012) conducted a focus group of mental health professionals to explore the participants' views on using intuition in practice. They defined clinical intuition at the outset as "automatic responses that are based on knowledge acquired through significant, explicit learning from textbooks and in clinical practice" (Witteman et al., 2012, p. 19). Their conclusions are that clinical intuition is concerned with feeling, combined with experience. The participants suggested three sources for their intuition: clinicians' observations, experiences elicited by the client, and training and experience. The mental health practitioners suggested they use intuition more frequently upon first contact with clients, when they feel uncertainty or doubt, or throughout the entire treatment process. According to the participants, intuition is a good source for hypotheses regarding treatment, but as a hypothesis, the intuition must be checked through other means. The participants also noted risks associated with using intuition, notably that it can lead to the wrong conclusion due to confirmation bias or projection.

Siegel (2013) conducted a study on therapists who use intuition in their work. She defined her participants as awakened therapists. She defined this term as "a therapist who lives a transpersonal life" (p. 68). Siegel reported that the therapists discussed working in the realm of spiritual resonance, which she defined as "an energy force originating from what might be referred to as Spirit" (p. 49). They rely on the "intuitive skills of alternative ways of knowing such as inner knowing, inner hearing and seeing, and kinesthetic senses in order to monitor subtle shifts in the energy field [between themselves and their clients]" (p. 57). This monitoring is an important component in assessment. The therapists additionally reported transmitting energy to their clients as part of the helping process.

The findings of these studies on clinical intuition bring greater understanding to what may be involved in the experience of clinical intuition and how it may differ from the phenomenon studied by cognitive psychologists. The repeated themes of connection and the role of the client in the process arise as important elements. The differences between the studies are also noteworthy. A great deal more research must be conducted before a corpus of work can begin to form a clear picture of what clinical intuition is and how therapists and counselors use it.

Psi Literature

There is a great deal of research on intuition that is not represented in the academic press. Radin (1997) has suggested that this reflects a bias against the nature of reality that is suggested by this work and not a reflection of the legitimacy of the research. Those who research such experiences use the term "psi" to refer to the subject of their experiments. These researchers hold that intuition is actually several distinct phenomena. This observation may account for the diversity of experiences relative to clinical intuition and may hamper a full understanding of this complex concept.

First written about by British psychologist Robert Thouless in 1942 (Radin, 2006), the term "psi" is used to describe telepathy, clairvoyance (perceiving distant objects or events), precognition (perceiving future events), and psychokinesis (mind–matter interactions) (Radin, 2006; Swann, 1987; Targ, 2012). Scientists refer to telepathy, clairvoyance, and precognition under the umbrella term extrasensory perception (ESP). Those three capacities, plus psychokinesis (PK) are often referred to as the "big four" foundational findings in the field (Braud, 2005; Tart, 2009). Charles Tart (2009) further divided PK into mind–matter interactions and psychic healing, in recognition of the extensive research supporting these phenomena over the last three decades (see, for example, Benor, 1993, 1994; Jahn & Dunne, 2011; Krippner & Villoldo, 1986).

Radin (1997) identified how the changing cultural understanding of physical reality has impacted the thinking about psi over four eras. He identified the first era as the age of *anima mundi*, the living universe, when psi was seen as natural communication between soul and spirits. Era two, the classical scientific era, spanned from the seventeenth through the mid-twentieth centuries. In this era, physical reality was viewed mechanically (Targ & Putoff, 1977). Since time, space, and matter were believed to be fixed and absolute, independent of observer influence, scientific understanding of psi was impossible. In era three, the current quantum era, psi can be explained as a reflection of the participatory nature of physical reality. Participatory reality is a worldview in which space, time, energy, and matter are relative, complementary, and dependent on observation (Radin, 2006).

Radin (2006) went on to speculate that era four will be an "Integral Age," when physical reality will be understood as "actively participatory" (pp. 242–243). By this he means that there will be greater understanding of how exactly humans participate in the co-creation of reality. This will include a better understanding of how matter is influenced and can be shaped by observation and conscious intention.

Psi research in the current era is centered on the belief that "Virtually all contemporary research on receptive psi (telepathy, clairvoyance, and precognition) is founded on the assumption that psi is essentially an information transference process" (Braud, 2005, pp. 50–51).

This conclusion both undergirds and is supported by a growing corpus of research in parapsychology. A meta-analysis of quantitative psi research has confirmed the effects of telepathy, remote viewing (perceiving distant objects or events), precognition and presentiment (perceiving future events and emotions connected to those events), and telekinesis. Williams (2017) noted that while he did not conduct a formal meta-analysis of presentiment, statistical significance has been demonstrated across studies.

The relationship between psi scholarship and psychotherapy is longstanding, even if at times uncomfortable. Jung embraced what was considered occult, participating in séances and exploring Eastern philosophy, astrology, and synchronous events (Ullman, 1974).

Freud was a member of both the British Society for Psychical Research (SPR) and its American (ASPR) offshoot (Ullman, 1974). Founded in 1882, the SPR describes its mission on its website as the "first society to conduct organized scholarly research into human experiences that challenge contemporary scientific models" (www.spr.ac.uk/about/our-history, 2/7/18). Since the early days of both the British Society and its American offshoot founded by psychologist William James, psychiatrists and psychologists have continued to play leading roles in both societies. As influential members, they have been contributors in developing the major themes in psi research (Ullman, 1974). Ullman pointed out that it was psychiatrist Frederic Myers who coined the term "telepathy," which has been a focus of much of the literature on psi. Acknowledging the importance of the clinical setting in understanding psi, Ullman wrote that it provides a "rich store of information concerning the emotional atmosphere in which psi occurs, the personality dynamics at play, the relative roles of patient and therapist, and the clinical criteria for the recognition of the telepathic dream" (Ullman, 1974, p. 247).

The interweaving of psi scholarship with psychology may be manifest by understanding an evolution within the psychotherapy disciplines that corresponds to the four worldviews explored by Radin (2006). Accordingly, one may look at Freud's work as an example of second-era mechanistic thinking. As noted above, Freud demonstrated an interest in telepathy, but given that his work was coeval with the rise of logical positivism, he ultimately adopted the mechanistic perspective of mental functioning. This can perhaps be most clearly seen in one of his earliest contributions, "Project for a

Scientific Psychology" (1953). Using the classical laws of matter and energy described by Newton, Freud developed his model of the id, ego, and superego as a theoretical structure of the mind that paralleled a "clockwork that functions according to deterministic, causal principles" (Winer, 1994, pp. 13–14). The emphasis is on the individual mind. This perspective limits the ability to perceive, let alone understand, any psi phenomena that may operate in the clinical encounter.

One may interpret the changes that occurred in psychotherapy theory in the 1950s as the result of the era two shift in understanding the nature of reality. Therapists began to move toward conceptualizing therapy as a "two person" (Winer, 1994) system rather than as the therapist observing the internal machinations of a client's mind. This era saw a rise in the importance of the therapist/client dyad and use of the relationship as the vehicle of therapeutic change. Empathy emerged as a therapeutic strategy, the matrix for therapy (Winer, 1994).[1] Object relations, self psychology, and relational theories as well as family and group therapy developed, reflecting deepening understanding of connection while broadening the context of change. They demonstrate growing awareness that the fundamental nature of reality is more like a piece of fabric connected with interwoven threads than like mechanisms of a clock (Bohm, 1980; Capra, 1977; Radin,1997).

Era three psychotherapy practice is developing as reflected in growing interest in and acknowledgment of intuition as an expression of human capacity and a tool of effective practice.

The writers have found that therapists who experience high degrees of psi abilities are still, for the most part, unwilling to speak openly of their experiences unless they are assured of confidentiality.

Based on Radin's (2006) speculation about an era four worldview, one may anticipate that in era four therapists will be able to seamlessly integrate psychotherapeutic theory with psi abilities. Furthermore, the clinicians' understanding of their patients may not be limited by time or space. Thus we see that the understanding of psychotherapy based on the psi worldview is moving from the cognitive psychology perspective that intuition is dependent on cognitive processes that are interior to an individual mind and more a reflection of the capacity to connect to a unified field of intelligence.

As noted, many psi researchers share the position that intuitive insights are the result of receiving subtle information from a field of consciousness that connects everything (Dossey, 2013; McTaggart, 2002; Targ, 2012). The field is nonlocal and operates outside of mechanistic principles of space and time. Field theory, particularly quantum field theory, provides an explanatory structure to make sense of phenomena that otherwise are inexplicable, such as precognition or telepathy. This relational view of intuition has gained the interest of psychotherapists.

The cumulative knowledge established in psi research since the early days of psychotherapy helps to explain phenomena that clinicians have experienced all along but that could not be explained by theory as it was understood at the time. Seeking to understand their experiences, clinicians have made significant contributions to research on the nature and structure of anomalous experiences in psychotherapy, participating in research that establishes both the variety of intuitive experiences and their usefulness in clinical settings. Such contributions are being made by therapists of all disciplines. These include psychiatrists, such as Benor (1993, 1994), Ehrenwald (1978), Eisenbbud (1982, 1983), Grof (1976, 1988), Orloff (1996, 2009), Schwarz (1965), Weiss (1988), Weiss and Weiss (2013), as well as psychologists, including Braud (2005), Krippner (1979), LeShan (1975), and Villolldo and Krippner (1987), and social worker Virginia Satir (1988).

The psi research emanates from an understanding of the nature of reality that is starkly different from much of the research and theory explored above. While the psi literature has historically been marginalized in the peer-reviewed academic journals traditionally consumed by psychotherapists, there appears to be a growing interest in a possible détente. It is also noteworthy to interrogate the space between the views of academics who produce those journals and the front-line everyday psychotherapists who participated in the study explored in this book.

Sinclair's Typology

In 2011, Marta Sinclair edited a comprehensive volume that integrated research on intuition from a number of diverse sources. This included the psi research, the psychology studies, and the research conducted in the field of management. The stated point of the text was to bring together differing perspectives, highlighting the areas of agreement as well as differences between these sources.

Sinclair (2011) used a basic definition of intuition: "direct knowing" (p. 13). She synthesized a great deal of research and concluded that in looking at intuition, there are a number of discrete aspects of intuition that have been studied. One of these is that it seems to serve several different functions. Many of the differences between the functions of intuition center on where the information comes from and how it is processed. These factors suggest three types of intuition. The first is intuitive expertise, which is based on pattern matching between a current situation and past domain-specific experiences and is associated with very little affect. Intuitive creation is associated with a higher level of affectivity. It combines domain-specific information, general experience, as well as stimuli to which the intuitive has or has had cursory exposure. Finally, intuitive foresight is the least-understood function of intuition. This form of intuition incorporates a broad scope of information from the present context, and perhaps a sense of possible future information.

Of particular note here is Sinclair's (2011) suggestion that intuition centered on interpersonal interaction is a distinct subset of the functions of intuition. She pointed out that this area is relatively poorly studied. She reflected that this may be due to the implication of a transpersonal interaction and the presence of nonlocal information. She acknowledged that some interpersonal intuition may be based on microexpressions and nonverbal communication. This does not, however, account for how people can know something in relation to people who are not in their proximity.

Summary and Discussion

As this chapter demonstrates, there are a number of different perspectives regarding intuition. In synthesizing these perspectives, three different theories emerge. Certainly, the theories need not be mutually exclusive: intuition in general and clinical intuition specifically may be more than a singular phenomenon. Nonetheless, the three theories that are currently represented in the literature include two cognitive theories: the heuristic model, which purports that intuition is a "quick and dirty" problem-solving strategy that is highly prone to error due to emotion-laden retrieval bias (Kahneman, 2011); and that it is the implicit application of tacit learning (Plessner et al., 2008).

An alternative explanation is represented in the work of psi researchers and psychotherapists: that is, intuition may be a form of communication. This theory includes two different explanatory models: that the unconscious communication is based on subliminal microexpressions and nonverbal cues or that it is the result of the activity of a co-created field.

One of the ways one may conceptualize the difference between the cognitive psychologists' theories and that of the psi researchers and therapists is the degree to which clinical intuition may be interactive. The former posit a one-person model, or a process that occurs in the mind of the individual intuitive. The latter suggest that intuition can be an interactional phenomenon in which two people play contributing roles in the process.

With these issues in mind, we turn to the experiences and understanding of the therapists who shared important incidents surrounding their professional use of intuition. What do they experience? How do they use it? Where does it come from? What other factors, events, practices, etc. may be associated with it? Their stories contain significant pieces to this complex puzzle.

Note

1. For a further discussion on the distinction between empathy and compassion, see Marilyn Stickle's article "The Expression of Compassion in Social Work Practice" (2016); the main point of the article stresses the limits of empathy and offers compassion as a more emotionally sustainable matrix for therapy: "[C]ompassion activates positive affect and regions associated with affiliation."

Works Cited

Agor, W. H. (1989). The logic of intuition: How top executives make important decisions. In W. H. Agor (Ed.), *Intuition in organizations: Leading and managing productively* (pp. 157–170). Newbury Park, CA: Sage.

Alperovitz, S. (2013). Nonverbal communication in analytic work. *Journal of the American Psychoanalytic Association, 61*, 363–377.

Ammaniti, M., & Trentini, C. (2009). How new knowledge about parenting reveals the neurobiological implications of intersubjectivity: A conceptual synthesis of recent research. *Psychoanalytic Dialogues, 19*, 537–555.

Arlow, J. A. (1979). The genesis of interpretation. *Journal of the American Psychoanalytic Association, 27* (suppl), 193–206.

Arnd-Caddigan, M., & Pozzoto, R. (2006). Truth in our time. *Qualitative Social Work, 5*, 423–440.

Arnd-Caddigan, M., & Pozzoto, R. (2011). The politics of "twoness": Policy clinical judgment, and evidence-based practice. *Social Work in Mental Health, 9*, 122–136.

Bass, A. (2015). The dialogue of unconsciousness, mutual analysis and the use of self in contemporary relational psychoanalysis. *Psychoanalytic Dialogues, 25*(N), 2–17.

Beebe, B., Knoblauch, S., Rustin, J., & Sorter, D. (2005). *Forms of intersubjectivity in infant research and adult treatment*. New York, NY: Other Press.

Belenky, M. F., Clinchy, B. M., Goldberger, N. R., & Tarule, J. M. (1986). *Women's ways of knowing: The development of self, voice, and mind*. New York, NY: Basic Books.

Benor, D. J. (1993). *Healing research: Holistic energy medicine and spirituality* (Vol. 1). Oxfordshire: Helix Editions, Ltd.

Benor, D. J. (1994). *Healing research: Holistic energy medicine and spirituality* (Vol. 2). Oxfordshire: Helix Editions, Ltd.

Berne, E. (1977). The nature of intuition. In P. McCormick (Ed.), *Intuition and ego states: The origins of transactional analysis* (pp. 1–31). San Francisco: TA Press. (Original work published in 1949).

Betsch, T. (2008). The nature of intuition and its neglect in research on judgment and decision making. In H. Plessner, C. Betsch, & T. Betsch (Eds.), *Intuition in judgment and decision making* (pp. 3–19). New York, NY: Lawrence Erlbaum Associates.

Bion, W. R. (1962). *Learning from experience*. Lanham, MD: Rowman and Littlefield. [Reprinted in 1977 in *Seven Servants*. New York, NY: Jason Aronson.]

Bion, W. R. (1970). *Attention and interpretation: A scientific approach to insight in psychoanalysis and groups*. London: Tavistock. [Reprinted in 1977 in *Seven Servants*. New York, NY: Jason Aronson.]

Bohm, D. (1980). *Wholeness and the implicate order*. New York, NY: Routledge.

Boston Change Process Study Group. (2010). *Change in psychotherapy: A unifying paradigm*. New York, NY: W. W. Norton.

Braud, W. G. (2005). The farther reaches of psi research: Future choices and possibilities. In M. A. Thalbourne & L. Storm (Eds.), *Parapsychology in the twenty-first century: Essays on the future of psychical research* (pp. 40–63). Jefferson, NC: McFarland.

Brown, L. J. (2009). From "disciplined subjectivity" to "taming wild thoughts": Bion's elaboration of the analyzing instrument. *International Forum of Psychoanalysis, 18*, 82–85.

Campbell, J., & Pile, S. (2015). Passionate forms and the problem of subjectivity: Freud, Frau Emmy von N. and the unconscious communication of affect. *Subjectivity, 8*(1), 1–24.

Capra, F. (1977). *The Tao of physics: An exploration of the parallels between modern physics and Eastern mysticism*. New York, NY: Bantam Books.

Charles, R. (2004). *Intuition in psychotherapy and counselling*. London: Whurr.

Chiesa, C. (2014). On the seashore of an endless world, children's play: Using transactional analysis in play therapy with children. *Transactional Analysis Journal, 44*(2), 128–141.

Damasio, A. R. (1999). *The feeling of what happens: Body, emotion and the making of consciousness*. London: Vintage.

Deutsch, R., & Strack, F. (2008). Variants of judgment and decision making: The perspective of the reflective-impulsive model. In H. Plessne, C. Betsch, & T. Betsch (Eds.). *Intuition in judgment and decision making* (39–53). New York, NY: Lawrence Erlbaum Associates.

Dossey, L. (2013). *One mind: How our individual mind is part of a greater consciousness and why it matters*. Carlsbad, CA: Hayhouse.

Ehrenwald, J. (1978). *The ESP experience: A psychiatric validation*. New York, NY: Basic Books.

Eisenbbud, J. (1982). *Paranormal foreknowledge: Problems and perplexities*. New York, NY: Human Sciences Press.

Eisenbud, J. (1983). *Parapsychology and the unconscious*. Berkeley, CA: North Atlantic Books.

Emoto, M. (2004). *The hidden messages in water* (David A. Thayne, Trans.). Hillsboro, OR: Beyond Words Publishing, Inc.

Farber, S. K. (2017). Becoming a telepathic tuning fork: Anomalous experience and the relational mind. *Psychoanalytic Dialogues, 27*, 719–734.

Ferro, A., & Basile, R. (2009). The universe of the field and its inhabitants. In A. Ferro & R. Basile (Eds.), *The analytic field: A clinical concept* (pp. 5–29). London: Karnac.

Fortuna, T. (2015). Unconscious communication. *Empedocles: European Journal for the Philosophy of Communication, 6*, 121–126..

Freud, S. (1920/1989). Beyond the pleasure principle. In P. Gay (Ed.), *The Freud reader*. New York, NY: W. W. Norton.

Freud, S. (1933/1989). The question of Weltaschauung. In P. Gay (Ed.), *The Freud Reader*. New York, NY: W. W. Norton.

Freud, S. (1953). Project for a scientific psychology. *The standard edition of the complete works of Sigmund Freud* (Vol. 1, pp. 295–343). London: Hogarth Press.

Freud, S. (1961). On beginning the treatment. In J. Strachey (Ed. and Trans.), *The standard edition of the complete works of Sigmund Freud* (Vol. 14, pp. 166–204). London: Hogarth Press. (Original work published 1915).

Friedman, H. L., & Hartelius, G. (2013). Editors' introduction: The promise (and some perils) of transpersonal psychology. In H. L. Friedman & G. Hartelius (Eds.). *The Wiley Blackwell handbook of transpersonal psychology* (xxv–xxxiv). Malden, MA: Wiley Blackwell.

Gallese, V. (2009). Mirror neurons, embodied simulation, and the neural basis of social identification. *Psychoanalytic Dialogues, 19*, 519–536.

Gilligan, C. (2011). *Joining the resistance*. Cambridge: Polity.

Gooch, S. (2007). *The origins of psychic phenomena: Poltergeists, incubi, succubi, and the unconscious mind.* Rochester, VT: Inner Traditions.

Glockner, A. (2008). Does intuition beat fast and frugal heuristics? A systematic empirical analysis. In H. Plessner, C. Betsch, & T. Betsch (Eds.), *Intuition in judgment and decision making* (pp. 309–325). New York, NY: Lawrence Erlbaum Associates.

Golafshani, N. (2003). Understanding reliability and validity in qualitative research. *The Qualitative Report, 8*, 597–607.

Gore, J., & Sadler-Smith, E. (2011). Unpacking intuition: A process and outcome framework. *Review of General Psychology, 15*, 304–316.

Grof, S. (1976). *Realms of the human unconscious*. New York, NY: E. P. Dutton.

Grof, S. (1988). *The adventure of self-discovery*. Albany, NY: State University of New York Press.

Hartelius, G., Rothe, G., & Roy, P. J. (2013). A brand from the burning. In H. L. Friedman & G. Hartelius (Eds.), *Transpersonal psychology* (pp. 3–22). Malden, MA: Wiley Blackwell.

Heinneman, M. B. (1981). The obsolete scientific imperative in social work research. *Social Service Review, 55*, 371–397.

Hofer, B. K., & Pintrich, P. R. (1997). The development of epistemological theories: Beliefs about knowledge and knowing and their relationship to learning. *Review of Educational Research: Washington, 67*(1), 88–140.

Hogarth, R. M. (2001). *Educating intuition*. Chicago: University of Chicago Press.

Hogarth, R. M. (2010). Unpacking intuition: A process and outcome framework. *Psychological Inquiry, 21*, 338–353.

Horton, C. (1974). Psi-conducive states of awareness. In E. D. Mitchell (Ed.), *Psychic exploration: A challenge for science* (pp. 616–638). New York, NY: Cosimo Books.

Jahn, R., & Dunne, B. (2011). *Consciousness and the source of reality*. Princeton, NJ: ICRL Press.

Jarreau, A. (2012). Intuiting the unknown: Listening with the unconscious mind. *Modern Psychoanalysis, 37*, 66–81.

Jeffrey, A. J., & Fish, L. S. (2011). Clinical intuition: A qualitative study of its use and experience among marriage and family therapists. *Contemporary Family Therapy, 33*, 348–363.

Jones, E. (1957). *The life and work of Sigmund Freud, volume 3 the last phase*. New York, NY: Basic Books.

Jung, C. G. (1972). *Typologie*. Olten: A. G Walter Verag. (Original work published 1921).

Kahneman, D. (2011). *Thinking, fast and slow*. New York, NY: Farrar, Straus and Giroux.

Kohut, H. (1971). *The analysis of the self.* New York, NY: International Universities.

Krippner, S. (Ed.). (1979). *Psychoenergetic systems: The interaction of consciousness, energy and matter*. New York, NY: Gordon and Breach Science Publishers.

Krippner, S., & Villoldo, A. (1986). *The realms of healing*. Berkeley, CA: Celestial Arts.

Kruglanski, A. W., & Gigerenzer, G. (2011). Intuitive and deliberate judgments are based on common principles. *Psychological Review, 118*(1), 97–109.

LeShan, L. (1975). *The medium, the mystic, and the physicist*. New York, NY: Ballantine Books.

Lieberman, M. D. (2000). Intuition: A social cognitive neuroscience approach. *Psychological Bulletin, 126*, 109–137.

Marks-Tarlow, T. (2012). *Clinical intuition in psychotherapy: The neurobiology of embodied response*. New York, NY: W. W. Norton.

Mansfield, V., & Spiegleman, J. M. (1996). On the physics and psychology of the transference as an interactive field. *Journal of Analytic Psychology, 41*(2), 179–202.

Maxwell, J. A. (1992). Understanding and validity in qualitative research. *Harvard Educational Review, 62*, 279–300.

McTaggart, L. (2002). *The field: The quest for the secret force of the universe*. New York, NY: HarperCollins.

Mega, L. F., Gigerenzer, G., & Volz, K. G. (21015). Do intuitive and deliberate judgments rely on two distinct neural systems? A case study in face processing. *Frontiers in Human Neuroscience, 9*. doi:10.3389/fnhum.2015.00456

Moore, B. E., & Fine, B. D. (Eds.). (1990). *Psychoanalytic terms and concepts*. New Haven, CT: American Psychoanalytic Association/Yale University Press.

Munowitz, M. (2005). *Knowing: The nature of physical law*. Oxford: Oxford University Press.

Noy, P. (1982). A revision of the psychoanalytic theory of affect. *Annual of Psychoanalysis, 10*, 139–186.

Orloff, J. (1996). *Second sight*. New York, NY: Warner Books.

Orloff, J. (2009). *Emotional freedom: Liberate yourself from negative emotions and transform your life*. New York, NY: Three Rivers Press.

Perry, W. G. (1970). *Forms of intellectual and ethical development in the college years: A scheme*. New York, NY: Holt, Rinehart, and Winston.

Petitmengin-Peugeot, C. (1999). The intuitive experience. *Journal of Consciousness Studies, 6*(2–3), 43–77.

Piha, H. (2005). Intuition: A bridge to the coenesthetic world of experience. *Journal of the American Psychoanalytic Association, 53*(1), 23–49.

Pilard, N. (2015). *Jung and intuition: On the centrality of forms of intuition in Jungian and post-Jungians*. London: Karnac.

Plessner, C., Betsch, C., & Betsch, T. (Eds.). (2008). *Intuition in judgment and decision making*. New York, NY: Lawrence Erlbaum Associates.

Radin, D. (1997). *The conscious universe: The scientific truth of psychic phenomena*. New York, NY: Harper One.

Radin, D. (2006). *Entangled minds: Extrasensory Experiences in a quantum reality*. New York, NY: Simon & Schuster.

Ray, M., & Myers, R. (1989). Practical intuition. In W. H. Agor (Ed.), *Intuition in organizations: Leading and managing productively* (pp. 247–261). Newbury Park, CA: Sage. (Originally published in 1986 in *Creativity in business*. Doubleday).

Rea, B. D. (2001). Finding our balance: The investigation and clinical application of intuition. *Psychotherapy, 38*(1), 97–106.

Reik, T. (1948). *Listening with the third ear*. New York, NY: Grove.

Reiner, A. (2004). Psychic phenomena and early emotional states. *Journal of Analytical Psychology, 49*, 313–336.

Rock, A. J., Storm, L., Irwin, H. J., & Beischel, J. (2013). Parapsychology. In H. L. Friedman & G. Hartelius (Eds.), *Transpersonal psychology* (pp. 401–416). Malden, MA: Wiley Blackwell.

Rodwell, M. K. (1998). *Social work constructivist research*. New York, NY: Garland Publishing.

Rogers, C. (1980). *A way of being*. Boston: Houghton Mifflin.

Rosen, H. (1996). Meaning-making narratives: Foundations for constructivist and social constructionist psychotherapies. In H. Rosen & K. T. Kuehlwein (Eds.), *Constructing realities: Meaning-making perspectives for psychotherapists*. San Francisco: Jossey-Bass.

Rosenbaum, R. (2011). Exploring the *other* dark continent: Parallels between psi phenomena and the psychotherapeutic process. *Psychoanalytic Review, 98*(1), 67–90.

Sands, S. H. (2010). On the royal road together: The analytic function of dreams in activating dissociative unconscious communication. *Dialogues, 20*, 357–373.

Satir, V. (1988). *The new people making*. Mountain View, CA: Science and Behavior Books.

Schmid, B. (1991). Intuition and the possible and the transactional creation of realities. *Transactional Analysis Journal, 21*(3), 144–154.

Schore, A. N. (2005). A neuro psychoanalytic viewpoint: Commentary on paper by Steven H. Knoblauch. *Psychoanalytic Dialogues, 15*, 829–854.

Schwarz, B. E. (1965). *A psychiatrist looks at ESP*. New York, NY: Signet Mystic Books.

Seligman, S. (2009). Anchoring intersubjective models in recent advances in developmental psychology, cognitive neuroscience and parenting studies: Introduction to papers by Trevarthen, Gallese, and Ammaniti & Trentini. *Psychoanalytic Dialogues, 19*, 503–506.

Sharpe, E. F. (1937/1988). *Dream analysis*. London: Karnac Books.

Siegel, I. R. (2013). Therapists as a container for spiritual resonance and client transformation in personal psychotherapy: An exploratory heuristic study. *The Journal of Transpersonal Psychology, 45*(1), 49–74.

Sinclair, M. (Ed.). (2011). *Handbook of intuition research*. Cheltenham, UK: Edward Elgar.

Smith, N. W., & Smith, L. L. (1996, January). Field theory in science: Its role as a necessary and sufficient condition in psychology. *The Psychological Record, 46*(1), 3–19.

Spitz, R. A. (1965). *The first year of life*. New York, NY: International Universities.

Stern, D. B. (2013a). The interpersonal field: Its place in American psychoanalysis. *Psychoanalytic Dialogues, 25*, 388–404.

Stern, D. B. (2013b). Field theory in psychoanalysis, part 2: Bionian field theory and contemporary interpersonal/relational psychoanalysis. *Psychoanalytic Dialogues, 23*, 630–645.

Stern, D. B. (2013c). Relational freedom and therapeutic action. *Journal of the American Psychoanalytic Association, 61*(2), 227–255.

Stern, D. N. (1985). *The interpersonal world of the infant: A view from psychoanalysis and developmental psychology*. New York, NY: Basic Books.

Stickle, Marilyn. (2016, February). "The Expression of Compassion in Social Work Practice." Journal of religion and spirituality in social work: Social thought. *Taylor & Francis Group, Inc, 35*(1–2), 120–131.

Swann, I. (1987). *Natural ESP: A layman's guide to unlocking the extra sensory power of your mind*. New York, NY: Bantam.

Tahka, V. (1993). *Mind and its treatment*. Madison, CT: International Universities Press.

Targ, R. (2012). *The reality of ESP: A physicist's proof of psychic abilities*. Wheaton, IL: Quest Books.

Targ, R., & Putoff, H. (1977). *Mindreach: Scientists look at psychic abilities*. New York, NY: Delacorte Press.

Tart, C. (2009). *The end of materialism*. Oakland, CA: New Harbinger.

Thouless, R. H. (1942). Experiments on paranormal guessing. *British Journal of Psychology, 33*(1), 15–27.

Trevarthen, C. (2009). The intersubjective psychobiology of human meaning: Learning of culture depends on interest for co-operative practical work—and affection for joyful art of good company. *Psychoanalytic Dialogues, 19*, 507–518.

Ullman, M. (1974). *Psi and psychiatry in psychic exploration*. New York, NY: Cosimo.

Vaughan, F. W. (1979). *Awakening intuition*. New York, NY: Anchor Books.

Villolldo, A., & Krippner, S. (1987). *Healing states: A journey into the world of spiritual healing and shamanism*. New York, NY: Simon & Schuster.

von Franz, M. L., & Hillman, J. (1980). *Zur typologie C. G. Jung*. Tellbach-Oeffingen: Verlag Adolf Bonz GmbH.

Waelder, R. (1960). Basic theory of psychoanalysis. New York, NY: International Universities Press.

Weiss, B. L. (1988). *Many lives, many masters*. New York, NY: Simon & Schuster.

Weiss, B. L., & Weiss, A. E. (2013). *Miracles happen: The transformational healing power of past-life memories*. New York, NY: HarperCollins.

Welling, H. (2005). The intuitive process: The case of psychotherapy. *Journal of Psychotherapy Integration, 15*(1), 19–47.

Williams, G. (2017, Summer and Autumn). Psi and the problem of consciousness. *The Journal of Mind and Behavior, 34*(3/4), 259–283.

Williams, S. (2006). Analytic intuition: A meeting place for Jung and Bion. *British Journal of Psychotherapy, 23*(1), 83–98.

Winer, R. (1994). *Close encounters: A relational view of the therapeutic process*. Northvale, NJ: Jason Aronson.

Witteman, C. L. M., Spaanjaars, N. L., & Aarts, A. A. (2012). Clinical intuition in mental health care: A discussion and focus group. *Counselling Psychology Quarterly, 25*(1), 19–29.

2 Therapists' Understanding of Their Intuition

The field of psychotherapy has been conflicted from the beginning about how to understand intuitive experiences. Labeled variously as mental telepathy, the sixth sense, extraordinary knowing, and second sight, the confusion around what to call intuitive experiences reflects the fundamental problem of language inherent in our discussion. On a deeper level the confusion is related to understanding the source and nature of intuition. In this chapter, we will address how therapists define clinical intuition, what it is, and where it comes from. We will highlight how clinical practice understands intuition as a distinct way of listening and a valid way of knowing.

We asked seasoned clinicians how they define and use intuition in practice. The definition distilled from our research is: intuition is the acquisition of information about the client and/or course of therapy, attained by means other than overt communication, including how to use it to further the client's well-being and goals in psychotherapy. The therapists discussed their understanding of where this capacity comes from and their explanations of how it works. The focus is on intuition as a process: how to identify it and how to describe the continuum of intuitive experiences.

Across disciplines, intuition has been described as the "third wave" of knowing following the first and second waves of instinctual and intellectual knowing. Research on intuition is being conducted throughout the world in diverse fields including neuroscience, business, medicine, psychology, and meditative and spiritual traditions. In line with the examination of intuitive processes across disciplines, the picture that emerges is that while intuition has not been acknowledged broadly in psychotherapy, clinicians are incorporating this multifaceted phenomenon in increasing numbers (Lifescience Foundation, 2013).

The explanations for intuition therapists offer span from the esoteric to the uniquely personal aspects of their life experience. Some express the belief that their intuition is derived from a transpersonal source, that there is something beyond the individual that accounts for the phenomenon. This is variously identified as divine, an impersonal force, or a higher self. Other clinicians think intuition is the result of an ontological connectedness that allows for the exchange of information. Some clinicians experience intuition as a form of energy and believe that their intuition is information carried through the movement or transfer of energy. Several therapists indicate that they believe intuition is the result of a subtle information exchange between people.

On a more personal level, therapists describe intuition as the result of accumulated knowledge, wisdom, and practice experience. This includes knowledge of the neurological and biological aspects of the human body as well as understanding of the psychological, social, and spiritual aspects of life experience. Clinicians also suggest that intuition is the ability to quickly access acquired information that comes through learning and observation without reflection.

Some clinicians are comfortable not having an explanation for the phenomenon, simply labeling it a mystery. The most robust idea in this category is that intuition is related to a connectedness that permeates everything. These related ideas are expressed broadly in the literature on intuition. Clinicians hold this view in spite of wide variation in religious and spiritual orientations, including atheism. Understanding of connectedness is a main theme in clinical understanding as reflected in our research and across the literature on intuition (Dossey, 2013; McTaggart, 2002; Targ, 2012).

While there is a wide range of explanations given, therapists agree that intuition is a natural human capacity available to everyone, developed more highly in some than in others. It is clear based on current research, that the understanding and use of intuition has profound practice implications.

A Transcendent Source

It is important to note at the outset that many of the therapists the authors interviewed were committed to a specific religious tradition, to which they alluded in the interviews. Many of them, however, disclosed that while their spirituality is important to them, they do not follow a specific religious tradition. Some identified as distinctly not spiritually oriented. Many of those who profess a specific religious orientation and those who are more generally spiritual indicated that they attribute intuition to some kind of transpersonal source. For some, the source is deistic; for others, it is not. There are also prominent examples of therapists who explicitly do not attribute intuition to any sort of higher power.

Elizabeth provided an example of deistic inspiration. For her, she is a medium for a transcendent source: "I feel almost like a channel for a higher self or God or whatever you want to say. . . . I just think that in addition to my life experiences, that it's God-given. It's a gift." Lena echoed the belief in a transpersonal source but added that she must open to receive the intuition: "Where it comes from. . . [is] being open . . . it was described by a mystic as a third eye being the eye through which I experience God, God is looking at me." Lena's nod to the mystic tradition here is an important discovery; she seems to be suggesting that the same faculty that enables her direct (but unspoken) communication with God is also of use in her encounters with other people. This speaks also to how many of our participants expressed that their spiritual worldviews were models for their intuitive experiences with patients.

Deborah's understanding of her intuition is also informed by her religious worldview. She is noticeably influenced by the Catholic doctrine of a "Communion of Saints," in which there is communication between the living and dead through a shared faith. For Deborah, intuition is not only God given but also works through the Holy Spirit, saints and angels, and the souls of the departed:

> I think it comes through intuition as well as a higher power, divine. The saints and angels are out here. Those people who—my mother, my God, the saints and angels are helping me to find the Holy Spirit. They're helping.

Deborah's expansion of a transcendent source to that of a community rather than a single deity offers room for speculation on how she may see this intuitive faculty working in the social (and therapeutic) world. Does her relationship to a spiritual community offer an alternate model of communication that can be roughly translated to our common use of the word "intuition"?

Felicia's understanding of her source of intuition offers a possible way into the subject of how the transcendent world of the spiritual relates to the material world. For her, there is a nearly direct equivalence between "spirit" and "nature" ("I think it comes from the spirit . . . Nature is spirit . . . that's where spirit is. . . "). She goes further to state that her intuitions are directly manifested from the spiritual world into physical sensations, described at one point in the interview as lines of music coming into her mind. She confirms: "I think that's spirit . . . I think that's intuition." Felicia's connection to nature further suggests that she feels there is something innate about how intuition works and that it may be a fundamental part of our connection to the natural world and others.

Ellen referenced an impersonal force for good, a theme elaborated by Ann. "Almost like there is a universal force that's working towards healing, and I align myself with it." She gave an example of an intuitive experience, explaining, "maybe that was a gift from beyond." Later she described an experience in which she had entreated her deceased grandmother to give her a sign. The next morning as she was walking by a stream, a hawk practically grazed her head. She noted that her dog did not bark at the hawk. She explained the experience as:

> A communication from beyond to me that I'm open. . . . when I say "intuition," that sometimes I think it's information, maybe, that's being shared from beyond—I don't know—or from this stream of knowing that's up there that we can sometimes access. . . . If I can just key into that flow, then I can produce. . . . I guess I do believe that there is a force and that prophets like Jesus, Buddha, and Muhammad, and sure there are countless others we don't know about even, that they were connected somehow. They keyed, and they got it. I believe that there is a life force and that it is good. . . . it's a force for love.

The unifying thread throughout these personal philosophies on the transcendent source of intuition is that it is connected to a higher power or unifying force that they understand variously as God, celestial beings and spirits, or a higher self.

A Universal Connection

Many clinicians discussed their view that intuition is the result of an all-encompassing connection, or oneness, or that everything is part of a larger whole. This view is reflected by Lena:

> Intuition comes as a result, I think . . . I'm part of something much bigger than myself . . . We're all part of—I feel like we're all part of something bigger. . . . I know they're [clients are] part of something that I'm also connected to. . . . I know we're meant to be here discussing this right now, because I have something to teach them, and they have something to teach me . . . That's what I mean by oneness. . . . I just felt like I was part of something bigger than myself. . . . I'm a channel. . . . We're not all separate. . . . You're part of something bigger.

In reflecting her belief that she is a channel, Lena places herself in an interconnected world that forms a unified whole. Perhaps she sees intuition as simply the shared communication among individual parts. Or perhaps her ontological philosophy that she's "part of something bigger" offers a bolder view on the porous nature of consciousness and identity: i.e. our thoughts, behaviors, emotions—who we are—is in part created by our interaction within the larger world.

While many of the professionals endorsed the belief that intuition is connected to a higher power, it is important to note that some of them pointedly eschewed this perspective. Sarah is a counterexample for this view. She was clear. "I don't think of it as spiritual. I think of it as just a fact of our universe." She prefers instead a more secular understanding of her experience with a universal intuition: "I feel like . . . we are all part of a collective unconscious, and that we can tune into that or not tune into it. I tune into it." Her use of the term "collective unconscious" as an explanation for human connection conjures Jung's use of the same term. The idea is that humans have a shared unconscious, an internalized universal understanding of what it means to be human that is both historical and transcultural. Sarah's point, in saying that she chooses to "tune in" to the collective unconscious, is that intuition is a recollection of meanings that we all share. And, in that, there seems to be a level of understanding that isn't overtly communicated.

Several therapists described a similar understanding of connection as Lena. Brenda expressed it as, "I believe that everything is related." Dinah framed universal relatedness as "oneness," suggesting that intuition is due to "being at one with everything." David affirmed a sense of connectedness. "I've had that sense forever. . . . we're all connected." Each of these therapists is using their own language to describe connection that is deeply felt.

The theme of ontological oneness, connectedness, or being part of a larger whole arose repeatedly among the therapists in this study. To be sure, there are nuanced differences in the specific nature of their experiences. Sarah's point that there is a choice that can be made whether to tune in or not tune in to connectedness underscores the individualized experiences in this category. This is a common theme across literature on intuition: namely that oneness or connectedness is a robust explanation for intuitive capacities.

Energy

Bridging the gap between somatic sensations and emotional (affective) states, many therapists experience intuition as "energy" and understand the movement of energy as the explanation for intuition. Some of the clinicians in the study suggest that intuition is the result of receiving and interpreting energy. Alejandro reflects this way of knowing. "I think it goes beyond emotion and beyond the rational and beyond intellect. I think there's some energy, I guess that's the best word to use."

Alejandro's uncertainty about where to place energy in the emotion–reason continuum is instructive on the nature of intuitive experience: it can be more easily felt than articulated or placed in a system of thought. His emphasis that intuition goes "beyond" traditional categories of consciousness also highlights the challenge of easily pinning intuition down to a single phenomenon that can be named and classified.

Though explaining intuition as a form of energy is a challenging endeavor, some of our therapists have concrete theories of its relationship to the hard sciences. Jeff offers an explanation that places intuition within the electrical impulses of neuroscience.

> Brainwaves and energy . . . we can read them by placing leads on your scalp . . . obviously, we're not shoving needles through the scalp and the skull and into the brain. Those waves emanate. I think it's electricity that goes to your scalp, but who knows what goes beyond that? We don't know how to measure. That, I don't think, is so woo-woo, spacy, out there, crazy at all. . . . When somebody's sitting this close to you, I think you can feel some vibes . . . It could be energy.

Jeff is referring to the use of functional magnetic resonance imaging (fMRI) to measure and map the brain's activity. His explanation extends Alejandro's theory of intuition as felt energetically in a single body (or brain) to that of a *connection* between people.

Grace and Natalie also understand their intuitive ability to be due to awareness of energy. Grace reflected, "I think a lot in terms of energy . . . Maybe it's like a sixth—literally the sixth sense of some capacity that we have for tuning in, that we mostly probably don't—that is an energetic piece of us." Grace's suggestion that intuition is a "sixth sense" is intriguing and should spur further conversations on the nature of intuition, as it shows up as a common theme not just amongst our therapists but in other studies on intuition as well.

Natalie offers an interesting addition to the concept of intuition as energy; she sees energy as a medium for information: "I see it as some sort of energy source that is there, whether you're aware of it or not. I think it has a lot of information, if you're able to sort of tap into it."

As we've touched on, the therapists who understand intuition as a form of energy, many also caution against "negative" energy as a downside. Lauren sees this as a matter of being "too open" to it.

> . . . what I mean about being open to it [intuition] so that it can come through—there are these energy fields that we have where we can have energy coming in or not. . . . You can have energy opening you up. I've been told by [name redacted] and that group, they say, "Your energy field is too open. It's too open. You have to learn to close yourself more because you're taking in too much stuff." . . . I've had experiences with entry by other energy systems coming in.

From Lauren we learn about an important aspect of intuition. Viewed from the perspective of energy and of making a choice to open to it or not, it is also possible to open to it too much. In doing so, Lauren finds that she is affected by others' energy systems negatively impacting her.

Accumulated Knowledge, Experience, and/or Wisdom

Clinicians also suggest that their intuition is the product of their experience and learning coming together, including clinical and life experience in general. Elizabeth was among the clinicians who provided this explanation. She offered,

> I think it comes from experience, a lot of it, and a lot of information, knowledge, wisdom that you have compiled over the years. This is something that I feel much more acutely now than I did in the past because I have compiled so much experience and knowledge and wisdom that I'm—it's one of the best things about getting older. I feel like there's just so much there for me to draw upon. It gives me a confidence that, when I was young, I may not have had.

She suggested that due to close work with people as they process their experiences, clinicians may gain vicarious wisdom. "We're constantly having people think about what it is that they're experiencing, their thoughts, their ideas—all the different theories they could be using and strategies, all that kind of thing." Elizabeth's inclusion of the full range of human experiences that serve as a foundation to intuitive understanding incorporates the broad factors that contribute to deep wisdom and effective use of intuitive impressions.

Other clinicians highlighted the importance of training and experience. Sharon referenced the social work knowledge base as an important element in the mix. She said, "I think the knowing is understanding what I'm hearing from the patient as related to the social work knowledge base." Her point is that for her, intuition is an ability to recall relevant information from her knowledge base and apply it in new situations.

Brenda also understands her intuition, in part, as an ability to easily recall past training. "Some of it is experience, too." For Ann, "Sometimes it feels like it's just a coming together of what I know and my experience." Jessica also expressed this idea, adding that the process is unconscious: "Basically, it's [intuition is] a pulling together of information I know and I have, subconsciously or something, I'm pulling it together in my brain and it's just presenting as though it were a picture."

These therapists suggest that their intuition is—at least in part—the result of accumulated experiences. This amalgam includes wisdom gained through personal experience and through vicarious experience with their clients. The multiple sources that feed intuition—the fund of information acquired as well as experience—may be processed outside of the conscious awareness of the therapist. The integrative nature of intuition is reflected in the synthesis of what has been learned, experienced and is known as it is relevant in the context of the patient's life in the therapeutic moment.

Conscious Processes

Clinicians shared an understanding of intuition that includes information held on a conscious level. The conscious part of the process is comprised of information acquired through client records, observable client behaviors, and application of theory. Lena gave a case example in which her intuition was in part related to her use of more explicit sources of information: "With him [a client] I had benefited from reading his paperwork that came with him. It gave me some information."

Ellen appears to combine analysis of objectively observable behavior with a more intuitive process. She shared a case example that she identified as an instance of using her intuition that a client was suicidal. As she processed the experience in the interview, she concluded that

> . . . her behavior was different, because . . . I don't think she'd ever called me before. She certainly is not the type of person that would call me on Sunday, so you could just say I put all the clues together that there was something wrong.

Thus, while she experienced the information as intuitively derived, she was able to note that there was an aspect of the process that included processing more overtly observable behaviors and comparing these to her sense of the client's previous patterns of behavior.

Lena indicated that in some cases, formal theory is linked to intuition in the clinical encounter.

> Well, as far as Cognitive Behavioral, I'm an observer to behavior. I observe behaviors that sometimes have not been integrated cognitively by my clients. As far as Cognitive Behavioral, I'm looking for error. I'm picking up on not only what they're saying, but what they're doing that tells me that there's a disconnect and that there's not an awareness . . . Family systems. That's a very visual thing for me. . .

This quote suggests that Lena uses overtly observable behavior, coupled with the application of either cognitive-behavioral or family systems theory. She sees these more conscious elements as informing what she ultimately experiences as intuitively derived information. Lena's coupling of theory and intuition also shows how therapists don't see intuition as an isolated capacity; it's both a complement to and a check on theory and manualized therapy. In this way, the clinicians have discerned that there may be more overtly acquired information—including the client's observable behavior, records, and formal theory that coalesce into the information that they ultimately process intuitively.

An Interpersonal Process

Many clinicians suggest that intuition is not the result of the individual therapist's activity alone but equally depends on the participation of their client. This experience is differentiated from a sense of universal connection, focusing on the process that unfolds between the therapist and the client. The clinicians described this process with terms like "unconscious communication," "resonance," and "attunement." There was widespread agreement that they experience their intuition—at least in part—as an interactional process.

Justin explained his intuition in these terms:

> I might have termed it resonance . . . or maybe transference and countertransference . . . I think it's something about the interaction between the two [therapist and client]. That there's something that—there's something in the relational field. I guess that's how I see it. That the clients will be experiencing thoughts and feelings, and then that's going to trigger something in the therapist and vice versa.

In this way, Justin understands that intuition is a dynamic process, in which information isn't necessarily attained all at once but can develop over time. Brenda also suggested that there is some form of unconscious communication going on between the client and therapist during an intuitive exchange. She stated,

> I don't think that they [clients] are necessarily conscious of [it] but . . . I think there is a deep feeling that they have that I'm feeling, and maybe we use the word intuiting, cuz I'm there. They're transmitting, projecting, whatever term you wanna use. I can feel it. . . . I really think with two people or with more than two people, there really is unconscious communication. . . . it's in-between us somehow.

Brenda elaborated that this communication is not fully explained by metacommunication. Discussing transparency and authenticity in the clinical encounter, she explained how these factors relate to intuition: ". . . well, if the channel is open. Maybe that's really the bottom line . . . I think . . . it's unconscious. . . . I think people just feel—people just feel each other. They just do."

Deborah offers the term "transactional" to describe this understanding of intuition: for her, intuition is a "reciprocal process between the patient and the therapist." She believes what is communicated in the reciprocal process is the "unthought known," a term that other therapists used as well. Alejandro is perhaps the most explicit in his explanation of intuition as "unconscious communication" in conveying a similar concept.

Jeff suggested that intuition may be "something emanating from them [the client] or between me and them." Later he reiterated the relational nature of his clinical intuition. He stated that

> I probably have less intuition with clients I don't like as much and don't feel as close to. There are times when they're emitting verbally and in other ways so much toxic negativity I have to get behind cognitive Plexiglas. I don't think that's a good setup for intuition. . . . I think there has to be a mutual trust and a clinically appropriate sense of closeness for it to flow well.

The concept of cognitive Plexiglas introduces an understanding of Jeff's that he can protect himself, at least in part, from toxic negative energy by distancing himself cognitively from his patients.

Janet and Samantha also addressed the concept of a connection between themselves and their clients as an explanation for intuition. Janet noted that the client plays a role in this, in that they must be open to the process. She said, "the connection between the client, and what's happening with them, and their openness, and whether defenses are down allows me to access my intuition."

Samantha used the term "connectivity" to describe the two-person nature of her intuition: a connection between client and therapist. She specified that this connection requires the client to actively participate in the process for it to be effective: "It's reaching for someone to have them hopefully reach back. Connectivity. . . . I think in therapy, if the client's unable to connect, then they may not want to share for feeling that they may be being judged."

These two clinicians are pointing out that connection is a choice that clients make in whether to connect to a particular therapist or not. This points to a theme among our therapists that, to a certain extent, intuition is a participatory process that one (or both) parties choose to engage in. This contrasts with intuition that either comes easily or "unbidden," though the two understandings aren't mutually exclusive.

Perhaps the most dynamic understanding of this category, some clinicians explain intuition as part of an interpersonal process that inhabits the "space between" themselves and their clients, or the shared experience in which they are involved. This shared experience, whether it is termed unconscious communication, attunement, or connectivity, is key to their understanding of intuition. This observation is consistent with the suggestions made by clinicians that intuition may be associated with the transfer of information through an unknown medium or through energy. The distinction here is the source of that medium: whether it comes from a transpersonal source or simply as a product of the interaction of two people. The most promising part of this definition, in terms of therapy, is that it points to a certain amount of trust in "opening up" and that a therapeutic alliance has been formed.

A Natural/Normal Capacity

Some therapists use the term "gift" to describe their intuition while remaining clear that the gift is not unique or special, there is agreement that intuition is a normal human capacity that is available to everyone.

Elizabeth describes intuition as a "gift" and "normal" simultaneously: "I think it's a normal gift that you can recognize and reinforce repeatedly and have great respect for." Her emphasis on reinforcement, however, asserts that though intuition is a natural capacity in everyone, it still takes work to develop it.

Not all our therapists feel that intuition is equally available to everyone. Rather, it is a gift that approaches more the definition of a talent: Lena, Brenda, Lailla, Sarah, and Ellen elaborated on the perspective that was widespread among the therapists that intuition is a universal human capacity, but not everyone accesses or uses it. Lena indicated,

> I know everybody. . . [has intuition], but whether or not they're in touch with it . . . It's already there . . . you mentioned the word "trust" earlier. Teaching people to trust themselves, to open themselves up. . . . everybody has some intuition that they may or may not be in touch with.

Brenda specified that the gift may be developed. She stated,

> I think everybody has a capacity. I think the capacity can develop. To help that capacity develop, one thing is to model our own use of seeing the world big picture. One thing is to model our own use of intuition.

Lailla stressed that the gift is a potential that requires connecting in order to be actualized. She put it this way:

> I look at clinical intuition as part and parcel of this phenomenally complex configuration of who we are, as human beings. . . . We have the potential

> for it. It's there, innate. Whether it comes to the surface and we become aware of it and we use it—[depends on if] we are connected with ourselves.

Sarah also believes that orienting, or "tuning in" to this normal capacity is important to actualizing it.

> . . . we all have that capacity, but we all—we don't always use it. . . . It's there for everybody. I just tune into it. Right? I mean, that's true for all of us. . . . I think it's there. I think it's latent in some people, but I still think it's there.

Clinicians expressed an understanding of intuition that it is both a gift and a normal human capacity that may or may not be accessed or developed. For some, the gift emanates from a transpersonal source. For others, the origin of the "gift" is unspecified. There is widespread agreement that while the capacity is available to everyone, it may not be accessed or developed equally among all people.

Neurological

In the age of neuroscience, one may anticipate that therapists who described their views understand intuition in terms of neurological or more generally biological processes. Katherine and Grace suggested that mirror neurons may be implicated in intuition. Katherine stated, "I think it's just maybe our connection with other humans and mirror neurons." Grace echoed the explanation: "Well, I'm sure that there's some kind of neurological mirror neuron thing. . . "

From a biological perspective, Lailla gave an example of her use of intuition. Her client was describing an anticipated visit home to see his sick father. As her patient was describing the visit, Lailla got a mental image of people sitting at a table in a sunny kitchen. Her explanation for where this image came from was distinctly biological:

> The face, with my patient, I pay attention to what's going on. . . . That must have triggered a very subtle, in a very subtle way, . . . the group of neurons back there that had been involved when I was very little.

These therapists suggest that intuition may be, at least in part, explained by biological/neurological processes. Interestingly, in their descriptions of these processes, be they the activity of mirror neurons or other neurochemical processes, their explanations remain rooted in a two-person perspective. That is, the biological operations of intuition are triggered by or in some way involved with the material discussed by the client.

Bio-Psycho-Social-Spiritual

Therapists understand intuition as a complex phenomenon that is the culmination of several processes or factors interacting. These may be a combination of transpersonal and personal, nature and nurture, or bio-psycho-social-spiritual. Lailla was perhaps the most eloquent in describing this mixture of elements.

> . . . it's an unconscious meaning, a conscious meaning . . . it's a bio-psycho-social thing. . . . our life experiences literally construct, sculpt our nervous system. Our nervous system, in turn, constructs our life experiences. . . . my approach to these things is bio-psycho-social. It's complex. It doesn't honor one over the other. They are all important. That's who we are. Not one single area can do the whole job. All of that informs how I look at any subject, including intuition.

Lailla's integration of the complexity of factors that contribute to intuitive understanding reflects her ability to see the importance of each part that makes the whole of human experience. She is describing the essence of the intuitive process, openness to seeing the whole through its parts.

Brenda saw the combination of factors in intuition in terms of nature–nurture: "I think it's in combination. I think it's multiply determined. I think there's a genetic component. I think there's a life history." Brenda focused on understanding the complexity of biological and psychosocial aspects of experience serving as a basis for providing intuitive information.

A few of the participants added a spiritual dimension to the combination of factors that contribute to intuition. After identifying both considerable learning and experience as well as a transpersonal source for her intuition, Elizabeth suggested, "For me, it was the combination of the spiritual and the technical and the educative." Ann suggested,

> Sometimes it feels like it's from another place. Higher. If I'm dipping into the stream of . . . shared knowledge of the universe. Sometimes it feels like it's just a coming together of what I know and my experi-

> ence. . . . Sometimes it's probably a combination of all of those things and what the—just something in the other person, the client.

Elizabeth and Ann both connect intuitive knowledge to experience that spans the sacred and universal to the everyday of both therapist and client. They demonstrate an appreciation for levels of connection that contribute to understanding while giving them direction in their clinical process.

These excerpts suggest that therapists understand their intuition as a complex phenomenon that results from the coming together of many factors. These can be summarized in the label "bio-psycho-social"—or for some, "bio-psycho-social-spiritual." The important thing to gather from these complex assemblages of intuitive understanding is that it expresses itself differently in each person, even if some parts are experienced as universal.

Unknown

Many of the participants were comfortable with simply not knowing the source of their intuition. They discussed the mystery of the as-yet unknown. Elizabeth reflected,

> I think there's millions of dimensions. There's so much we have no idea about. I have great respect for that. . . . I just think that if you think about the whole universe, it's just so unfathomable. We're just this little teeny-weeny grain of sand. This is all we know, what we see. We're very three-dimensional, and there's probably many more dimensions. We could be coexisting on many different planes. I don't know. I just think it's worth saying that there's all of this out there that we don't know, and we have this little bit of a grasp of this thing called intuition. This is something that is not hocus-pocus. It's real and it's something we need to try to figure out.

In this passage, Elizabeth demonstrates her ability to think broadly about the universe and the impact that living on one of many possible worlds may have on intuition. She brings her thoughts back from what is unknown to the importance of understanding what we can know and the reality of intuition.

Lailla also expressed a respect for the unknown. In discussing the relationship between formal theory and clinical intuition, she concluded her observations with the recognition that there is simply much that we don't know.

> Well, I think theory, by definition, . . . means organizing a bunch of diverse things in a comprehensible way. I think that theory, to me, is there to be changed. . . . I think there's still a lot of things about intuition that we don't know . . . I'm open to finding out, but ask me how did I know about my friend's illness and death, and that my father was not doing well. I have no idea.

Dinah is perhaps the most confident in her understanding of intuition as a physical force. In her description of attunement, she understands that intuition is the result of others literally transmitting information, sometimes at a distance. She stated, "It's a gift to be able to pick up somebody sending you something from another country that I can feel." She went on to narrate an example. When she was in England, she had a dream wherein her sister told her that their father had died. Upon awakening, she learned that he had indeed died in a car accident in the United States. She explained, "Now that I've read more about the paranormal, I understand my sister came, somehow, to tell me that this had happened. At the same time." She recognized later in the interview that this process requires both parties to participate: "I guess it takes two tuned-in people to get attuned, of course!"

Dinah also indicated that she believes that inexplicable things are possible in the world:

> I think it's airy, but I think when I had my first dream about my father [that he had died], it was scary. I couldn't trust it. I couldn't believe it actually happened. I checked the dates, and checked the dates, and checked the dates. Then I said, "I believe people can move objects." I believe that a dog can follow its master from England to France and find it. I believe anything can happen.

It should be noted that Dinah's understanding of intuition as a paranormal function isn't unique among the therapists (the results were mixed on this category), yet she is uniquely confident in discussing this aspect of her intuition.

Alejandro, conversely, is comfortable not knowing the source of intuition, though he believes it's a dominant part of his thinking. He only suggests that it is a highly complex phenomenon and may in fact be several discrete phenomena. The complexity—possibly multiplicity—of the phenomenon places it beyond our current level of comprehension.

> . . . you start thinking of something greater than yourself, and very tiny and very well how do I know this stuff? . . . intuition is one of those

> things that they always say we use nine, ten percent of our brain and thoughts. There's 91 percent of us, be that brain, be that energy, be that wisdom, be that abilities, skills. Incredibly, incredibly, I think, sharp skills and things that other people may use or may have used in the past. . . . Intuition I think is the same. I think there is something that is 25—it's like what they call cancer. I think cancer is 20,000 things. I think intuition is a lot more. . . .

These clinicians related that they do not know where intuition comes from or what exactly it is. Partly because the phenomenon is so complex and partly because current understanding is so rudimentary, they are content in trusting their intuition without an explanatory model.

Summary and Discussion

Clinicians shared several different ways in which they understand their intuition that are consistent with others who have researched intuition. In some instances, they ascribe a transcendental (beyond-human) source to their experiences of intuition. This conforms with the findings of Jeffrey and Fish (2011), whose participants discussed a spiritual dimension to their intuition. Charles (2004) also reported a significant role for spirituality in the intuitive experiences of her research participants.

In other instances, the participants cited some unitive factor as an explanation. This factor was not understood to represent something beyond, but more between the therapist and client. The understanding affirms Jeffrey and Fish's (2011) findings. One of their participants made a statement that is very close to the understanding of some of the therapists who contributed to this book: "I think everything is connected" (p. 357).

Some of the participants understand their intuition to be related to the flow of energy. One participant elaborated that she believes that this energy carries information. This fits entirely with the finding cited in Chapter 5 (Forms of Clinical Intuition) that many of the participants have the subjective experience of feeling energy, the movement of energy, and/or shifts in energy.

Another common understanding among therapists in this study is that intuition is the product of accumulated knowledge, experience, and wisdom. This finding accords with learning theories of intuition noted in Chapter 1 (Current Knowledge and Perspectives), as well as the findings of Witteman, Spaanjaars, and Aarts (2012), who adopted a learning theory of intuition in their research. To review briefly, the learning theories of intuition hold in common the proposition that intuition is the result of having tacitly acquired information through repeated experience then implicitly or unconsciously processing this knowledge in a given circumstance to arrive at a split-second judgment. Some participants in the current study have suggested that they understand their intuition to be the result of prior learning and experience. Another corollary on acquired information through repeated information between this study and others is that Witteman, Spaanjaars, and Aarts found that for their participants, training and experience were viewed as important sources of intuition.

Three participants noted that they were aware of using consciously acquired information in the process of arriving at an intuitive insight, instead of, or perhaps along with, tacitly acquired information. The explicit information included the therapist's observations of the client's behavior. Witteman et al. (2012) found in a focus group that therapists referred to three different views regarding the source of their intuition. One of these views was that observations, or what they can explicitly see, informed their intuition. Along with observation, the therapists who contributed their expertise included knowledge from client records as part of the complex amalgam that culminates in knowing without knowing how they know.

The Jeffrey and Fish (2011) study also found that the therapists they interviewed understood intuition to be a two-person phenomenon. That is, they had the experience that the clients could make access to intuitively derived knowledge more or less difficult to acquire.

Our research findings conform for the most part to the studies we have referenced that were conducted in order to learn how clinicians understand intuition. In addition to these studies, there is a great deal of research on intuition that is applicable to psychotherapy practice including how it can be explained, where it comes from, and understanding about what causes it. Until there is broader understanding of the worldview reflected in quantum science and articulated in psi research as it relates to psychotherapy, it is important to be aware of the vast resources available to readers who want to explore and integrate intuitive processes.

Implications of Therapists' Understanding of Intuition

1. The source of intuition comes from the transcendent.
   Implication: Practitioners define the source of intuition in different ways; clinicians can work with their own understanding of the source.
2. Intuition reflects a unitive factor.

Implication: Viewed from the perspective of connection, intuition may be experienced as an all-encompassing connection that everything is part of a larger whole or oneness.

3. Intuition is experienced as energy that moves and carries information.
   Implication: The ability to tune in to, receive, and experience energy provides an important source of intuitive information.
4. Intuition is the product of accumulated knowledge, experience, and wisdom.
   Implication: Intuitive experience is supported through knowledge, life experience, and wisdom.
5. Intuition builds on conscious processes.
   Implication: Observing client behavior and knowledge obtained through client records and through other direct means contributes to intuitive processes.
6. Intuition is part of an interpersonal process.
   Implication: Intuitively derived knowledge is made more or less difficult to acquire based on the client's willingness and readiness to engage.
7. Intuition is a natural, normal human capacity.
   Implication: It can be developed by consciously choosing to pay attention to it, increasing awareness of the ways it personally unfolds, and learning to trust it.
8. Intuition is reflected in neurological/biological processes.
   Implication: Awareness of current understanding of neurology and biology informs intuitive processes.
9. Intuition is a complex phenomenon that includes biological, psychological, social, and spiritual elements.
   Implication: In its complexity, intuition involves all aspects of human experience.
10. Intuition is part of the mystery of life.
    Implication: Intuition is not dependent on any particular understanding of its origins or how it works; accepting it as part of the mystery of human experience does not impede its use.

Application of Understanding in the Therapeutic Setting

1. Start by making the decision to include intuition in your practice; it is a natural capacity that can be developed. Whether you are new to applying it professionally, have been working with it for some time, or have advanced practice skills, the principles are the same.

2. Remove intellectual barriers or biases against its use: remember there is nothing to fear. You are working on a set of skills that are grounded in decades of research.
3. Build clarity in your understanding of the source of intuition. Develop a narrative that explains the phenomena to you.
4. Connect with that source, asking for help according to your spiritual, cultural, or intellectual tradition.
5. Cultivate your connection to that source as you deepen your capacity to be fully present in mind, body, and spirit. Integrate your whole being.
6. Trust your impressions.
7. Develop your capacity to pay attention to their subtlety; they are the basis of developing intuitive capacity.
8. Establish ways to verify the accuracy of your impressions by asking questions, observing the unfolding clinical process, or simply holding them as hypotheses for later clarification.
9. Learn to use your intuition regularly. Skills develop over time.
10. Support your deepening intuitive awareness through balance in the physical, mental, and emotional aspects of your life. Your own peace and happiness are reflected in your ability to access your intuition.

Works Cited

Charles, R. (2004). *Intuition in psychotherapy and counselling*. London: Whurr.

Dossey, L. (2013). *One mind: How our individual mind is part of a greater consciousness and why it matters*. New York, NY: Hay House, Inc.

Jeffrey, A. J., & Fish, L. S. (2011). Clinical intuition: A qualitative study of its use and experience among marriage and family therapists. *Contemporary Family Therapy*, *33*, 348–363.

McTaggart, L. (2002). *The field: The quest for the secret force of the universe*. New York, NY: HarperCollins Publishers.

Targ, R. (2012). *The reality of ESP: A physicist's proof of psychic abilities*. Wheaton, IL: Theosophical Publishing House.

The Life Science Foundation. (2013). Retrieved January 3, 2015 from www.lifesciencefoundation.org/07Ways06.html#w61

Witteman, C. L. M., Spaanjaars, N. L., & Aarts, A. A. (2012). Clinical intuition in mental health care: A discussion and focus group. *Counselling Psychology Quarterly*, *25*(1), 19–29.

3 How Therapists Use Intuition in Therapy

In their book *The Use of the Self in Therapy* (1987), family therapists Virginia Satir and Michelle Baldwin write about a shift in the therapist's understanding from the role of a neutral observer to a fully engaged participant. To illustrate their point, they compare the use of the self of the therapists to that of a musician:

> I think of the instrument as the self of the therapist: how complete one is as a person, how well one cares for oneself, how well one is tuned into oneself, and how competent one is at one's craft being in tune with the self in order to accurately hear and understand the patient.
>
> (p. 24)

Satir and Baldwin's holistic view of the therapist and their dynamic engagement with patients can help us understand the goal of this chapter: i.e. how therapists go from an *awareness* of intuitively derived information to making *use* of it in practice.

The therapeutic relationship becomes a dynamic exchange between the therapist and patient. Having learned to trust her own experience, the therapist is receptive to the intuitive impressions she receives, tuning in to a level of communication with the patient that is beyond words and feelings.

The therapist's ability to listen intuitively is reflected in feeling and responding to the patient's rhythm, their timing, awareness of changing themes, and recognizing their texture and tone. In this way, the therapist takes in the essence of the patient in what Siegel (2010) describes as attuning "into our own inner world." Siegel (p. 34), elaborating further, uses the metaphor of dance as "reveal(ing) the deep reality that we are part of a larger whole, that we need one another, and, in some ways that we are created by the ongoing dance within, between, and among us" (p. 56).

Whether in the metaphor of music or dance, a relationship is developed that is neither hierarchical nor linear. By establishing connection in this way, the therapist comes to know the patient in ways they otherwise would not have. In the words of Evelyn Underhill,

> We know a thing only by uniting with it; by assimilating it; by an interpenetration of it and our selves . . . Wisdom is the fruit of communion; ignorance the inevitable portion of those who . . . stand apart, judging, analyzing the things which they have never truly known.
>
> (*Practical Mysticism*, p. 7)

From the moment of first contact between clinician and patient, whether by phone or in person, intuition informs the treatment process. In joining the patient by listening to the words spoken and simultaneously allowing awareness of how it feels to hear *this* patient in *this* particular moment, the therapist endeavors with goodwill and nonjudgment to understand. It is the ability to have singular focus on the client in this way that the therapist reaches a level of attunement that supports intuitive decision making.

From a research perspective, Bhugra, Easter, Mallaris, and Gupta (2011, p. 410) found that psychiatrists use a "complex combination of experience and intuition, training and evidence," with intuition being one of the most important factors in making decisions about symptom presentation and diagnosis (407). Novice clinicians reported relying more on an analytical approach than expert clinicians, who rely more on their intuition (403). Research by Srivastava and Grube (2009) also found that intuition is an important component of psychiatric diagnosis. They concluded that it is not clearly inferior to other diagnostic tools, recommending that it "should be used to modify, guide, and suggest diagnosis, including in the determination of the genuineness of self-report independent of diagnosis" (99). They point out that intuitive decision making may also be important in emergencies when time does not allow for alternative diagnostic approaches (104). These studies support the role of intuition in diagnostic and treatment decisions. The distinction Bhugra et al. found between novice and expert clinicians in their reliance on intuition may be more than a difference in experience levels; it may reflect different levels of awareness of and trust in their intuitive capacities. With time and experience, therapists learn that they can trust their intuition as a valid source of information.

Building on initial impressions, intuition continues to inform treatment decisions by supporting the development of a collaborative working relationship. The therapist actively engages in building internal resonance with the content of the conscious and unconscious messages the client is communicating. The therapist's integration of these messages reflects attunement that provides a context of safety for the patient. As the patient speaks, the therapist develops deepening awareness of the patient's inner world through the images, words, feelings, and knowing experienced in their presence. This includes the underlying themes that the patient is communicating that may be just outside of awareness. Beyond the words spoken, patients open the door to their inner world, reflecting the complexity of underlying feelings, emotions, and personality patterns. Therapists use intuition to listen to these multiple levels of information that are being communicated and to solidify a positive therapeutic relationship.

Articulating intuitive thoughts with good timing helps provide clarity and insight for both patient and therapist in the building of relationship resonance. Intuitive impressions can be introduced naturally and easily as part of the conversation when the therapist is seeking to refine understanding of the patient. Intuition is particularly useful when the patient agrees with and builds upon the observations the therapist has made refining their shared understanding.

Therapists also use intuition to support patients in their ability to explore alternative ways of thinking and experiencing their lives and relationships. This provides data relevant to diagnosis, direction, and length of treatment. Patients' ability for self-reflection, feelings of agency and empowerment, and desire for and commitment to change each factor into the outcome of treatment.

As patients' feelings of agency grow in the therapeutic relationship, trust deepens and material that may never have been discussed is articulated, perhaps for the first time in the patient's life. This is a positive indication that the therapeutic alliance is strong and deepening. In trusting that all thoughts that arise are important, the therapist can confirm that there is forward momentum. This form of free association supports intuitive insights that strengthen patients' self-knowledge and inner cohesion.

Intuition allows for individualization of sessions by allowing them to unfold in their own way. Doing so reflects the ability of the therapist to have an authentic relationship in which the needs of the patient are honored as central to the direction each session takes. By trusting the patient and the process, therapists teach by way of example. In turn, patients learn to trust themselves, the therapist, and the therapeutic process. The depth of what is shared with the therapist reflects how safe the patient feels.

Therapists found that intuition helps them decide on a direction for treatment, both in the moment to guide a specific session, as well as between sessions. For the therapists in this study, finding direction when the treatment process was stuck was noteworthy. This is very close to the findings of the Witteman, Spaanjaars, and Aarts (2012) study. Their mental health professionals relied on intuition when they felt uncertainty. Likewise, Welling (2005) hypothesized that intuitive clues are particularly useful with therapeutic impasses, when the therapist is caught up in the idiosyncratic functioning of the patient, when neither theory nor rational thinking can resolve it.

The therapists found additional benefits in using intuition that have not been explored in previous research. The list of possible benefits is quite impressive. Given that a few of these findings have also been uncovered in previous studies, a small corpus is beginning to build. The overall direction the collected research is taking is toward recommending clinical intuition as a valuable practice tool and a subject of a great deal more research.

Bove and Rizzi (2009) use the term "nonconscious" to describe the implicit nature of intuition to distinguish that it is not "unconscious" and related to "repressed" material (39) but rather that intuition serves as a tool, enabling the therapist to "consider carefully what is occurring so as to maintain a profitable link between explicit and implicit, verbal and nonverbal, aware and non-aware aspects of process" (p. 44).

The intuitive timing of comments or questions includes awareness of developing insight that is shared when the patient seems likely to be able to understand the meaning they encapsulate. Intuition plays a role in developing awareness of overarching patterns of thought and behavior that are often key to the removal of barriers to accurate perception. As the patient develops clarity about thought patterns that have clouded current perceptions, increasing freedom is experienced. Behaviors that originally developed as ways of coping with emotions including trauma, conflict, and longstanding patterns of abuse and neglect come to light, as do the mechanisms that were triggered to manage them. As clarity develops, confusion dissolves, resulting in new behaviors. Choices can now be made from an inner sense of freedom that comes from living in the present.

Bove and Rizzi (2009) address the intuitive capacity of the therapist as a healthy "nonconscious" aspect of the relationship that underlies the entire process, creating a relational healing environment. The usefulness of the therapist's intuitive capacity to access layers of experience that cannot be retrieved by the patient alone goes to the heart of the therapeutic task: to identify and remove barriers to health (Satir & Baldwin, 1987).

Perceiving the Hidden

In treatment, a therapist can use intuition to help determine what is "hidden." This may be unarticulated/unconscious needs, experiences, or feelings the client may be defending against. Therapists are able to know what is not being said or surfaced in treatment through the use of their intuition.

One way that intuition may accomplish this "uncovering" is by overriding intellectually derived conclusions. Jeff discussed this in relation to knowing what his client may be feeling. He states that while his intellect suggests that the client may be experiencing something in particular, his intuition may give him a more accurate understanding of his client's underlying feelings: "It's often been . . . that my intellect says, 'I think they're crying about this,' and then an intuition will say, 'OH, maybe it's that thing they told you many sessions ago about this or that.' "

Intuition can fill in gaps in terms of knowing something that the client is not consciously aware of, or is unable to articulate. Lena had worked on a battered women's hotline prior to becoming an LCSW. She explained how she used her intuition to understand what was not apparent with her clients.

> . . . on the hotline, . . . I didn't even have the person in front of me. I had to deal with them as—where they were and intuit many times their reason for calling. Many times they didn't know. They knew they called because they knew something happened. They weren't sure. They just knew they were in a dark place. They were having nightmares and sleeplessness and PTSD-like symptoms. They saw the Victim Assistance Network. It's now called something else. They just called this number, cuz they thought somebody could help them. Being part of somebody's initial efforts to reach out and deal with something that they weren't even really quite—they weren't cognitively in touch with. They knew something was wrong. . . . I would be able to formulate questions that would assist them in telling—cuz I wasn't gonna tell them why they called . . . I don't think I could have done the work without that ability to intuit through many, many levels of experience. What I'm experiencing from the person.

In some cases, the hidden material may help therapists understand how the client's internal experience contributes to dysfunctional behavior. For Ann, the ability to use intuition to see beyond what the client was presenting, to understand what the client may be experiencing internally, helped her to be able to work effectively with particularly difficult clients. She gave this example:

> I was working with a woman who's very personality-disordered, really difficult, really—everything you did was wrong. I mean, difficult to work with. Just pushed you away and denigrated you and dismissed you and everything. I just had this gut sense of this terrified child in there and terrified person and tried to stay—to stay connected to that in the midst of it.

Several therapists discussed how intuition helps them know important material that the client is not saying. Sarah referenced this use: "It's not what they say [that] makes me connect to an intuitive feeling, more than filling in the blanks, what they don't say." In some cases, this is because the client is purposely withholding information. Brenda related a case example in which she was able to access this kind of material:

> They were pretty newlywed. It seemed like there was something weird about the wife's relationship with the father-in-law. It just came to me as they were sitting there . . . That there was something sexually way off . . . I just felt like there was something sexually very incestuous going on. It was borne out when they were talking . . . the husband described his wife and his father—they were on a family picnic. They went off in the woods holding hands.

She later stated that with intuition, "You can tell when somebody's holding back from you or not." Samantha also uses intuition to apprehend something that the client is withholding. She related that it helps her, "Maybe sensing or knowing that something's not completely relaxed or quite right with somebody, that they're feeling something that they're just not sharing, and they don't have to tell you. . . "

Sometimes this sense comes as an awareness that something is not right, or that something is "off." Sharon gave an example of having such an experience.

> . . . you're listening, and all of a sudden it [intuition] says, "uh, something is wrong with what I'm hearing. There's something else." . . . I question "where is this really going? Is something else going on here that's not revealed yet?"

She went on to describe how her intuition alerts her that something is not right. "I'm thinking, 'Mmmm, something's not right here. Something doesn't feel right.'" She elaborated that with a specific client, this feeling led her to "challenge what I was hearing." By acting on her feeling of unease, she discovered, "Indeed, he [the client] was drinking."

Another common experience among the therapists is the intuitive sense that something is missing. Jennifer discussed this feeling. She said, "There's a sense here that maybe something's missing from the story. . . . Or maybe there is some sort of substance abuse going on I'm not getting—it's a piece that—it's like a sense."

A few of the therapists indicated that one class of information that they may gain about a client are those feelings against which the client may be defending. Brenda explained that sometimes intuition gives her a sense that "I feel like the person is really defending against some strong feeling." David gave a more involved explanation:

> There are times when I'll say to someone, "I just had a very strong feeling." I usually use the word "feeling." "It doesn't seem to fit with how you're talking to me about what's going on." My experience is that when that happens in here, it's often because it's hard for the person that I'm sitting with to have that feeling himself . . . That's a launching pad for talking about what came to me in a way that was not verbally communicated.

The ability to know the internal state of the client, what they need, how they feel, or what they are experiencing, can be extremely helpful in the clinical encounter, especially when this material is not surfaced directly in the consulting room. By using intuition, the therapists were able to understand their clients and the relevant issues beyond what they could ascertain through overt communication.

Perceiving Dynamics, Patterns, and Overarching Themes

Intuition may also help therapists understand dynamics, or patterns that are relevant to the client's functioning and/or the clinical process. This ability to step back and see the larger processes helps clinicians see the big picture and more effectively note changes.

The interviewer asked Justin to describe how he uses intuition clinically. He responded, "when I would start to see patterns with clients. . . " Brenda articulated a similar experience, using the term "big picture" to describe her ability to intuitively grasp overarching themes. She said,

> I think . . . part of being intuitive—is I look at someone or a situation, and I feel like I can get the big picture pretty quickly . . . For example,

> when I do couples work or family work, it comes in very handy. I can just see what's going on. I can see the pattern of how they're interacting and how they're using each other.

Ellen conceptualizes the target of therapeutic change to be whole systems. She described how her intuition helps her to understand how the relevant systems are operating within a specific case: "I can see how systems work sometimes that I don't know that other people would see that, and go 'what is it?'" She gave an example of a couple in treatment. She intuitively grasped that an issue, which had been identified as the husband's problem, was actually related to the wife's functioning: "She was the one that needed all the help." Ellen stressed that a previous therapist had not been able to determine this underlying dynamic. The identification of the dynamic had a profound effect on the client and rendered the therapy process highly productive.

One of the specific patterns that a therapist noted was enactments. Deborah stated that her intuition is important in alerting her that she and the client are engaged in this kind of patterned dynamic.

> When I begin to feel something that the other party is experiencing and when I feel that way know that it's usually . . . a repeated, old-history situation that we're into. An enactment kind of way of being, something that's getting enacted that needs to be talked to.

Intuition can be helpful in giving therapists information that goes beyond what the client is able to share and beyond the client's experience. This includes seeing larger patterns or dynamics, or how systems are operating within a given case. Understanding such core patterns allows the therapist to target change in a way that will have maximum impact.

Knowing Aspects of the Client's Past

Related to larger dynamics or patterns, intuition may help therapists gain insight into relevant aspects of a client's childhood, or how a client's past may be influencing present dynamics. Elizabeth had a startling example of intuition helping her understand how an event in a client's past related to his current situation.

> There was a gentleman that I was seeing, and he had a lot of anxiety and fear. For some reason, my instinct was telling me to tread back and

> find out when there were other times in his life that he experienced the same sensation. We went back, back, and he was—we talked about the various times. Then we went back to a time when he was a young adult . . . When we were talking, at some point, I got this really clear image of him at a lake. He was flailing in water and panicking and terrified that he was going to drown. Obviously, he didn't.
>
> That's as far as I got with it, but it was really clear, so I asked him. I said, "Have you ever had any incidents while you were on vacation?" I didn't want to say I had this picture in my head of you're almost drowning. It popped up in his head right away. He was telling me about it. It was that same sensation that anytime that his life was really being threatened, or he felt it was being threatened—I'm sure it wasn't that major in subsequent years, but. . . [the dynamic] played over and over and over again.

Other examples are perhaps less dramatic. Ann related, "Well, often, when I'm working with people who've been through abuse, I see them as a—as a child, I can see their family situation or what I imagine it to have been." She gave an example of an administrator who worked at a hospital in which the participant had worked. She described the woman as "very harsh." She elaborated, "I had this just immediate sensation. She wasn't loved enough. It just came into my head. Ah, someone did not love her enough."

These examples suggest that therapists might successfully use intuition to help them understand how their clients' pasts may be operating in or influencing the present, opening the potential for deepening the therapeutic dialogue.

Building Rapport

Understanding the client more deeply, beyond what they are able to articulate, builds the therapeutic alliance. The therapists supported this insight and explained that intuition can help them enhance the therapeutic alliance, develop rapport, and/or respond empathetically to their client.

One way that intuition helps with rapport is by quickly getting to what is most important to the client. Elizabeth noted this ability when she reported that her intuition helps her cut to the core issues, which in turn builds rapport: "I can . . . make someone feel really relaxed because they feel very understood. It goes along more quickly because I teach social work, and you have to develop rapport."

Another way intuition builds rapport is by helping patients feel understood. As such, intuition is therefore an important element in empathy. Jeff discussed this feature.

> . . . having intuition. . . [is] centrally a part of our work. It enables the client and the therapist to build a stronger rapport. . . . it brings forward a different kind of relationship with the client, a much more at ease relationship with the client. . .

Lailla also addressed this aspect of clinical intuition. She related that intuition helps her both "understand [the client], [and] demonstrate they're understood." This theme was echoed repeatedly in the interviews. Jessica observed,

> I think it's a satisfying realization [for the client] that I get it, . . . "Yeah! That's exactly what I feel like. Yeah. That explains it." It's that— . . . empathic attunement . . . It's comforting maybe . . . It feels like, "Yes. You know exactly—yes, that's exactly it. You get it." . . . [it helps in] developing a client–therapist relationship and developing a sense of trust. All of that is very important. I think this adds to that . . . in that the client feels like yeah, I really get exactly what they're feeling or what their experience was like. . .

Katherine indicated that intuition is helpful in reflecting the client's experience, which helps them feel cared for. She stated, "I'm able to say something and the client comes back and says, 'exactly.'" The interviewer asked her directly if she thinks it enhances the clinical process. She responded, "Yeah, I think so . . . because I think they're trying to express something maybe deep within themselves and I'm showing them that I really understand. I think in the moment they feel cared for and understood."

For Jennifer, the strength of the therapeutic alliance, which is dependent on intuition, allows her to know when she can take risks to help move the treatment forward.

> I feel like I can take risks without offending, that we can work—I can, in a way, pitch something. . . . I can explore more easily. . . . There's a sense of even if I'm off a little, she would cue me. . . . There is an efficacy and efficiency as well as a strong bond.

Samantha discussed how this rapport that is built on intuition has a distinct clinical advantage:

> I think using intuition with that person to have them feel safe and be able to connect, they'll share more with me. Then I can maybe get deeper to the root and find out if they seriously are in trouble or need hospitalization or if they're suicidal.

Intuition is used to help clients feel understood, to strengthen the therapeutic alliance, and to build rapport. This is accomplished by enabling the therapist to see beyond what the client is consciously aware of or able to discuss. Consciously deciding to access information intuitively helps therapists understand and communicate with clients to strengthen the therapeutic relationship.

Self-Disclosure

Whether or not to disclose personal information is an important decision in the course of treatment with the potential for impacting the therapeutic alliance in both positive and negative ways. Discernment about the reasons for self-disclosure is an important skill. Therapists in this study shared their experiences with intuitive insights informing their decisions.

Therapists are taught that the decision to self-disclose should be based on the client's needs, but how do you know the effect your self-disclosure will have on your client? Katherine related that she uses intuition to determine whether self-disclosure is therapeutic in a given moment or not. She said, "I think I just know when it would be maybe safe to share and other times not . . ." Natalie also noted the usefulness of intuition in deciding when and what to self-disclose:

> . . . sometimes I'll use my intuition and I'll share something personal, either a feeling I'm having as they're talking, or some experience that seems to fit in. I often will use my intuition in helping me decide, is that something I should self-disclose, or not? . . . I think when I do that, I'm being really authentic. . . . I'm always surprised at how sometimes they'll thank me for sharing what I shared.

Diagnosis

Some of the therapists indicated that they use their intuition to alert them to possible diagnoses. Grace stated, "I've just started seeing a woman, and I knew as soon as she walked in the room that her traumatic history was just walkin' in there with her." Sharon indicated that she uses her intuition to help with differential diagnoses: "When it comes down to differential diagnosis, . . . something would sling me in one direction or another to inquire on a symptomatology." Finally, Dinah and Sarah both indicated that people with personality disorders often trigger an intuitive sense. Dinah observed, "I can feel somebody very narcissistic right away."

Individualizing Treatment

The therapists who discussed clinical intuition felt strongly about manualized treatment protocols and the dehumanizing effect of overrelying on these methods for treatment. They reported that their intuition helped them to individualize treatment: to deliver what a specific client needs in a manner that is more likely to be usable by that client. Grace is one such example:

> Well, certainly [I use intuition to create] spontaneous interventions . . . because it's not like I approach them formulaically, like, "okay, every time we're gonna do this," or, "At this moment in the session, this is what happens." That's always arising out of something I'm sensing and hearing, is like, "Oh, oh, I think we could go somewhere with this."

Justin described a termination that did not unfold as terminations are described or prescribed in texts. He allowed himself to conduct the session based on his intuitions of what the client needed at the time. Upon reflection, he determined, "I think that was the right way to go, because it did end up being fruitful. It was a good session." He elaborated on using intuition to individualize treatment:

> I think it was intuition that was telling me, "You don't wanna do what . . . you have been trained to do . . . No, that's really not gonna work in this situation. I don't think it's best clinically, but I think we can get more out of it if we just go with what we have today." I think that was the intuition.

Lena also uses her intuition to guide her to meet the unique needs of each client. She related,

> I have to utilize intuition all the time to figure out how to engage them in a process that will work within their—the way they operate in the world.

> It's different for every single person. I don't have a methodology that is a one-size-fits-all. If I'm not intuitive about each person walking through my door from the time I have an intake with them, I would be lost.

Another way intuition can enhance treatment is by helping the therapist determine which theory to use at any given time. David uses his intuition to help him determine which theory may be most beneficial to his client. He observed, "My intuition guides my use and the application of theory." This suggests that clinicians who use intuition know and can implement multiple theories. The vast majority of the therapists who discussed their clinical use of intuition with us endorsed an integrated approach to treatment.

Clinicians noted that they use intuitively acquired information to help them meet each client as an individual, enabling them to shape their interventions in ways that are most beneficial to each client with thoughtful timing.

Inform the Direction of Treatment

Very closely related to individualizing treatment, the therapists in this study use intuition in the clinical encounter to help them determine the direction to take with a client, as well as using intersession intuitive knowledge to help guide the direction of the next session. They found that intuition was particularly helpful in moving treatment forward when they felt stuck.

Janet provides an example of a therapist who uses intuition to help her decide on a direction for therapy within a session. She stated that when she works on an intuitive level the work is "very deep," and "then I can come up with what I wanna say next, how I want to interact with that part that has now become a stream."

Justin described how he uses his intuition for most aspects of treatment, including helping him to direct the session:

> I mean, a thought will arise, or a feeling will arise, and then that will often instruct where we're going in the therapy. . . . I mean [it informs] everything, about assessment, about treatment, about plan . . . where we're going in the session. . . . the thoughts and feelings that arise for you as a direction to go. . . . Sometimes I'm aware of saying something like, "I'm having a thought," and floating that out and seeing what the

> client does with it. I think I tend to say that more. Sometimes I might say, "I'm having this feeling that—" and so I might float that out there that way. Other times, I might not be sharing it with the client. . . . but it still might inform where I might go in a session.

When Justin discussed teaching students and early-career therapists about using intuition, he replied,

> [teach them] to pay more attention to what are the thoughts that are arising. What are the feelings that are arising? Maybe what are the sensations that are arising? Then from that, how they might then make that transition to what to do with that and how that might inform decision-making and might be a guide, in terms of where the session may go.

Sarah discussed how she will have intuitive insights between sessions that help her find a direction for the next session. She finds that intuitive insights come when she writes her treatment notes. "When that happens, I always underline it, so that when I look at the note . . . before the next session, I always—I emphasize that." Jennifer also uses intersession intuition. When she sets her attention on a client between sessions, she may have an experience in which she realizes, "Oh, you know what? That's something I want to go back to," or "I think I want to see if this works."

Several of the therapists in the study suggested that they use their intuition to help them find a direction when the treatment feels stuck. Elizabeth described this common experience:

> when I see a client, if I'm having a difficulty with it. . . [I will use intuition] and have some clarity about what direction I need to go in. Then when I'm with the person, oftentimes, it's just right.

Jeff put it in these terms:

> When I'm working with a client, and I'm—maybe I'm really stuck on where we're going, or what we're doing, I use intuition, and then I usually ask the question, "You're saying to me, that there are times in your marriage, where you feel lonely?" . . . I think that something will come to me, and I have an "Ah ha, this feels like, this feels like sadness," or "this feels like trauma." Then I will ask the question about that. . . . we use intuition to move forward in our work. . .

Grace experiences her intuition somatically. She described how she uses her physical reactions "to tell me where there—where something might feel stuck or uncomfortable. Then we might work with that, so check that out. . . "

Intuition can also help with the direction of treatment by alerting the therapist where not to go, when not to act or respond, when not to pursue a thread or intervene. Lena and Natalie shared this experience. Lena highlighted the fact that sometimes her intuition leads her away from pursuing a specific track. "Would the intuition be saying, 'do this,' or maybe the intuition would be saying, 'Don't do this.' " Sometimes her intuition informs her "when to say nothing at all." She related a case in which a youth presented as uncooperative and disengaged. She intuitively felt that she should not press him. She stated, "The intuition I had was not to tell him what to do, not to push him, not to do anything at all, except accept him for who he was." The judgement was fruitful: she chose to refrain from pursuing him, and the young man engaged and completed a successful treatment.

Natalie shared that her intuition helps her decide whether or not to address some of the information that she has intuitively accessed in regard to underlying or larger issues: "I can choose, once I'm aware of it, I can figure out, do I need to use it? Should I not use—you know, that thing."

The therapists related that their intuition helps them move treatment forward when it begins to feel stuck. It also helps them determine a direction to take a particular session. The direction may be based on a choice of where not to go or what not to do in any given situation. Intersession intuition helps them determine a direction for future sessions.

Being on the Right Track

Intuition may also help clinicians determine that treatment is proceeding on the right track. Janet stated that when she has an experience that she identifies as intuition, "When that happens, I think that's when I'm able to sense that some kind of wisdom, or some sort of message . . . a sense of what feels right. . . " Janet shared this experience:

> I can't say it's always right, but the times when I've been able to access it, it feels like I'm on the right track, on the right wavelength. I may not know in that moment; I may not know that day in that hour, that my intuition and how I'm able to communicate that had an impact in the way that I hoped it would, but sometimes get that feedback. . .

Janet suggest that intuition helps her move the treatment process forward in a productive manner, sensing when it "feels right." She describes her experience as one of intuitive sensing of wisdom and connection with her patient who she comes to know as "being on the right track."

A Possible Future for the Client

Hope is an important part of any treatment process. Not only must the client have hope in order to move forward, but the therapist must also from time to time draw on hopefulness in order to continue the forward momentum. Intuition can help therapists gain some insight into a possible future for the client, engendering hopefulness as well as a target state that the therapist and client can work toward. As important as hope is, a therapist's ability to discern a possible future may also warn therapists of potential problems that may lie ahead for the client.

A few of the therapists related that they use intuition to help them anticipate what may happen in the future. For Elizabeth, this was a devastating awareness.

> I remember on one particular occasion, it was rather unique, a woman was sitting with me, and I had this voice in my head that said, "This woman's going to die." She was perfectly fine, and she did. . . . It was very unsettling. The poor woman was sitting there, telling me about a problem she was having with her boyfriend, and I'm sitting there thinking, this woman's gonna die. It took me a while to recollect myself so that I could be attentive.

While this was unusual for Elizabeth, anticipating the difficult circumstances that may lie ahead undoubtedly offered perspective on her patient's current concerns. Elizabeth's experience of her patient's imminent death is important because it helps link intuition to premonition. Premonition, as Dossey points out, literally translates to "forewarning." Elizabeth's ability to open herself to intuitive messages offers an explanation of how receptivity is a key component to deciphering precognitive impressions.

For other therapists, having an awareness of a possible future was a more hopeful, positive experience. It allows them to help clients move toward that perceived improvement.

David explained,

> I think I have a strong sense that things can get better. I will communicate that to a patient that I'm working with. I might say, "You don't have to believe this right now. You might not even be able to take this in right now. I can hold the optimism or the hope for both of us for right now." . . . in other words, that that person could get better, and have a better life, and struggle less.

Dinah also suggested this use. She said, "We're 'placeholders,' and we're kind of 'hope merchants.' . . . I do [intuitively] see the potential."

Summary and Discussion

The therapists in this study explained that they use intuition to inform almost every aspect of treatment. The therapists are able to gain understanding of their clients, especially acquiring insights into things about which the client is unaware or unable to articulate. They also gain awareness of dynamics and patterns that are important to the client's functioning. This may include aspects of the client's past that are relevant to their current situation.

Perhaps, in part due to the deep understanding intuition imparts to the therapists, they are better able to build a therapeutic alliance. They feel better equipped to determine when and what to self-disclose, as well as make differential diagnoses. They use intuitive insights to individualize treatment and determine a direction treatment might take both within and between sessions. Intuition may also alert therapists that treatment is proceeding appropriately. Finally, therapists can use intuition to ascertain a possible future—for better or worse—that may be before their clients.

These findings confirm the findings of existing research. In relation to a deeper understanding of the client, Charles (2004) found that therapists use intuition to help them attune empathetically to their clients. Welling (2005) made a similar point. He noted that clinical intuition may add to the efficiency of the therapeutic process by saving time, as important information may be available that would otherwise be obtained later by ordinary means.

Our study found that intuition helps therapists decide on a direction for treatment, in the moment to guide a specific session as well as using intuition while reflecting on clients between sessions to decide on a direction for the next session. For the therapists in this study, finding direction when the treatment process was stuck was noteworthy. This is very close to the findings of the Witteman et al. (2012) study. Their mental health professionals relied on intuition when they felt uncertainty. Likewise, Welling (2005) hypothesized that intuitive clues are particularly useful with therapeutic impasses, when the therapist is caught up in the idiosyncratic functioning of the patient, where neither theory nor rational thinking can resolve it.

The therapists found additional benefits to using intuition in the clinical context that have not been explored in previous research. The list of possible benefits to using clinical intuition that they have identified is quite impressive. Given that a few of these findings have also been uncovered in previous studies, a small corpus is beginning to build. The overall direction the collected research takes is toward recommending clinical intuition as a valuable practice tool, and a subject of a great deal more research.

Given the potential benefits intuition may confer on the psychotherapy process, therapists may be well-advised to build their intuitive capacities. This begins with an open mind. A sense of experimentation, exploring the potential meaning and testing the utility of passing senses, is the first step. Many of the possible subtle stimuli that warrant attention are discussed in the following chapters.

Trust is another important component of enhancing clinical intuition. This trust, as will be explored, must be premised on a high degree of self-awareness and a deep, genuine caring for the client. Even under these conditions, the necessity is to trust but verify. Wondering with a client if an intuitively derived insight is relevant can serve to surface material that may not have arisen otherwise, without imposing an agenda on your client. Being open to the possibility of intuitive insights has great potential to benefit virtually every stage and aspect of psychotherapeutic treatment.

Related Research

Our findings confirm existing research. In relation to a deeper understanding of the client, Charles (2004) found that therapists use intuition to help them attune empathetically to their clients. Welling (2005) made a similar point. He noted that clinical intuition may add to the efficiency of the therapeutic process by saving time, as important information may be available that would otherwise be obtained later by ordinary means.

The therapists in our study found that intuition helps them decide on a direction for treatment, in the moment to guide a specific session as well as using intuition while reflecting on clients between sessions to decide on a direction for the next session. For the therapists in this study, finding direction when the treatment process was stuck was noteworthy. This is very close to the findings of the Witteman et al. (2012) study. Their mental health professionals relied on intuition when they felt uncertainty. Likewise, Welling (2005) hypothesized that intuitive clues are particularly useful with therapeutic impasses, when the therapist is caught up in the idiosyncratic functioning of the patient, where neither theory nor rational thinking can resolve it.

Implications of Therapists' Use of Intuition

Participants found intuition useful across the treatment process. To recap, intuition is useful in working with clients in:

1. Perceiving the hidden
   Implication: Intuition provides the therapist with clues that access thoughts and experiences that may be intentionally or inadvertently hidden in the patient's presentation.
2. Perceiving dynamics, patterns, and overarching themes
   Implication: Intuition helps in understanding the client's experience, what s/he is feeling, and the underlying dynamics and patterns, both conscious and unconscious.
3. Knowing aspects of the client's past
   Implication: Intuition provides information from the client's past that is relevant to issues being addressed in the present.
4. Building rapport
   Implication: Intuition is a key tool in relationship building.
5. Decisions about self-disclosure
   Implication: Intuition supports the therapist's inner work of determining appropriate self-disclosure decisions.
6. Establishing diagnosis
   Implication: Intuitive impressions and awareness support connecting complex symptoms into a whole to support arriving at an accurate diagnosis.
7. Individualizing treatment
   Implication: The intuitive process is directed toward discerning the nuances of each person's unique life experience and the reasons for seeking treatment.
8. Informing the direction of treatment
   Implication: As connection develops in the therapeutic dyad resonance builds, intuition aids in directing treatment pathway decisions that are co-created.

9. Being on the right track
   Implication: Relationship resonance informed by the intuitive capacities to see, feel, hear, and know clearly grows so that both therapist and client experience therapy as working effectively.
10. Seeing a possible future for the client
   Implication: The clinician may anticipate the potential growth and difficulties the patient may experience in the future based on an intuitively informed assessment of current thoughts and behaviors projected into the future.

Application of Intuition in the Therapeutic Setting

1. Clear your mind of judgments and expectations; allow impressions to arise.
2. Trust that they hold important information; don't second-guess them.
3. Allow the free-floating thoughts that come up to fill in the gaps in your understanding.
4. Familiarize yourself with your intuition by observing the clarity that develops when you integrate the logic of the left brain and the creativity of the right brain.
5. Memorize the feeling of accurate, validated intuitive impressions.
6. Recognize how you feel when you are working in an intuitive state of awareness.
7. Build your awareness of the clinical dialogue that occurs when you are in this creative state.
8. Develop your ability to feel the energy in clinical process; what impasse feels like, when you feel stuck or your patient indicates they don't feel their issues are being addressed.
9. Pay attention to how you resolve the blocks to forward momentum and what has occurred that has created a shift in energy.
10. Learn to identify how you experience the different types of intuitive process: clairvoyance, clairaudience, clairsentience, and claircognizance.

Works Cited

Bhugra, D., Easter, A., Mallaris, Y., & Gupta, S. (2011). Clinical decision making in psychiatry by psychiatrists. *Acta Psychiatrica Scandinavica, 124*(5), 403–411.

Bove, S., & Rizzi, M. (2009). Listening to intuition: Reflections on unconscious processes in the therapeutic relationship. *Transactional Analysis Journal*, 39(1), 39–45.

Charles, R. (2004). *Intuition in psychotherapy and counselling*. London: Whurr.

Dossey, L. (2009). *The power of premonitions*. New York, NY: Penguin.

Satir, V., & Baldwin, M. (1987). *The use of the self in therapy*. Binghamton, NY: Haworth Press.

Srivastava, A., & Grube, M. (2009). Does intuition have a role in psychiatric diagnosis? *Psychiatric Quarterly, 80*, 99–106.

Underhill, E. (1915). *Practical mysticism*. PDF version. Found online at http://www.anglicanlibrary.org/underhill/UnderhillPracticalMysticism.pdf.

Welling, H. (2005). The intuitive process: The case of psychotherapy. *Journal of Psychotherapy Integration, 15*(1), 19–47.

Witteman, C. L. M., Spaanjaars, N. L., & Aarts, A. A. (2012). Clinical intuition in mental health care: A discussion and focus group. *Counselling Psychology Quarterly, 25*(1), 19–29.

4 Focus of Therapists' Attention

There's an epiphany at the close of the Rumi poem "Only Breath" in which he promotes "disciplined silence" as a way of understanding another person: "There is a way between voice and presence / Where information flows" (line 17; ll.15–16; Coleman Barks translation). There, the reader is left, in typical Rumi fashion, with enough questions about what that silent space between "voice and presence" is to ponder how it applies to their own practice.

Rumi's "disciplined silence" speaks to the topic of this chapter on focus and intuition. In the context of our research, the shift is a movement of attention by the therapist from logical discourse to focusing on the experience of listening and being in the presence of our patients. From this perspective, we are introduced to the inner-, inter-, and transpersonal elements of focus in intuitive practice.

Rumi, as he makes a symbolic distinction between the day as rational thought and the night as silent reflection, describes the elements of focus we hope to introduce to intuitive practice: the therapist quiets the mind, empties it of thought, detaches from outcome, and focuses attention on the patient, waiting for impressions to take shape. As they do, thoughts form and begin to make connections that become the focus of intuitive awareness. When the therapist speaks, conveying what is learned, the patient feels understood and gains clarity. The therapist at the same time, and in a parallel way, comes to know the patient with greater clarity through her own spoken words (Rumi describes this as "a powerful right arm of words sweeping down" in "The Night Air"; ll.55–56, Barks); this conveys an understanding of timing: impressions build, connecting what the patient is expressing with what is seen and felt by the therapist, until a moment of clarity is experienced by the therapist, who feels that it is time to speak. This moment of insight has been described as having a "consensus set" of feelings including excitement, a feeling of warmth, harmony, and enthusiasm (Agor, 1996). Over time, each therapist learns to recognize their own set of feelings connected to the moment of intuitive insight. It is felt in the body and easily expressed.

Paying attention to our intuitive impressions from our first point of patient contact alerts us to what lies ahead. Often our first experience is over the phone. Awareness of our feelings as we process the content of the conversation gives us information about the dynamics we will encounter and the likelihood of success in treating this particular patient. This has been demonstrated in research on first impressions (Gladwell, 2005; Goleman, 1998) where people were able to accurately sense within seconds of an encounter what their ongoing experience will be. The importance of this research is that intuition did not need to be developed, it was there as a natural capacity, accessed by shifting focus of attention from conscious thought to inner awareness.

While intuition is a general ability we all have, individual skill is developed by learning to quiet our minds, trusting the impressions we receive, and not allowing conscious thought to interfere with our perceptions (Swann, 1987, p. 321). Understanding comes through observation. This includes both metacommunications and paralinguistic behaviors as well as observations coming from the inner experience of the therapist. These inner experiences occur both in the patient's presence and between sessions. Therapists have varying levels of skill and their own unique abilities of observation. Learning to trust personal variations of experience reflects developing mastery of the intuitive process.

Therapists also have the ability to release focus and to enter a stage of awareness that is described as a trancelike state. This develops spontaneously and deepens both detailed observations and the broader patterns that connect them. It is the equivalent of a flash of insight that within seconds provides detailed images of the patient's inner world including deeply held beliefs, feelings, life experiences, their pain, disappointment, and fears. It may include diagnostic information and a treatment prescriptive. A good example of the ability to access this level of information can be found in the work and writings of Edgar Cayce. He regularly went into trance states and did "readings" of people who wrote to him asking for his help in the diagnosis and treatment of their medical conditions. Cayce induced deep trance states as the vehicle for his intuitive work. Clinicians who described entering trancelike states have mastered the ability to continue *active* engagement with their patients while accessing a deeper intuitive state.

Therapists in our study also described experiencing transpersonal states of awareness, in which the focus of their experience naturally moved beyond the personal identity of either themselves or their client. This is variously identified as higher self, God, and collective unconscious. These states of awareness are described in Bucke's classic work *Cosmic Consciousness* (1901), where they are extended to include experiences of transcendent realization, illumination, and an awareness of man's connection to the infinite. Transpersonal states of awareness occur spontaneously in psychotherapy and are focused on meaning that is relevant in the lives of their patients.

Our research demonstrates that clinicians, many of whom are not familiar with the intuition literature, focus regularly on their inner awareness, having learned to do so without benefit of clinical training or discussion with their peers. Their clinical examples parallel the findings described widely in psi literature and in the work of intuitive practitioners that include awareness of the many levels of their clients' behaviors, of their own internal experiences, and of the dynamic process between themselves and their clients.

The clinicians who participated in our research addressed six categories that reflect their focus of attention when they are having an intuitive experience: (1) they pay attention to subtle cues associated with metacommunication or paralinguistic behaviors; (2) they have prophetic dreams and experience what they describe as the client's spirit and their client's energy; (3) they become aware of internal cognitive, affective, and somatic states; (4) they focus on the clinical relationship; (5) they are aware of the physical and social environment; and (6) their attention is drawn to the transpersonal that can follow a suspension of focus. For purposes of research and discussion, focus of attention has been broken down into categories, though it is important to remember that the intuitive process is holistic and seamless.

The Therapist's Focus: Inner Experience

Working intuitively is in the capacity to focus on inner awareness, attending to the thoughts, feelings, and somatic experiences engendered in the presence of the patient. The therapist's ongoing self-awareness is the capacity to continuously attune to this subtle information.

Elizabeth indicated that she remained aware of her discrete, passing internal experience as she interacts with clients, as well as having a more general degree of self-awareness. This illustrates two aspects of self-awareness that are related to clinical intuition: first, awareness of the self in the moment and second, awareness of the self in interaction with this patient in this particular moment. The experience of the therapist of being in the presence of each client invokes a signature internal feeling that distinguishes each treatment relationship. Awareness of the images, words, and feelings experienced in the patient's presence are intuitive signposts that inform understanding.

On another level, awareness of one's general way of being becomes important. Elizabeth was clear that there are a few questions that are important to answer: what are the aspects of self that you tend to avoid? And what areas of experience have you not fully integrated? Elizabeth's example suggests that the ability to access and inspect these aspects of self, as well as immediate experiences, are important tools of discernment.

Deborah's experience of self-awareness suggests another important element of clinical intuition: she spends time centered on self-awareness as an intersession experience. Between sessions, she will think about the client and observe herself. That is, by watching how she reacts as she brings up thoughts about her client, she brings awareness to her internal experiences. Thus, awareness of internal processes both during and after sessions can be important ways to enhance clinical intuition.

Therapists monitor their internal experiences very closely in order to register intuitive information. Self-awareness during a session, as an intersession experience, and as more global self-awareness is also associated with clinical intuition.

Focus on the Client: Metacommunication

Metacommunication or paralinguistic communication includes body language and vocal inflections. It includes the barely perceptible tightening of facial muscles to large shifts in posture and all of the ways one holds one's body and moves; it can also be tiny changes in the pitch of one's voice to large changes in volume, coupled with degree of force and rhythm in voice and movement. Metacommunication, more simply is about how people communicate in subtle but nonetheless objectively measurable ways. Some of these changes occur below the threshold of conscious perception, but they are nonetheless grounded in the physical realm: they can and have been recorded at speeds that make them more readily observable. Several of the participants noted that they pay very close attention to these aspects of communication that usually occur on a nonconscious level.

For example, Elizabeth indicated that intuition is triggered by looking at someone's face. By focusing on another's face, she is able to "read someone's intent." She gave a more fine-grained description of reading faces: "the look on their face and in their eyes." Elizabeth's attention to faces reflects her development of reading visual cues; this is the "seeing" component of intuition.

> Lena feels that she also has an extraordinary ability to listen. She jested, My ears, sometimes I feel like they should be shaped like Spock's, because I feel that they're just perked up, listening to tone of voice, tenor of voice, pace of breathing, silence, . . .

As well as her ability to listen closely, she observes behaviors,

> I observe behaviors that sometimes have not been integrated cognitively by my clients. . . . I'm picking up on not only what they're saying, but what they're doing that tells me that there's a disconnect.

Lena's comparison to Spock concretizes her listening experience, reflecting her development of the "hearing" component of intuitive awareness.

While Lena referenced listening carefully, Sarah was more explicit about listening and watching her clients. She gave pointed advice to those who wish to develop their clinical intuition:

> . . . people who listen very carefully and listen beyond the exact words, can develop intuition. . . . noticing body language, tone of voice, noticing choice of words, noticing themes that keep—that appear and reappear, all contribute to using intuition.

In this example, Sarah demonstrates the combination of two avenues of intuitive awareness, pointing out that she pays close attention to both what she sees and what she hears.

Grace also focuses on her clients' metacommunication. She elaborates on her intuitive process, pointing out that rather than simply observing it, "I'm pulling in a lot of sense experience . . . tone of voice and how a person is moving in their body." She makes the distinction between simply looking at a person and an intuitive process that integrates the sensory experience of being in that person's presence.

Metacommunications and paralinguistic behaviors give therapists a great deal of information about their clients beyond what is explicitly said. All of the ways that information is subtly communicated are relevant to the intuitive process: facial expressions, body language, movement, gestures, and vocal qualities like rhythm, volume, and rate.

Beyond Metacommunication: "Other" Client-Generated Phenomena

While metacommunication and paralinguistic behavior are subtle, they are nonetheless observable and measurable. Participants also discussed focusing on something they believe their clients are broadcasting from a distance that is not directly observable. The therapists describe their experience of energy that feels tangible when in direct contact with patients who are sitting in the room as well as when they are not. Energy communicates subtle information that can come in any form and from any distance.

Dinah gave a good example of how information can be communicated through prophetic dreams about the deaths of loved ones and an instance in which she and her sister showed up at a family gathering dressed almost identically. She stated, "It's a gift to be able to pick up somebody sending you something from another country that I can feel." She is describing information communicated to her from a distance through no visible means (energetically) that informs her about matters that are consequential and those that are less important.

Jessica and Grace both gave examples of how information is communicated when in direct patient contact. It operates in the same way as information that comes from a distance: it is an inner awareness of communication taking place. Jessica reflected this in her description of tuning into herself in order to access subtle information that her client is communicating. Grace is also aware of her internal experiences during therapy that are coming from the client. At different points in the interview, she identified what she was taking in from the client as both their spirit and their energy. She stressed that what she is experiencing internally comes from the client and that it is clearly something extrasensory: "Can I feel the person that's sitting next to me? How do I feel it if my eyes are shut? How do I know they're there?"

Jessica stated that her focus is split between her client's metacommunication and her internal processes: "Whatever feeling you get from working with the client over time, notice it. . . . if that feeling is being engendered in you, it's probably being engendered for other people. . . " The word "engendered" is important in this quote: she is suggesting that she can discern the difference between her own feelings and those that come from the client. Jessica addresses the issue of discernment in developing intuition, learning to distinguish between a personal thought and a deeper awareness of the patient.

Experience Between the Client and Therapist

Therapists addressed subtle experiences they have with their clients, including feeling a connection to their energy or spirit. Likewise, some described a subtle process, an experience between the client and the therapist in which they engage and contribute equally. This includes concepts like connection, alignment, the space between, and parallel processes.

Elizabeth discussed her experience of sitting with a client: "It's very interactional. It's an ongoing thing." In describing the connection, she indicated that the client has to "allow me to open them." And stated that "they have to feel it."

Deborah repeatedly referenced the "reciprocal process between the patient and the therapist" as being at the core of her clinical intuition. She elaborated, "It's in-between us somehow." Thus, she focuses on a transactional, reciprocal process that is bidirectional.

Jennifer used the term "connection" to describe placing her attention on processes that occur between herself and her clients.

> . . . it's more a connection I feel—it's like I feel like we are a mirror, like there's a simpatico or there's a mirroring. She's [the client] just taking me in as well as I'm taking her in. . . [it's] how aligned you feel with someone . . . it's that flow. . . . It's an exchange.

Janet used the concept of space between herself and her client to describe the connection. She focuses her attention on how she experiences what she calls "the sense of space" and "the space between us [the client and herself]."

Justin used the terms "resonance" within a "relational field" to describe the interaction between himself and his clients that he attends to.

> A lot of what I see as happening has to do with thoughts and feelings that are coming up for the client and me. . . . I might have termed it resonance . . . there's something in the relational field. I guess that's how I would see it. That the clients will be experiencing thoughts and feelings, and then that's going to trigger something in the therapist and vice versa.

He used terms like "space" and "field," which suggest a distinct phenomenon. As noted in Chapter 1 (Current Knowledge and Perspectives), several people who have explored intuition understand the experience as occurring within a field: an area of mutual, reciprocal influence.

These descriptions of what occurs in the relationship between therapist and patient suggest a vibrant, active connection that is felt by both. Their engagement includes thoughts and feelings that mirror one another, resonating in an easy flow. This experience is felt energetically and can bring therapists a sense of spiritual connection to their client.

Environment

Two of the therapists also discussed the importance of being able to attend to the environment, be it physical or social. Dinah focuses on external or environmental cues. She discussed "atmospheric clues, and weather cues, and all of that, too." She added, "You see things in . . . the environment." She is aware of how the environment and more specifically the weather affect her, and she is alert to the impact it has on her patients as well. People respond to weather patterns, atmospheric pressure and light and dark. The changes can be experienced across a spectrum from changes in mood to more profound states of anxiety and depression.

Sharon talked about a general awareness of one's surroundings and the social environment. Growing up in an urban setting, she learned to be consciously aware of the people around her and to process their intentions intuitively. She stated that,

> . . . there's a sense of knowing what's around you, being aware . . . it's "something, possibly, is going on here. Watch out. . . . Who just passed me? Who is behind me? I need to look around. Watch out. . . ". . . . look beyond what you see.

Dinah and Sharon's accounts suggest that when focus of awareness is brought to the environment, either physically as reflected in the weather or socially as reflected in the people around you, important information is available. Their personal experience and understanding reflect broader patterns in the collective consciousness that they can easily attune to with their patients.

Trance/Transpersonal

Two of the participants also suggested that the transpersonal is a focus of their attention. That is, they focus on something beyond the personal identity of both self and other. This is variously identified as higher self, God, and collective unconscious. The experience may be preceded by a trancelike or empty state.

Elizabeth suggested this sequential attention. She says that she first enters a trancelike state or emptying out. In this "empty" state, she can then access a transpersonal phenomenon. She is careful not to identify this phenomenon too sharply, calling it either her higher self or God.

> It would be an emptying out and then thoughts . . . it feels almost as if I'm in a trance state. I feel almost like a channel for a higher self or God or whatever you want to say. . . . When it's working really well, it is almost like a spiritual trance-like experience.

Sarah stated that she, too, turns her attention to something transpersonal. She experiences this phenomenon as the collective unconscious: "We are all part of a collective unconscious, and . . . we can tune into that or not tune into it. I tune into it." Thus, she appears to focus more purposefully on the transpersonal in the course of her intuitive work.

The understanding that Elizabeth and Sarah are communicating reflects high levels of intuitive awareness. They access this naturally flowing state by focusing their attention beyond the immediate to an experience they describe as the collective unconscious, the higher self, God, "whatever you want to say," with similar outcomes. They access direct knowledge of their patients, also referred to as a unified field, a "sea of consciousness-and-energy" that connects everything in a "single, unified experience" (Pierce, 2013).

Sarah describes a "tuning in" process that she enters by choice. Elizabeth elaborates on a similar experience by describing the sequence of the shift in more detail. She enters a trancelike state that she experiences as "emptying out" and then she has intuitive impressions ("thoughts"). To her, the information she receives comes from an intelligent source outside of herself. She feels like the conduit, a "channel" for the information made available to her. The tuning in that Sarah and Elizabeth are describing reflects high levels of consciousness that enable them to access transcendent states of awareness.

Summary and Discussion

The experiences of the participants in our study suggest that the ability to focus on multiple aspects of the clinical situation are important to intuition. Therapists tune into many things, including their own personal processes and experiences, aspects of their clients' physical and vocal actions, as well as something more abstract. They also attend to the interactive process or therapeutic field between the client and therapist, the environment, and a nonfocus or emptying, which may precede the advent of the ability to focus on a transpersonal phenomenon.

These multiple forms of focus are highly consistent with Geller and Greenberg's (2012) description of therapeutic presence. Colosimo and Pas (2015) described the therapist's attention while being fully present as being on "shared intersubjective space" in a "deep state of communion" between therapist and client (p. 110). This requires the therapist to be open and linked to the client.

Many of the participants confirmed Marks-Tarlow's (2012) theory of intuition, in that they noted giving very close attention to the metacommunicative and paralinguistic behaviors on the part of their clients. Marks-Tarlow, following the work of Alan Schore (2005), has posited that intuition is associated with "visual eye-to-eye messages, tactile and body gestures, and auditory prosodic vocalizations . . . facial expression, posture, and tone of voice" that are "implicitly processed in the right brains of two communicative partners" (Schore, 2005, p. 833). Interestingly, Charles (2004) suggested that much of the metacommunication and paralinguistic behaviors that are processed nonconsciously may not, in fact, be intuition. She suggested that nonverbal communication and neurodynamic stimuli may in fact be sensory and not intuitive. Nonetheless, the participants in the present study were clear that they attended to these behaviors very closely and that doing so was associated with the acquisition of intuitively derived information.

But beyond this, the therapists who shared their own intuitive process suggested that they may focus on something that comes from the client that appears to not be communicated through vocal features, gestures, body language, etc. This "something else" was identified by Grace as "soul," or "energy." This observation conforms with the form intuition may take for several of the therapists in this study (see Chapter 5 on Forms of Clinical Intuition).

The therapists have honed their self-awareness. They appear to be able to access the processes and contents of their internal experiences. Training their attention on themselves appears to be an integral aspect of intuition. This coincides with Honorton's (1974) observations. He reviewed the psi research that had been conducted on the intuitive experience, noting that the internal experiences of the participants were important aspects of the episode.

A few therapists noted that they attended to a process or "space" between they themselves and their clients. One therapist used the terminology "analytic field," which is in concert with the work of Stern (2013). As reviewed in Chapter 1 (Current Knowledge and Perspectives), the analytic field was described by Stern as the mutual influence of analyst and analysand, consisting of an unconscious reciprocal exchange of information. This suggests placing one's attention on the process between two people influences intuition.

Dinah and Sharon both experience their ability to focus on environment to be associated with their intuition. For Dinah, the environment was the physical environment: atmospheric and weather. For Sharon it was the interpersonal environment: the people surrounding her.

Elizabeth stated that she can also release focus, experiencing a trance-like state or emptiness. This is close to the findings in Petitmengin-Peugeot (1999). Her participants reported that their intuition is accompanied by an "absence of conscious gestures" (p. 62) and "panoramic attention, not focused on any special object . . . involuntary attention, not directed towards any specific goal" (p. 67). This is suggestive of the emptying out that Elizabeth noted.

Elizabeth also indicated that the trancelike state may be accompanied by an awareness of a transpersonal source. Sarah, likewise, turned her attention to a transpersonal phenomenon when she was using her intuition. This coincides with Rogers's (1980) observation:

> There is nothing I can do to force this experience, but when I can relax and be close to the transcendent core of me, . . . behaviors turn out to be right. . it seems that my inner spirit has reached out and touched the inner spirit of the other. . . .
>
> (1980, p. 129)

Based on the data from the study, intuition appears to be impacted by the ability to focus on several different stimuli. It may be that the ability to focus in several areas at once is an important ability. Conversely, intuition may be associated with the ability to release focus, and experience an "empty" or trancelike state. These observations have important clinical implications.

Implications of Therapists' Focus of Attention

Where you train your focus during therapy may help you access intuitively derived information. To recap, when engaged in an intuitive interaction in your clinical practice, your focus may be on:

1. Self-awareness
   Implication: Importance of the therapist's ability to process internal thoughts, feelings, and bodily sensations while maintaining focus on how they are related to the client
2. The client
   Implication: Importance of focusing on the client's metacommunication and paralinguistic behaviors while deepening attention to something more, such as soul or energy
3. The therapeutic relationship
   Implication: Importance of maintaining focus on the client while monitoring internal experiences and the therapeutic alliance, including the degree of connection, alignment, and parallel process
4. The environment including the weather and the interpersonal environment
   Implication: Importance of how the weather, seasons, and the physical environment effect clinical sessions as well as the interpersonal environment between patient and therapist. This includes the office environment.
5. Apprehension of things at a distance in both time and space
   Implication: The focus of intuitive knowing extends beyond the clinical hour; things can be seen and known that are not physically present and can be occurring outside the clinical setting. They may have occurred in the past or may occur in the future.
6. Feeling the energy of the exchange between patient and therapist both in session and between sessions
   Implication: Awareness of energy as a focus of attention is an important aspect of intuitive knowing. All matter is energy and, as such, emits information.
7. The importance of the ability to release focus, "emptying out," and transpersonal experience.
   Implication: The whole is more than the sum of the parts. The ability of the therapist to release focus including on the patient, on one's own inner awareness, and the therapist–client relationship can cultivate a state of consciousness that transcends the individual parts. When they did so, participants noted an experience of a transpersonal source that enhanced their intuitive abilities.

Application of Focus in the Therapeutic Setting

1. Focus your attention on your patient, register your impressions; allow yourself to trust that they are important no matter what form they take.

2. Determine if the information is applicable to what the patient is currently focusing on or if it informs your intuitive understanding about the patient in a more global or different way.
3. Continue to pay attention to your focus of attention. If it remains stationary, it will continue providing you with additional information until you decide what action to take, if any. When your attention shifts, follow it; the moment of action has passed. If the information is important, your attention will return to it again.
4. Decide how best to act upon information that continues to re-enter your awareness; it is important. When your focus of attention shifts back to the intuitive impression repeatedly, it is important.
5. Focus on the therapeutic relationship and expand your ability to take in what's occurring within you as well as with the client, and mind the interplay or space between or field that encompasses you and your client.
6. Connect from the deepest part of yourself, with empathy, compassion, and deep caring. "Feel into" the pain, sorrow, and disappointments of patients as well as their hopes, joys, and achievements.
7. Consider how practices of self-awareness can develop your intuitive skills: meditation, self-reflection, personal therapy, and supervision by intuitively informed clinicians.
8. Try the "what if?" experiment: that is, you can approach a session with the playful notion of "what if I can experience or take in something from my client that I cannot see or hear or describe in physical terms?"

Works Cited

Agor, W. (1996). *The logic of intuitive decision making: A research-based approach for top management*. Westport, CT: Quorum Books.

Bucke, R. M. (1901). *Cosmic conscious* [republished in 1970]. New York, NY: E. P. Dutton and Company, Inc.

Cayce, E. (1982). *The Edgar Cayce primer*. New York, NY: Bantam Books.

Charles, R. (2004). *Intuition in psychotherapy and counselling*. London: Whurr.

Colosimo, K. A., & Pas, A. E. (2015). A rational model of expressed therapeutic presence. *Journal of Psychotherapy Integration, 25*(2), 100–114.

daSilva, R. (2017). Ingo Swann: *Man of miracles: A personal memoir in four parts*. Self-published.

Geller, S. M., & Greenberg, L. S. (2012). *Therapeutic presence: A mindful approach to effective therapy*. Washington, DC: American Psychological Association.

Gladwell, M. (2005). *Blink: The power of thinking without thinking*. New York, NY: Little, Brown and Company.

Goleman, D. (1998). *Emotional intelligence: Why it can matter more than IQ*. New York, NY: Bloomsbury.

Honorton, C. (1974). Psi-conducive state of awareness. In J. White (Ed.), *Psychic exploration: A challenge for science* (pp. 616–638). New York, NY: G. P. Putnam's Sons.

Marks-Tarlow, T. (2012). *Clinical intuition in psychotherapy: The neurobiology of embodied response*. New York, NY: W. W. Norton.

Pierce, P. (2009). *Frequency: The power of personal vibration*. Hillsboro, OR: Beyond Words Publishing.

Pierce, P. (2013). *Leap of perception: The transforming power of your attention*. Hillsboro, OR: Beyond Words Publishing.

Rogers, C. (1980). *A way of being*. Boston, MA: Houghton Mifflin.

Rumi, Jalal al-Din. (1995). *The essential Rumi: Coleman Barks translation*. New York, NY: HarperCollins.

Schore, A. N. (2005). A neuropsychoanalytic viewpoint: Commentary on paper by Steven H. Knoblauch. *Psychoanalytic Dialogues, 15*, 829–854.

Stern, D. B. (2013). The interpersonal field: Its place in American psychoanalysis. *Psychoanalytic Dialogues, 25*, 388–404.

Swann, I. (1987). *Natural ESP: A layman's guide to unlocking the extra sensory power of your mind*. New York, NY: Bantam.

Forms of Clinical Intuition

5

The participants in our research initially answered the question "what is intuition" in the same way most people would: "just knowing." Yet when the conversation deepened, they were able to describe the forms their intuition takes in great detail. This suggests that intuition is more easily *felt* than expressed in language. This chapter articulates those forms: from somatic sensations (through the five senses) to affective (emotional) states.

Clinicians relayed that they have more than one kind of experience that they understand to be intuition: physical sensations, emotions, seeing pictures, hearing words, knowing things that have not been directly communicated by their patients. However, most identified one or a few dominant forms that the experience takes. Individual intuitive experience differs in a way that parallels learning styles. For example, visual forms of experience reflect preference for pictures and images, auditory experience for sound and music, kinesthetic experience for physical sensations, and olfactory (smell) and precognitive experiences. Given the fundamental linguistic nature of psychotherapy we might assume that verbal forms of intuition are a shared preference among practitioners.

Further, though most of them are unaware of the literature on intuition, their use of it in clinical practice parallels decades of research on what it is and the forms that it takes, namely: seeing, hearing, feeling, and knowing. Information can come in any sensory form. This suggests that intuition is innate and overlooked in favor of logical thought. When clinicians were assured of the confidentiality of our interviews, they were able to talk with depth and clarity about their intuitive experience.

The feeling and meaning that clinicians experience in relation to the forms that intuition takes reflects the ability of our participants to make sense of and to use the intuitive impressions they receive. This suggests that they have learned to include their inner experience of their clients along with rational thought.

The vocabulary we have for intuition in a clinical setting is surprisingly scarce. This explains why our participants most often described intuition vaguely as "just knowing." A glance at the etymology of the word is helpful: the Latin *in*-[ward] + *tuērī* (to look), to look inward, and by extension, to contemplate. The word's history, rooted in our sense of sight, points to intuition as a capacity related to the bodily senses rather than reason. This is confirmed further by popular descriptions of intuition: when asked how we know something, we may describe having a "gut feeling," a hunch, a creative inspiration, or just knowing that we are making the right decision or taking the right course of action; the standard definitions of intuition. Intuition takes a turn, however, in the eighteenth century, in which philosophers, led by Kant's response to Newton's theories on time and space, defined intuition as an "immediate apprehension by sense" (OED). This shift in meaning from intuition as a lingering contemplation to an immediate (and unmediated) thought is instructive: intuition is the direct arrival of information; it is knowing the "thing itself," free of distortion and bias.

Participants also discussed their intuition as working at a distance, connecting them to their family members and important friendships in their lives as well as experiencing the presence of the spirits of deceased loved ones. The experience of spirits was also described as extending beyond those known in life to others, including those connected to their patients.

There are two additional, general statements about intuitive experiences that therapists shared. The first is that the form that intuition takes is often such a commonplace experience, or so subtle, that one may not even register the event. The second is that intuition is not sought but rather comes spontaneously. While it is unbidden, the therapist's awareness of it enables them to connect information that had not previously been integrated. This suggests that an awareness of the forms that intuition takes is worth understanding so that subtle, unexpected insights are registered and integrated into the clinical dialogue.

Common/Subtle

A theme from our research is the ineffability of the intuitive moment. For some therapists, the lack of a formal vocabulary for intuition keeps them from fully integrating it into practice. Jessica's experience with intuition is symptomatic of the problem. She uses intuition but has never labeled it as such and therefore misses the opportunity to identify it and develop her ability to use it more effectively. It was simply information, the source of which she never questioned or reflected upon.

> . . . I didn't define what I just described to you, a visual image that's a metaphorical representation of a client's situation—it never occurred to me that that was an intuition. It just never struck me as anything that was relevant. it was just something that I just ignored.

Jessica demonstrates the importance of defining the intuitive process as a valid and important way of understanding common / subtle experiences that inform clinical process. When intuition is acknowledged as real and becomes part of training curricula, therapists will have the benefit of using a common practice language based on research and training.

Jeff expresses another, perhaps more troubling aspect of the problem: ignoring his intuition entirely and losing what he may learn from it. He described his intuition as "very gentle," or a "soft thought," and because of this, he stated, "I think I probably ignored it for years."

The subtlety of intuition, as reflected in Jeff's practice experience, stresses the importance of acknowledging and defining it. Intuitive processes are a natural resource residing in each of us that provide critical information relevant to the focus of our attention. Though intuition may run in the background of experience and not be acknowledged, it can also be brought into the foreground and understood as a process of acquiring critical information fundamental to therapeutic processes. Acknowledge. Define. Use.

Unbidden

Besides being commonplace and subtle, many of the therapists indicated that the experience was unbidden, sudden, or came without effort. Elizabeth, for example, indicated that it was "like a flash in the pan." Deborah used the term "spontaneous." Natalie stated, "It just sort of pops in my head. It's like there's no sort of pre-thinking before . . . It just sort of comes to me." The spontaneous nature of intuition points to a difference between logical thought and intuitive processes. Logic is linear perception that is based on thinking of things as separate and disconnected; it is based on cause and effect, requiring effort to see connections. Intuition, on the other hand, is based on understanding connection; it is spontaneous, effortless, and efficient.

In some cases, the unbidden nature of a thought is dramatic. Sarah relates,

> Last week, a woman I've been seeing sat down in the chair, and I looked at her, and I thought, "her husband's dying. This work is gonna be so painful." Then she started the session by talking . . . about the difficulty she was having [at work]. Then she paused and said, "That's not why I'm really troubled today. My husband told me he's dying."

The unbidden nature of Sarah's experience speaks to an important aspect of intuition: receptivity. Though therapists may not be actively seeking intuitive information, they receive it; in images, through sounds, feelings, and sudden knowing, as reflected in Sarah's vignette. It is important to note that Sarah does not act on her impression immediately, but rather waits until her patient introduces it as the focus of discussion.

Knowing

Knowing, also described as "just knowing" by our participants, is reported as the most common experience by those who describe having a sudden awareness of some new knowledge or insight. The information may be quite striking or more ambiguous. Though "just knowing" is vague on its face, our participants were able to elucidate a key distinction that exists between *knowledge* as a logical process and *knowing* as an intuitive process. Knowledge comes from external authority and is based on logic that may link to a particular theory or practice paradigm. Knowing, on the other hand, draws on inner learning and wisdom. Knowing brings spontaneous understanding of what is most relevant and timely in the immediate situation.

For example, David is tentative in his intuitive insight, though it does provide him with a hint of useful information: "It's something that I don't know for certain, but it's close to knowing something more certainly." Alejandro expresses his intuition with more certainty, as "immediate knowledge of an idea, situation or thought without reasoning." Lena elaborated, adding a somatic component to the definition of knowing: "It's not just a knowing in the front, but it's through my entire being." Dinah goes further, defining knowing as forming a connection with a client, a sort of chemistry: "You can have a sense of being attached and knowing what's happening . . . Or you can be alienated, and not in a knowing space. So, for me, 'knowing' is a very positive state." Dinah, interestingly, points out the agency of the therapists and patients involved, who each either choose to connect or not. It's also important to note that Dinah feels that when she chooses to connect, her knowing is exceptional.

Ellen builds on our understanding of the exceptional nature of intuitive knowing by reflecting that it gives access to information that cannot be obtained through other means: "[it is] knowing things that other people don't know . . . through other means that other people don't know . . . means that aren't obvious to most people."

Sarah related a similar depth of intuitive experience,

> I often have the experience of not being . . . of knowing something before someone tells me. Now, some people describe . . . tell me . . . I've heard this today, in fact . . . "Oh, do you have ESP [extra-sensory perception], or do you use mental telepathy?" But I define it as intuition. I just intuitively know something that I haven't been told.

The nuanced description of knowing reflected in these interviews conveys a sense that intuitive knowing can range from tentative or ambiguous (and therefore not as useful) to strong and confident. It is important to note that Ellen and Sarah have the strongest impressions; this is perhaps because each of these clinicians were aware of their intuitive experiences early in life and learned to manage those insights in relating to other people. They therefore learned to translate their intuitive way of knowing into a way of working professionally, supporting our understanding that clinical intuition can be developed like any other ability.

Thoughts Without Thinking

The sense of knowing may include other subjective experiences. For some, this knowledge came in the form of a thought. The clinicians reported two different experiences: the majority of the participants were not aware of thinking prior to the arrival of the thought. Some of the respondents suggested that trying to think may countermand intuitively acquired information. One participant indicated that "contemplation" can trigger an intuitive insight.

There is a difference between thinking a thought and a thought you are receiving. This is the distinction between logic and intuition, the shift in awareness that takes place in moving from the intellect to direct experience. Logical thinking is very directive, very linear. For example, attempts to problem solve, to determine what you should do or say next to the client, thinking about how you can steer a client toward an understanding, or what recommendations you can make to help the client address their problem may represent one form of thinking. Thoughts represented by musings such as "I wonder what the client is getting at here" introduce logic. Reflecting logically about the process undermines intuitive ability (Gladwell, 2005), and you lose the flow. Likewise, if your internal dialogue begins to elicit emotions such as fear or anger, you have shifted from intuiting to reasoning (Day, 1996). Thoughts without thinking, on the other hand, align with the definition of intuition as direct apprehension.

Deborah begins to give shape to the difference between thinking and receiving an intuitive thought; for her it's a *negation* of thinking that enables the arrival of an intuitive thought. "It's not something I'm thinking about so much."

Sharon expressed her experience of the arrival of intuitive thoughts as a harbinger of danger: "There's something there that I just go to in my head. . Perhaps, its starts with, uh-oh, something . . . doesn't feel right . . . something, possibly, is going on here. Watch out." Felicia gives a concrete example of intuition as a diagnostic impression:

> I'm working with a man who is married and has a family, and is having some family problems now . . . I'm driving to work and I say, "Ah, sex addiction." That was an intuition. I hadn't thought, I hadn't looked at his record and thought, "I'll go back and see what sex addiction is," and clinically thought that.

While Felicia's insight is spontaneous, Brenda offers an explanation of how that process works:

> It's the not over thinking things. Okay. I have a feeling about the way this should go or the way these things work together, I'm gonna go with that. . . . it's like if you're dancing, and you start thinking, then you start getting—you're not flowing . . . it's muscle memory. There's something similar, something evocative, where it's just a very natural—the idea of reverie in the therapeutic process . . . I'm floating along in a reverie with this client and hearing him or her.

Brenda not only reiterates the important point that overthinking obstructs the efficacy of the intuitive process but also defines it as a heuristic process in which knowledge is stored as "memory" that can be quickly accessed with experience.

Brenda illustrates how intuition can come in the form of single words, images, and knowing as well as a way of working that becomes an experiential flow; a stream of connections. Brenda described her experiences of intuitive thoughts as having an auditory feel:

> It's . . . hearing, but not like hearing voices. Just I'll say the sentence in my mind. It's a thought, but it's a very powerful thought. "Okay, this is what you need to do." It's just a thought. The statement, declarative statement. Yeah.

Elizabeth has the experience of intuition as an unbidden thought and contemplates to clear her mind for intuitive awareness to emerge: "It can come in a very whimsical fashion where I'm not even expecting it, or it's just as the process of contemplation."

The therapists in this study indicated that they often experience intuition as the arrival of a thought. They included spontaneously receiving diagnostic impressions and warnings about dangerous situations, thoughts without thinking. Contemplation adds the understanding that it can help to clear the mind in preparation for receiving intuitive thoughts.

Affect

Along with knowing, intuition was often experienced among the participants as an emotion or affect. They frequently identified "feeling" one of the four pillars of understanding in psi research. As the term can indicate either emotion or sensation, its meaning was frequently identified as feeling emotions. Deborah identified intuition as something "felt." She elaborated, "affectively, . . . yeah, affectively felt sense . . . I begin to feel something. . . " Samantha identified "an awareness of an emotion." Brenda also endorsed the affective nature of her intuitive experiences. She was discussing her ability to "see through subterfuge." She continued, "I just had this feeling, this really strong . . . It was emotional. I'm very aware of that when it comes up."

Deborah identified the feeling that she has during an intuitive episode as an insight into her client's feelings:

> It is a feeling state for me. It is not something I'm thinking about so much. I make that clarification between feeling and thinking. . . . it comes into play when I feel something in an interaction with a patient

> or in a group. . . . Affectively felt sense . . . I begin to feel something that the other party is experiencing.

Lailla also discussed the affective nature of her intuitive experiences. In her example, the feeling is the sudden onset of anxiety:

> I have had a wonderful and blessed relationship with my father. . . . All the years that I was here [in the United States], it was amazing that I suddenly would feel like I would get anxious about my father, that is he okay? Something might be going on. . . . I would call, and lo and behold, something was happening to him. I had a very dear friend . . . I hadn't been in touch with him for decades. . . . I started feeling that I wonder how he is. I just started getting worried. . . . I finally saw in the paper that he had been very sick, from the date that I started feeling antsy.

The feelings the clinicians identified as intuition were varied and sometimes strong. One participant identified anxiety about a loved one's well-being, while another has the sense that her intuitive affects are related to her client's experience. The respondents in this study confirm the conclusions of many of those who have theorized and studied intuition: there is a strong relationship between intuition and affect.

Somatic

In many cases, feeling is somatic, that is experienced through the body and senses. Many participants identified a "gut feeling," or a "gut reaction." Sharon described the gut feeling as "a sense of a visceral feeling. . . . I feel a little tightness." David discussed an experience that others in the study identified, which is that they will often think about a patient and get a call from that person.

> I will start thinking about a patient that I have finished with, and then out of the blue I'll get a call from that patient. . . . More often than not, when I think about somebody I end up getting contacted by them.

Connecting thinking about a person and then receiving a call from them is one of the most common intuitive experiences and is connected to a "gut feeling," according to Radin (2006, pp. 142–145).

Participants also discussed other somatic experiences as intuitive. Elizabeth stated that her feeling is "more in my heart or in my stomach." Dinah identified a few somatic reactions as intuitive:

> [When] I'm with somebody who is narcissistic, I can feel my skin burning. I feel it on my skin, and I can feel trickles up my arm. It's a cutaneous kind of feeling. . . . I just feel it. I can feel it right here [pointing to her arms, cheeks, and the top of her head]. . . . On the other hand, when I feel good energy, my heart is looser. . . . Your chest can tighten; or your chest can be loose, and there can be space inside. When I'm feeling good with somebody, there's a lot of space in my body.

Samantha related that she knew as a child that she was more intuitive than most people. When asked about the experiences she had in childhood that led her to this understanding, she responded, "I would always get a sore throat, which I guess I know is now a lump in your throat. I guess, when something wasn't right, whether it be in school or with friends. . . "
Brenda identified another somatic experience.

This is an overwhelming feeling of fatigue.

> I think that I know [what the client is feeling] sometimes when I'm with a client, and this is very unusual, but it has happened enough now to clients I've had over the years. Where I feel like I'm going to fall asleep, and I'm really desperately struggling not to fall asleep. It's a terrible feeling.

David indicated that one form his intuition takes is a sensation "in my heart area . . . and in my head area." The therapists reported a number of different somatic experiences that they identified as intuition, although "gut feeling" was the most widely endorsed somatic experience (Radin, 2006). Other sites of sensations are the head, chest, arms, skin, and more general sensations like fatigue.

The relationship between mind and body is another focus of attention that arises in the course of gaining a better understanding of intuition. These therapists reflect an understanding of the mind–body connection and intuition as a holistic process. Brenda's "terrible feeling of desperately struggling not to fall asleep" could benefit from further intuitive analysis, as demonstrated by Grace in her description of combining both somatic and affective states of awareness:

> I definitely often feel a located sensation that feels emotional, or that it could be tied to emotion, like, my heart will get heavy; my heart will get spongy. I will feel a grip in my stomach, one of these kind of things. That grip could be a number of things, but it definitely calls my attention. . . . Sometimes I'll feel things in my heart area, and it could be guarded; it could be a stab of pain; it could be sorrow, like the heaviness of sorrow.

Grace articulates in more detail how somatic and affective feeling states are connected, describing her awareness and how she processes them. She describes what has long been known, that emotions have physical correlates; among them the fight-flight-freeze response and the dilation of capillaries in the face, resulting in the face appearing to turn red, when one feels shame. Awareness of the simultaneous registry of affective and physical experience provides important information that deepens intuitive awareness.

Energy

Though the clinicians experience intuition through the traditional five senses, they also introduced their experience of intuition as energy. The introduction of this concept adds to a broader discussion on how states of attunement and disharmony are experienced. Participants labeled energy variously as "resonance," "vibes," "chi," "movement," and "flow." This suggests that our participants are experiencing similar phenomena described in different ways. They also described experiencing "negative," "troubled energy" and the feeling of being "energetically drained" by their patients. The importance that our participants placed on energy suggests that they are aware of the subtle influences that inform their understanding of the client, both those that reflect a harmonious experience of the clinical encounter and those that reflect discordance.

There was a common experience among the clinicians: sensing energy or "vibes," or "resonating." For example, Natalie indicated, "sometimes I feel the energy." Justin discussed energy in terms of "chi." When he learned about somatic experiencing, he stated, "I realized—I started to realize that the kinds of things that I was experiencing it's really talking about this . . . this energy, or chi." Lauren stated, "I get terrible vibes." Alejandro simply stated, "I know there is energy."

Grace expressed her experience that the energy she felt was broadcast by others: "I think I'm picking up on her [a client's] energy shifting in and out of her body." Dinah also indicated the role of the other in her experience of energy. She used the term "resonate": "I don't resonate with narcissists, 'cuz they don't resonate."

While participants often made passing references to feeling energy, a few discussed them at greater length. For example, Lena described her experience of energy in nature: "When I see a stump of a tree that has been cut down, I will feel drawn to go stand on a stump. When I do, I feel this energy come through my body." Likewise, Ann related this narrative:

> I had someone come in to me for—to be a client . . . I just got this sense of very—gosh—extremely troubled energy, but at a very—that she had—didn't have much grasp of it . . . the energy that I felt when I was with her was just—it was like that sense of "I don't wanna touch this." . . . I just knew that was an energy that I could not be effective with.

Dinah experiences "movement in the universe," or "flow." She stated, "There's movement in the universe. Sometimes I feel like it's a great movement; and sometimes I feel like the universe is not moving well. It's just in a bad place. You can. . . . feel 'in the flow,' and a feeling of spaciousness."

Many of the participants in the study suggested that they have an ability to experience energy, vibes, resonance, and movement. Some understood the specific manifestations of these experiences to relate information coming from their client, or the broader environment. Practitioners may be familiar with energy concepts through any number of channels including alternative therapies practices, the martial arts, yoga, and meditation practices. This is a concept that, while supported in Eastern thought, is just beginning to be adopted in Western systems of psychotherapy. Energy psychology is based on understanding the fundamental nature of energy in health and healing.

Auditory

Some clinicians reported auditory experiences during and intuitive episode. For example, Elizabeth was with a client in session,

> . . . and I had this voice in my head that said, "This woman's going to die." She was perfectly fine, and she did [die]. I actually heard her voice . . . I know that it's my voice, but this was like another voice or my higher self.

Lena described, "a humming in my ears." However, this sensation is complex, seeming somewhat synesthetic:

> it's like a hum and a warm feeling behind my ears . . . When I say hum, hum's not even a good description . . . if you can put a temperature on . . . put a sound to warmth . . . so it's not really a hum, but it's like a hum . . . If you put a sound to warmth.

Brenda and Felicia both heard songs as a source of intuitive knowledge. Brenda stated, "Sometimes when you're sitting with someone and a song will come in your head? Okay. I haven't heard that song in years. There's something about the lyrics of that song that are probably helpful." Felicia had a similar experience:

> It was so often that a song would come. I consider that intuition . . . We [would be] in the middle of a discussion, and the client says something, and it reminds me of *The Sound of Music*. It reminds me of a hymn that we sing at church. Lines of music float into my head as I work with clients. . .

Ann gave an example of an auditory experience she had in which a snippet of an overheard conversation came into relief.

> I used to have an office also in [place name redacted], and there was a yoga studio attached to the office that one of my colleagues ran. I was at a period where I was very much worried about finances at that time. There were people out there chatting, and I couldn't understand their words except when this woman said, "Oh, the money's there. Don't worry. The money's there." Then I couldn't hear anything else. Now, I don't know what that is, if that's intuition or if that's just—'cause I really—I could not understand the words until this person said that. It was like oh, my gosh because it was like a—maybe that was a gift from beyond.

The auditory experiences the therapists discussed include hearing voices—both "outside" and "inside" their minds—hearing bits of a song, and hearing a "warm hum," or "the sound of warmth." When they have these experiences, they interpret them as meaningful information, their presentation reflects thoughtfulness and deep reflection.

Visual

Many clinicians reported having visual images that they interpreted as the arrival of intuitively derived information. Elizabeth described such an experience with a client:

> . . . when we were talking, at some point, I got this really clear image of him at a lake. He was flailing in water and panicking and terrified that he was going to drown. . . . it was really clear.

She decided to share this mental visualization with her client. "It popped up in his head right away. He was telling me about it [the near-drowning experience]."

Likewise, Dinah reported a mental image as an example of her intuition at work:

> One time I was very taken with someone, and I was standing in a department store, and I was thinking about him. I had a picture of him that was so clear. It was like I could see him in front of me . . . not a hallucination, but . . . in my mind's eye. It was so clear. Just at that moment, he called me on the telephone.

Lena's example of visually experienced intuition is a nonclinical example. Instead of a mental image, she experienced a distortion in her visual field.

> My husband of 30 years . . . I thought he was too old for me . . . he said he always knew he would marry me . . . When he first asked me to marry him, I said, "No," because he was too old for me. Then I went on a trip. When I came back, the whole . . . airport faded out . . . He came into focus. On the way home, I said, "I think I'm supposed to marry you." It was very visual. Visual like somebody's hitting me over the head and saying, "Yes. Yeah. This is who you're supposed to marry."

Ellen also experiences intuition as distortions in her visual field. She described this form: "I'd be in a session with people, and parts of their bodies would distort, like their heads would grow larger, or like somebody I'd see, his arms would shrink up, and he would not have arms." She explains the distortions as patients "living in their heads" or not having agency.

Lauren experiences intuition in a visual form when she mentally "sees" her clients as they may have been as children.

> With a client, the visions that I have with clients, I see them as children a lot of times. It's very amusing to me because I'll be sitting there and this guy is talking about how he didn't like to share. I can just see him as a kid. It's a funny sensation to see someone more as a child as they're talking. . . . Sometimes a child comes really through in that way.

Katherine also "sees" her clients' childhood experiences. She stated, "I can go back and see events. . . . I feel like I can see. . . [a client's] childhood." Although she was clear that "I never know if what I'm seeing is what actually happened, obviously."

David revealed that he sees auras with some clients. He related, "I'm surprised sometimes quite often about . . . what I see when I'm sitting with someone."

> It's an outline of the person that's sitting in front of me, and usually it's a white outline. Sometimes it's a wider outline than other times. Sometimes it's a brighter outline than other times. Today, two hours ago, very unexpectedly I saw and paid attention, and looked away, and looked back, and saw it again, and saw more, and then an hour ago, didn't really think about the previous hour. All of a sudden I thought, oh, I should look and see, and I saw again—I don't know what to call it—like, an energy field around. It was not as bright. It was not as deep.

Brenda has yet a different visual experience. She sees images of words in her mind.

> I actually will see the words, because I'm very visual. . . . Just the sentence. . . . it could be one word. It could be "accept." Accept the situation. It could be "love this person." It's usually very direct.

There are many different ways participants described visually experienced intuition. They may see images that are relatively simple, like a snapshot, or a more dynamic scene like a video. They may see visual distortions or see their clients as children. Like auditory experiences, sometimes the images are internal: seeing in the mind's eye. Sometimes they appear more external, like auras. Like the auditory experiences, these therapists embraced the experience by trying to understand its meaning.

Olfactory

Only one participant discussed olfactory experiences, and these were not experiences she had had but rather those of family members. Ellen said, "My aunt smelled roses whenever anybody died. She would just smell a rose, and she'd say, 'Well, who died?'" She also stated, "right after my father died, my sister knew he [his spirit] was there because she smelled grass."

Unmediated Action

Some therapists seem to say or do things without a sense of agency over the activity. In several instances, clinicians stated that they don't know why they did or said something specific. For example, Lauren related, "I don't know what makes me do these things, but I know I do it."

Examples of taking action without seemingly thinking them through result in positive outcomes. They fit what has been described in research on states of flow as action-awareness merging, a state of involvement so deep that "action feels spontaneous and almost automatic" (Kawabata & Mallett, 2011).

Associations

Intuition arrives in the form of subtle, transitory internal experiences that are connected to the client. Awareness of these experiences comes by way of associations, as indicated by Deborah, "for me it gets engendered by association." That is, she allows herself to follow connections between what the client presents and what comes up in her and what the relationship between the two may be. She interprets this information as relevant to the client's experience and/or treatment process. Using the term "associations" was unique to Deborah. Yet her observation is quite astute in that she highlights the binocular vision required to notice, then use intuition in therapy: the therapist centers simultaneously on the client, as well as on the internal experiences that are arising from moment to moment within the therapist. Deborah's observation emphasizes the importance of paying attention to the small, internal transitory experiences you have while simultaneously noting what the client is working through in that moment.

Other Experiences Identified as Intuition Outside of Psychotherapy

There are a number of additional experiences that the participants identified as intuition; it should be noted that these experiences take place outside of psychotherapy. We have included them to broaden our understanding of forms that intuition may take. These experiences have alternately been described as spiritual and paranormal. We are interested in these stories because (1) they add more texture to the background of our participants and (2) because our clinicians have stressed before that their patients sometimes explicitly sought out a given therapist because of their comfort and sensitivity to the paranormal.

Elizabeth credits a near-death experience as the beginning of her connection to the spiritual realm:

> I had spirits visit me when I was a little girl [and later in life] . . . we lived across from a Civil War battlefield . . . we had a lot of spirit visitation there. They used to come one at a time and just hover over my person when I was laying down in bed . . . Then one time, my husband saw it, and he described it to me to a tee.

She explained how important it is to have her experience corroborated by another person. This confirms our earlier finding that people are more likely to share their intuitive experiences when they have support and encouragement from family, friends, and colleagues.

Lauren recalls an experience with the paranormal as auditory:

> As I was sleeping I heard this voice say, "Get up." I said, "I'm tired. Goodnight." I just rolled over. Then I heard a couple of voices and they said, "You've got to get up." I said, "Please, don't be so insistent. Let me sleep." I rolled over. Then I heard a number of voices and they were screaming at me, "You need to get up." I said, "Hey, don't you have somebody else to talk to tonight?" Went back to sleep. Then I heard this huge chorus of voices and they were screaming, "You've got to get up. You've got to get up. Look around. Look around. . . . I'm looking around and I saw a flame.

Dinah reported having had prophetic dreams of death:

> I was in England, and he [my father] was in [the United States] I had a dream that night. The dream was . . . it was so real, it was freakish . . . I

was standing with my sister, and my sister-in-law . . . in a little circle in my house of origin, and we were going to a party . . . I said to my sister-in-law, "What are you wearing?" She said, "I'm wearing my black dress with gold in it." Then I said to my sister, "What are you wearing?" She said, "I'm wearing blah-blah-blah-blah-blah. What's Daddy wearing?" She looked at me and she said, . . . didn't you know? Daddy's dead! He died!

Dinah later learned that her father had died. She related a second prophetic dream about the death of someone close to her:

And then I had another intuitive dream where my godmother died. I was lying in bed, and at 12:00 a.m. all of a sudden I sprung up and started crying, and the word "mother" came to me. I thought, "That's weird. My mother is fine." I went back to sleep. About 6:00 a.m. my mother called me, and she said, "[name redacted] died last night." She was my godmother. I said, "Really? What time?" She said, "Midnight." . . . I've had that happen a lot.

Ellen discussed seeing the spirit of a family member: "I saw my grandfather after he had died."

Seeing the spirits of deceased relatives and prophetic dreams are reported commonly in bereavement literature.

Ellen has repeatedly experienced a precognitive ability to "find people."

. . . . I can find people. I probably can't do it to anybody, but like my mother. She was coming up here, and she was going to an art show. She wanted me to pick her up in [name of city redacted] at 5:00. . . I just knew she was in an art museum somewhere in [the city], so I drove and figured it's the [name of a specific museum redacted]. Where else would it be? I just drove down to the [museum], got out of my car. Then it's just, this was a determination that I was just gonna find her, and walk into the [museum]. I walked in. All of a sudden, I didn't know what to do. This woman turned around, and it was my mother. I did that with a friend in a movie theater. . . . I needed to find my friend. She was in a movie theater. I commenced walking into the middle of the theater. Walked down and, all of a sudden, stopped, and I didn't know what to do, where I'd go next. The person next to me goes, [name, redacted], and that was her boyfriend, and there she was . . . if I have to find someone, . . . I could find them.

Ellen described another example of intuition taking the form of precognition:

> It's kind of like finding people, but it's not the same. My grandmother was in a nursing home, and one day, I woke up, and I just decided that I would go see her. No reason, and she was way across town, so I just went there. I had no idea how I was gonna get back. I didn't even know what bus came back there. I got a ride there, and then I walked in. I walked by a room, and I looked in, and it wasn't her. Then I couldn't figure out where she was, so I came back, and she was dying.

Sarah has experiences of thinking about family members when they are ill or hearing from people who were thinking of her just before a communication arrives from her.

> I texted my daughter last night. I said, "Everything okay?" and she texted me this morning. "How did you know I had a fever last night?" . . . I got a text from someone today, this—also this morning, that I had sent that person something, and she had been thinking of me that morning. Those kind of things. That happens all the time. I consider that intuition.

These examples suggest that a number of different psi or "paranormal" experiences have been noted among the therapists who contributed to this study. Some of these experiences are quite extraordinary, like seeing spirits, and others may be easily dismissed as coincidental, like thinking of someone just before they call. These experiences are reported widely in psi literature (Radin, 2006). Awareness of research on paranormal experiences strengthens therapists' ability to listen intuitively to the meaning these experiences represent to our clients.

Summary and Discussion

The therapists in this study described a number of different experiences that they interpreted as the harbinger of intuitively derived information. Many of these experiences are related to the senses: sounds, images, sensations, and even smells that are mental or internal. Some of these senses have an external quality: feeling the skin or seeing or hearing things that have the subjective feel of being "outside" the self.

There are experiences that appear to feel like they are independent of the clinician's agency. These include thoughts that arise without the experience of thinking and actions that feel unmediated by conscious choice.

Another important group of experiences involves affects or emotions. These can be strong at times. The therapists may interpret these emotions as being shared with the client. The therapists often experience an emotion when something is "wrong."

Yet another experience that many of the participants discussed was the feeling of energy. This can include the quality of the energy (e.g., "good," "bad"), the amount of energy (e.g., "strong,"), or shifts or changes in the energy.

Many of the experiences noted represent *qualia*, or the subjective aspects of sensory experiences. Because of the purely subjective nature of the phenomenon, they are difficult to describe and impossible to measure. Nonetheless, other qualitative studies on intuition confirm the experiences of the therapists in our research. Petitmengin-Peugeot (1999) reported that her participants often identified the form their intuition took as sensorial. These include internal images or, rarely, visual hallucinations; sensations (such as internal tensions, subtle sensations in the hand, etc.); sounds that may be interior or pronounced out loud, tastes, and smells. Petitmengin-Peugeot also identified thoughts without words, a feeling of certitude, and a feeling of coherence or meaning. Her participants, like some in the study we conducted, also reported the capricious, unpredictable manner in which these experiences arise. With the exception of the feeling of coherence or meaning coming into being, the experiences reported in the Petitmengin-Peugeot study were replicated by our research.

Likewise, Charles (2004) noted that intuition may be experienced as "a feeling, thought or bodily sensation, . . . an impression, a joke or a visual image" (p. 32). Thus, the findings in our study support previous findings and suggest that the experiences reported by the intuitive therapists who shared their experiences may be representative of the experiences of a larger group of people.

Whatever the nature of the experience, the therapists agreed that in most circumstances, intuition is unbidden, although one clinician indicated that it can arise as a result of contemplation. Another noteworthy experience is that whatever the form of intuition, it is often such a commonplace experience that the clinician did not necessarily register that he or she had access to information. One therapist who discussed this indicated that he would like to become more mindful of the process so that he can use it in a more targeted or purposeful way.

The fact that intuition may be unrecognized suggests that if it is possible to unconsciously use the information acquired intuitively, perhaps the use of intuition in the clinical process is more widespread than we can measure. In any case, therapists who wish to hone their intuitive capacities may do so by bringing the information to the conscious level. This may be accomplished by attending to subtle, common experiences. Noting them is a precursor to interpreting or exploring meaning that may be associated with these experiences.

Implications of Forms of Clinical Intuition

The therapists in this study described a number of different experiences that they interpreted as the harbinger of intuitively derived information. Many of these experiences are related to the senses: sounds, images, sensations, and even smells that are experienced as if with a sixth sense. They include a spectrum of experiences that range from subtle to dramatic.

1. So commonplace/subtle that intuitive insights may not register as important
   Implication: It is important to be aware of the forms intuition takes so you don't overlook them.
2. Intuition is unbidden, spontaneous.
   Implication: Intuitive insights are sudden/effortless; they cannot be forced.
3. Intuitive experiences occur on a continuum.
   Implication: Intuition can be barely perceptible to providing dramatic revelations, including whole scenes related to events that are occurring, that have occurred in the past, or will occur in the future.
4. Intuition comes in the form of "just knowing" through cognitive experiences, thoughts or insights.
   Implication: Learn to identify a sense of spontaneous knowing as intuitive information.
5. Intuition is experienced as a thought without thinking.
   Implication: Learn to distinguish between a directed linear thought and an intuitive thought that you are receiving.
6. Intuition is experienced as an emotion or affect.
   Implication: Be aware of how you are feeling and the intensity of your feelings; they are important intuitive states of awareness.
7. Intuition is experienced somatically as well as affectively.

Implication: Gut feelings or a feeling in your stomach, heart, or other organs, and sensations on or under your skin, all provide intuitive information.

8. Intuition can be felt as an energetic experience.
   Implication: While we think of ourselves as solid bodies, we are vibrating fields of energy. Awareness of how we feel in the presence of other people is an indicator of the impact of their consciousness on ours, including feeling resonance or feeling drained.
9. Intuition comes through sound, images, and the senses.
   Implication: These experiences reflect extrasensory ways of hearing (as if with a third ear) seeing (as if with a third eye), and smelling things (as if an extended olfactory sense).
10. Intuition may feel like unmediated action or speech.
    Implication: When you are in a deeply connected state, action and speech can be spontaneous and automatic.
11. Intuition comes to mind in indirect ways.
    Implication: Be aware of thoughts that arise in your awareness, whether they are symbolic or associative.
12. Intuition provides a feeling of coherence or meaning.
    Implication: Memorize the feeling of coherence so that you can return to it.
13. Intuition is reflected in synchronicities or "meaningful coincidences."
    Implication: When synchronicities occur, they are the result of intuition. Note and enjoy them.

Application of Forms in the Therapeutic Setting

1. Intuitive messages can come in any sensory form; check all your senses!
2. Learn to identify fleeting thoughts, physical experiences, and feelings and hold them in awareness.
3. Continue to reflect on these experiences to discern their possible meaning.
4. Set an intention to notice subtle experiences; intuition is often unbidden. Trust that your sense of knowing likely reflects an insight into your client and the therapeutic process.
5. Experiment with those unbidden thoughts. How does the open-ended play of thoughts differ from thoughts targeted toward a specific result? What kind of information does each yield?
6. Be aware of "gut feelings" and other somatic experiences.

7. Be aware of subjective experiences including body and mind; emotions have physical correlates.
8. Begin to think of feeling energy: this includes the quality of the energy and shifts or changes in the energy. This is reflected in how you feel in the presence of another person; do you feel hopeful, optimistic, or drained, confused, conflicted? Consider that you are picking up important information that is being registered in your own awareness.
9. Consider examples of unmediated action—doing something without reflection, or even a sense of agency—and how they may reflect your intuitive insights. Therapists we interviewed found them, over time, to be beneficial.
10. Consider your dreams or paranormal encounters. Are they connected to a patient you are treating?
11. Check in with your clients! They can help you confirm or challenge your intuitions; they may help you learn how to use those impressions if they are correct.
12. Flex your intuitive muscle; put yourself into environments that encourage intuitive thinking so that you can better recognize their forms. Choose to work with populations and people with whom you resonate.

Works Cited

Charles, R. (2004). *Intuition in psychotherapy and counselling*. London: Wiley.

Day, L. (1996). *Practical intuition*. New York, NY: Villard Press.

Gladwell, M. (2005). *Blink: The power of thinking without thinking*. New York, NY: Little, Brown and Company.

Kawabata, M., & Mallett, C. J. (2011). Flow experience in physical activity: Examination of the internal structure of flow from a process-related perspective. *Motivation and Emotion, 35*(4), 393–402. doi:10.1007/s11031-011-9221-1

Petitmengin-Peugeot, C. (1999). The intuitive experience. *Journal of Consciousness Studies, 6*(2–3), 43–77.

Radin, D. (2006). *Entangled minds*. New York, NY: Paraview.

Experiences and Practices Associated With Clinical Intuition

6

Therapists enter their psychotherapy offices with a lifetime of experiences and practices that shape who they are and how they work. Clinicians who have learned to trust and work with intuition in their personal lives bring that skill to practice. This chapter examines how the personal lives of therapists impact their development and the practices they engage to support their intuitive abilities.

The therapists we interviewed represent a broad range of early life experiences. Some experienced social or family circumstances during childhood that prompted them to see below the surface and to develop their intuition. Some used difficulties as a springboard to greater dependence on their intuition. In others, positive childhood experiences were credited with enhanced intuition. Some of their families normalized, valued, and modeled intuition, while in others it was devalued, ignored, or discouraged. Family-of-origin dynamics varied widely in their impact on the development of self-esteem, feelings of agency, and connection to a larger sense of meaning and purpose. In some cases, experiences supporting intuition came from other settings or extended family members, and for others a bit later in life when they found people who accepted, validated, and normalized intuition.

The practices therapists engage in to foster their intuition also support a strong positive sense of self, representing practices commonly associated with developing inner awareness and well-being. Personal psychotherapy; different forms of meditative, spiritual, and opening practices; reflection; spending time in nature; exercise; and reading all support intuitive development. The spectrum of abilities that clinicians bring to psychotherapy practice varies widely, reflecting personal talent and practice. Therapists who have developed their inner lives, having learned to listen and to be "taught from within" (Shinn, 1925, p. 11), have gained self-knowledge through life experience and have developed intuitive capacities long before they begin practicing professionally.

The experiences and practices clinicians associate with their clinical intuition are included in the next section drawn from the research data.

Cultural Acceptance

Cultural normalization of intuition may be a factor in being comfortable with acknowledging and using it. For example, Lailla is originally from the Middle East. She stated, "I come, really, from thousands of years of cultural meaning that intuition has been very central." Likewise, Alejandro was born in Europe and has worked and traveled in several European and Central American countries. He observed,

> I think going to Venezuela later on, and then traveling got me in touch with a lot of people who [are] more into intuition and things like that. I think Latin American—what we call less developed countries—are much more open to points or extremes sometimes, but to those things. Brazil is one of them. Venezuela was . . . I think traveling through Latin America, I learn more like that. It's more tolerated, I think. I think may have to, because there's a lot of . . . The African influence, the Christian and then the Native Americans. There's a ton of tolerance for that.

In cultures where the phenomenon of intuition is acceptable, it is more easily understood and viewed as valuable, eliminating significant barriers to its development. Through heritage and travel, these clinicians have experienced cultures that differ from the industrialized West, enabling them to acknowledge and accept their own intuitive abilities.

Experiencing Different Cultures/Changes in Community

While some of the participants came from or experienced cultures in which intuition was overtly accepted, others found that simply experiencing difference was important. Both moving repeatedly as a child and travel were important in the eyes of two participants.

Lena discussed her experience of changes that resulted from moving repeatedly.

> I think it comes from having been an army brat. I was always dealing with change and meeting new people and assessing my new surroundings. . . . I was expected to navigate a new situation, within the parameters of the Department of Defense and also my family, especially when we lived overseas.

Katherine explained how the experience of different cultures is related to intuition. It relates to her ability to take multiple perspectives.

> I've traveled a lot. I've lived in four different countries for 12 years of my life. I think learning other languages creates some different channels to understand people. . . . I think I can just see or feel things from different angles and different ways.

While for Lena moving repeatedly helped to develop intuition as a means to acculturate quickly, for Katherine the exposure to a multitude of perspectives or worldviews—realizing that there is not one way of being in the world that is "correct"—was beneficial. In both cases, the therapists credited a more nomadic childhood with enhancing their intuition. This observation may also play a role in Alejandro's experience, although his experience was more heightened in adulthood. These two therapists credit their exposure to cultural contexts of acceptance for their comfort with intuition.

Danger in the Social Environment

In some cases, therapists have found that exposure to danger has sharpened their intuition. Sharon found that living in a crowded urban environment where there was potential danger on the street honed her intuition. She related,

> I was born and raised in [a major metropolitan area] . . . I think there's a sense of . . . knowing what's around you, being aware . . . It's not paranoid, but it's "Something, possibly, is going on here. Watch out." It may be some, and too, a part of street smarts . . . Who just passed me? Who is behind me? I need to look around. Watch out for the pickpockets if I'm in Europe. . . .

Interestingly, both cultural support and cultural exigency appear to be valued by the participants as contributing to their development of intuition.

The Necessity to Discern Within the Family

For some therapists, the larger social environment was dangerous, which may have led them to develop their intuition. In other cases, it was difficulty in the family environment that rendered the ability to use intuition important. Some therapists who rely on intuition had the early experience of needing to remain alert and anticipate what was needed or about to transpire. Lena felt a duty to anticipate her disabled mother's needs. She related that this required her to learn how to read what other people required:

> I had to always be on alert as to how I was needed . . . I felt like my life was training me with this [using intuition] because of my mother's handicap. . . . I had always—when I was growing up, had always been in tune with what she needed. . . . it wasn't a big deal for me to tune into what people are—the need that they're not saying anything about. I think even before I went back to school and my training, I was trained to be discerning about what might be helpful or what somebody might need. . . . I feel like my whole life I've had to be in tune. I've had to anticipate needs of people. . .

It's important to note here that Lena credits this early relationship as her training ground for intuitive work.

Dinah experienced an unpredictable childhood environment in which hypervigilance had survival value.

> Well, in my house, you had to have a lot of intuition because you had to anticipate what was going to happen. I had a father who was very unpredictable. I think I learned, sort of, hypervigilance and watching people. You know how a dog just sometimes watches everything? I think I just learned to study people. There were a lot of people around. We lived near a lot of extended family. They all had their pathologies. They would get into fights over nothing. I was just sitting there watching and taking in. I developed a strong sense of intuition. . . . they used to call me "Rubber Neck," because I used to take in everything that was happening. That's strong intuit [sic]. You knew when to disappear. . . .

Dinah reflects upon a different role intuition can play in family dynamics: protection from conflict and unpredictability in the environment. Her focus on members of the family supported her developing discernment of when to disengage. In this sense, Lena and Dinah supported their developing intuition in opposite ways, each learning to engage or disengage as their circumstances warranted.

Intuition/Paranormal Experiences Were Normalized, Validated, or Modeled in Family of Origin

While some therapists found that danger or exigency heightened their sense of intuitive knowing, others had supportive experiences that heightened their awareness. Several of the therapists hailed from families in which intuition and other psi experiences were normalized and discussed with ease. Lena was validated for being intuitive both as a child and as a young professional.

> [Growing up] I don't think we necessarily used that word ["intuition"]. I know for example, my mom always encouraged me to trust my feelings. . . . There was the idea of being a female and what that meant and being a power as a female.
>
> That was really—that was definitely a point of discussion with my mom and me.

Ellen grew up in a family in which intuition and other paranormal experiences were commonly understood to be valid.

> [As a child] it was a conversation that you knew people from another life. People in the family would comment . . . like my mother and my father and my grandmother would say, "Oh, we knew him from another life." . . . When I was young, yeah, I saw my grandfather after he had died, and so that was a common topic of conversation. . . . It wasn't a big deal, but it was something that was said—I mean I said it when everyone was there, so that wasn't considered odd. . .
>
> I may not necessarily remember when I was little these things. It's more like when I was adult. Like my mother would say, well, my aunt smelled roses whenever anybody died. She would just smell a rose, and

> she'd say, "Well, who died?" Those kind of statements were not considered odd. My mother went to see a psychic at one point. It was just part of our life. . . . I don't know if my father had that in his family or not, but my mother's family, it was just rife. . . . It was just what our reality was. . . . It was just the way I was raised.

Felicia experienced a family environment in which a close family member had psychic abilities. This seems to have opened a door for Felicia to be comfortable with her own intuitive capacity.

> I can't remember that my family discussed intuition, but when I was about, probably about ten years old, my aunt, my mother's sister, lived with us for a year, and taught in our country school . . . Every night after dinner, after the dishes were done, we would sit down at the card table, and play the ouija board. . . . It was not probably every night, but a lot of the time, we did that. It was a really big activity for the year that she was there. I put that in the realm of the intuitive.

Lauren also had a close family member whose example helped her be comfortable with intuition: "Yes. I had a grandmother who was psychic. . . . I spent a lot of time with her. We'd sit out on the porch and she would talk about her psychic abilities . . ."

The experiences these clinicians describe—being told to trust their feelings, open family discussions about intuition and other paranormal experiences, and direct experience with psychic relatives—have validated the importance of intuition in the lives of these therapists.

In encouraging Lena to trust her own feelings, her mother supported her in the fundamental principle of intuition, learning to trust what is being felt. In Ellen's family, open conversation about intuitive experiences including the four pillars of psi—clairvoyance (seeing), clairsentience (feeling), clairaudience (hearing), and claircognizance (knowing)—moves validation of intuition to the level of experience. In this milieu, Ellen's report of seeing her grandfather after he died was embraced and became an important part of family lore, further supporting her openness to intuitive experiences. Felicia and Lauren had ongoing experiences with psi through their psychic relatives, an aunt and a grandmother respectively, that gave them firsthand knowledge of direct application of intuitive skills. These indelible experiences have opened their awareness to what is possible and modeled ways that intuitive information is available.

Supportive Parent(s)

Simply being supported by your parents—not necessarily for your intuition—may confer benefits on the use of this capacity. Two of the participants described having a good relationship with their parents. Brenda stated, "My parents, they were pretty cool. I remember thinking, 'I'm glad I have my parents.'" Lailla said, "Well, I have been blessed to have a wonderful relationship with my father. I think that my mother, as well, but more so my father."

Good relationships with parents during childhood support development of a positive sense of connection and well-being. Positive relationships are built on love and respect and, for children especially, reflect the experience of being seen and appreciated as the unique gift they are. This builds a foundation for the development of self-worth and self-esteem in children who learn to honor their own inner lives. Subsequently, when children grow up and choose to become psychotherapists, they bring these gifts of self-worth, self-esteem, and self-knowledge to clinical practice. They have learned how to be present for their patients and to transmit the support that they themselves have experienced.

Validated by Colleagues

In developing clinical intuition, it is helpful to have had the experience of being validated by colleagues, supervisors, or teachers regarding intuition. Therapists noted that they found these experiences to be very valuable.

Brenda shared the experience of being able to talk to a colleague about her clinical intuition. While they do not use the term "intuition" explicitly, the experience is nonetheless shared. She related,

> In my private practice, there's one other person I talked to. We just talked about the feeling we get. Also . . . where I work part-time, . . . They talk about, "I got this feeling. I got this sense." They don't necessarily say intuition.

David has seen auras in his clinical practice. He was able to discuss this with a couple of colleagues, one of whom took his experience seriously.

> [I have talked with] one colleague seriously and another one that I will joke about with it, but one colleague seriously who she's also

> a clinician, very well trained, very highly spiritually developed, actually, and has guided me a little bit in terms of maybe what's happening is this. Maybe that. If you feel like you're ready and want to develop more, let me know and we can think about that together. . .

Jeff is one of a few participants who is part of either a group practice or consultation group where talking about intuition is explicitly accepted. He related,

> . . . it's a very open group to spirituality, to intuition, to cutting-edge stuff. Yeah. We're always sharing that with each other. It's not a judgmental crew, so if I talk about something like this, nobody's gonna say, "What are you talking about?"

Felicia suggested that things are changing, and it is now more acceptable to discuss clinical intuition with colleagues. She said, "I think in many circles it's highly acceptable to use intuition."

Formal Training and Theory

Training experiences have proven to be both very helpful as well as potentially disruptive to the use of clinical intuition. One of the variables that arose is discussing training was the presence or absence of validation for intuition. Therapists who experienced validation of their use of intuition in their clinical training found the experience to be quite profound. Lena was validated for being intuitive both as a child and as a young professional during her training as a social worker. Asked when she had first noted using her intuition in a clinical encounter, Lena related,

> . . . as an undergraduate in a field placement, I remember I said something to someone in a group, and I said something very encouraging. Afterwards when we were—I was in supervision. The supervisor [said], "That was really good." It was just—and I didn't think about it. There was another time around the same time. . . . I was [co-leading a group with a graduate student]. Afterwards, we were talking about a group. This was after the first time I'd ever done a group. She goes, "Your clinical skills are really advanced. You've obviously been doing this a long time." I was like, "Oh, gee, Thank you". . . . I didn't say, "Oh, it was

> intuition." . . . I think she [my supervisor] got that it was intuitive. . . . I think it was reinforcing for me.

For Dinah, validation came in the context of training analysis. She said,

> . . . when I started in my analytically oriented therapy, I would, very honestly, tell my therapist everything. She knew every, every, every, everything about me. I'd tell her what was going on in a case, "I made this decision to go here; I made this decision to go there. Even though it sounds 'off of the tradition,' this is what I said." She'd say, "Oh, I would say the same thing!"
>
> So I had somebody who thought like I did, and sort of had the same sensibilities, and the same amount of ability to, sort of, know when to go forward and put on the steam, and when to be gentle; and when that was validated for me, then I knew that I had good senses, and that I could follow them [intuitions]. . . . It was important to find somebody who really felt the way I did.

Jennifer was validated by a supervisor, which she credits as helpful:

> I was in supervision for years—many, many years, maybe 15 or more, with a fellow . . . His approach was very grounded in the relationship. . . . I feel like that work with him really—he is with me, his voice, those experiences. That definitely informs, and intuition was something that we did talk about.

Validation of intuition during training is important in laying the foundation for its inclusion in ongoing practice experience. Whether intuition is acknowledged as a separate skill directly or implied when the clinician is acknowledged as having been able to gain important information, the result can be similar: the clinician learns to trust their process. Direct acknowledgment of intuition is useful, however, as it focuses attention on a whole field of knowledge.

Formal theory can also support intuitive processes. Deborah, for instance, found that the formal theory she learned during training was helpful in accessing her intuition. She did so by re-framing the concept of intuition as "associations" and discussed her first experience in working with her associations. In doing this, Deborah makes an interesting move: she explains,

> I was in a two-day institute where we explored our own feelings. I chose the guy who was the theory of the self. I thought this has gotta

> be interesting, so twelve or fifteen of us sat in our space and started exploring our own feelings about what was going on in the room in a process-oriented way. . . . He used self-psychological terms. He used empathy, attunement, mirroring.

This therapist was very clear and consistent that she understands intuition in terms of Intersubjective theory: she cited the importance of the theories of Stolorow, Orange, Benjamin, and Mitchell. Thus, for Deborah, formal theory is inseparable from the use of intuition.

Dinah also understands a specific formal theory to be central to her understanding and use of clinical intuition. In reference to Internal Family Systems, she elaborated,

> . . . through IFS, Internal Family Systems. . . . It's very spiritually oriented. There is a large meditative practice that's recommended. The people are very into Hakone, and mind/body things. The whole thing is, "Where do you feel it in your body? Where do you feel it?" It is a spiritual practice. . . . When you're really working with a patient, you get to a different vibrational level where you can feel very close to the person.

Justin understands the psychodynamic concepts of transference and countertransference to be linked to intuition. He stated,

> I don't think that I even thought of it as intuition. A lot of the methods in which I've been trained, I don't think they talk about it as intuition, but I think that's really what it is. Like I was saying in terms of the relationship, they might say transference or countertransference or things like that.

Jessica found that part of her training that was not tied to formal theory was relevant to the development of her clinical intuition.

> I think now that I'm really thinking about this theory and training and remembering some of the seminars from [name of institution redacted]—I was there in a two-year psychotherapy program, not psychoanalysis—I do recall—and I'm gonna paraphrase it. I don't recall exactly how this was worded by, I think, maybe more than one instructor—that if you're getting really a noticeable feeling of sadness or frustration or confusion or whatever it is with the client in the space, integrate that awareness in your work with the client.

For Lena, the aspect of her education that she cited as most crucial to her use of clinical intuition was the idea of putting the client first. She related, "My very first social work professor encouraged us to get out of the way. She would constantly say, 'It's not about you.' "

While some of the therapists in the study found parts of their formal training to be helpful to their use of intuition, many found it to hamper intuition. Ellen was among the latter.

> Well, I don't know that anything was necessarily said, but I imagine it probably wasn't. I did walk away with the impression that—well, I walked away, definitely, with the impression that there are certain rules you followed, and they didn't include anything that had to do with spirituality. I'm sure I didn't think—I never heard anything about intuition. I really thought I was—really, when I started, I was so outside the box. Now it's normal, the things that I did, like using meditation. Nobody did it. . . . I'm sure no one encouraged me to use all of my facilities and capabilities.

Elizabeth also felt that her formal training was unhelpful:

> I studied at a psychoanalytic institute. I can't think of a worse environment for that [developing intuition]. . . . the professors were all older women, very, very, very rigid people. . . . I think they communicated the theories, but I didn't appreciate how they were interactionally.

David was ambivalent about the relationship between formal training and intuition. He felt that the one aspect of his formal training that was helpful to his intuitive ability was in learning to go beyond the clients' overt communication to the "unthought known." Yet in spite of this aspect of his training, he generally saw his formal training as hampering his intuition.

> It [formal training] probably hampered [my use of intuition] somewhat, because in academic training there are particular theories to learn, for instance. People usually work hard to learn that particular theory. I can tell you it wasn't until I finished analytic training, which was here in this city, and at an institute that is known to be, I would say more middle of the road, not super conservative and not extremely open, either, but it wasn't until I finished that training that I really allowed myself to get back to what five years before I had gotten pretty good at, which was put it any way you want, intuition, trusting my gut, something. Training can interrupt it, I think, actually.

Like David, Grace found that one piece of training may have been helpful: specifically, trauma training. But for the most part, she feels that formal training tended to impede the capacity.

> Well, certainly, I did some learning on various techniques for trauma, . . . Specifically, [redacted name] does this—she's up in [city name redacted], and does some . . . trauma training that includes various kinds of, I would say, very right-brained kind of approaches. . . .
>
> I think professional training's—it's very analytical, keeps us out of our bodies, and so then we've lost our access . . . so I think that that's—and I'm not against it. I'm all for an integrated kind of—but if it stays there, words can sometimes get so in the way. Labels on things prevent us from actually knowing the thing, which is, of course, the irony of being in therapy, where most of what we do is talk, right? . . . Again, it's like how we use those words, and how we get into them. I do think a lot of academia is often disembodied, and I just think that that really. . .—then we're not learning to use this instrument we have for picking it up.

In spite of her experiences in school, she indicated that there are continuing-education workshops that touch on topics that may be relevant to intuition: "We also, now we have courses like, 'Using Meditation and Yoga in our Clinical Practice.' I've taken some of those classes."

The views of the professionals concerning a possible relationship between formal training and intuition were mixed. Some therapists felt that specific theories or practices that they learned during training were helpful in developing the use of clinical intuition. Others felt that there were aspects of formal training that fettered the use or development of this capacity. In the chapter on Current Knowledge and Perspectives, it is clear that many theoreticians from diverse schools of therapy support clinical intuition. There is a strong thread throughout the history of psychotherapy, from Freud to contemporary theorists that recognize the value of intuition in clinical work.

Developing Sense of Self

Sense of self may be conceptualized as a set (or grouping) of characteristics or traits, yet two of the therapists discussed this phenomenon more as a practice or experience: their focus was on generating a strong sense of self in general and as a professional. It appears to be related to an ability to "settle in" in order to facilitate intuitive work.

Felicia noted that her sense of professional self is tied to her intuitive capacity: "When I'm feeling at my strongest, in terms of my sense of who I am as a professional, is when my intuition flows more freely." This suggests that confidence is a key factor in the successful use of intuition. Jeff likewise suggested that his sense of self is important to his intuition. He noted that as he moves forward into the twilight of his career, he would like to explore and use his clinical intuition more. He reported,

> I think, for me, personally, coming out of my intellect more but not just being so emotional. . . . To use this internal compass in a way that's only recently presented itself to me. I think it's relaxing in my role as a therapist and in life in general. Wanting to track something in me. . . . I want more of me to inform my work, and I think I have that confidence this far into my career.

Jeff's use of internal compass is worth remarking here. A few of the therapists in this study suggested that the experience or practice of developing a strong positive sense of self, including the sense of professional self, were important to their use of clinical intuition. For many, their own therapy facilitated this process. Jeff and Felicia also point out an important point about the link between using intuition and professional confidence; it's possible that their confidence also brings a sense of job security and lack of fear in using intuition in practice.

It also appears in the narratives of such therapists that valuing intuition, inversely, is related to a strong, positive sense of self. These therapists seem to be suggesting that increased emotional or psychological health is related to greater comfort and ability to access intuition.

Ann is an example of someone who came to value her intuition in the process of her own therapy. For her, opening to her intuition was part of a healing process, and accessing her intuition was dependent on her coming to know and value herself.

> . . . I was always very sensitive and—which was not that great in my family. . . . I think I just—it was really probably through the process of my very first therapy, where I began to learn to value my sensitivity and my insights and then just having some feelings about people that proved to be right. I guess it really, for me, probably started with therapy. . . . it's really all a part, I think, of valuing yourself, knowing yourself, listening to your own voice, developing your own voice.

Katherine had a very similar experience. Intuition was not a topic of conversation in her family of origin. It was in the course of her own therapy that she opened to the phenomenon.

> Probably maybe through my own therapy. Dealing with my own anxiety and depression probably . . . I don't know if that ever was explicit. Yeah. I probably felt that. Yeah. Felt more comfortable with it.

These two therapists, in revealing that their personal therapy helped them value their intuition, suggest that opening to intuition is tied to overall self-awareness and self-acceptance.

Meditation, Mindfulness, Presence, and/or Prayer and Other Spiritual Practices

Meditation, mindfulness, presence, and prayer taken together constitute the largest category of practices that the clinicians in our study share. They were placed in a single category because these practices were often blended or overlapped in the therapists' conversations. Among them, meditation was the most widely discussed.

Elizabeth uses meditation specifically to invite intuitive insights. She explained, "When I see a client, if I'm having a difficulty with it, I may review the case, and then I'll go into a minor meditation and have some clarity about what direction I need to go in."

Katherine described how her meditation practice helps her access her intuition.

> . . . the more relaxed I am, the easier it [intuition] would come to me. If I were at a day-long meditation retreat, it would be easier to access after I had gone deeper into meditation than if I'm just rushing around doing errands or being busy. . . . to me, going slower is going deeper. Just you don't miss the signals that might come because there's not so much craziness and noise—excess noise.

Elizabeth tied meditation to another spiritual practice that is unique to her religious orientation. This is "putting someone in the light."

> . . . [There are] so many different types of meditation. . . . . One of the things that's part of being a Quaker is that you hold people in the light.

> That basically is, you put a light of the spirit around someone to enhance their lives in some way or another. I sometimes will hold ideas to the light so that I have somewhat of a detachment to it, but I can see it more clearly so that—sometimes, I'll do it that way. I might meditate on a concern and then really focus on it and then think about what is it about it that makes me uncomfortable about that concern, and then come up with one particular concern and then hold it at a distance and look at it. . . . At times, when I'd be working with someone, I would consciously hold them in the light to help them . . . It was a very deliberate process.

Sarah also meditates. She linked meditation to creativity, which she ultimately recognized as beneficial to her intuition: "I meditate. I practice Transcendental Meditation, off and on, and that—I think that makes me more creative. All these things help me be more creative, I think, and that fosters intuition. . . " It is important to note that while Sarah meditates, she also noted that her intuition was robust before she began the practice.

> I think of my childhood, when I wasn't doing any of the above, and I felt very connected to an intuitive process. That's why, I mean, now I think the meditation, for example, enhances my intuition, but I don't consider it—I don't consider that I wouldn't be . . . intuitive, if I didn't meditate.

Some therapists used the terminology "presence" and "being fully present" to describe a practice related to their intuition. For example, Jennifer reported that she engages in self-care, including exercise, healthy eating, and good sleep hygiene. She reported that her self-care "helps me be present." She continued: "I'm more intuitive when I'm present." She also discussed a meditation practice in the context of spiritual practice:

> I was born and raised Catholic, but I'm not a practicing Catholic. I do spiritual reading and I meditate. I like to say I try to meditate, because it's so hard. I work at it pretty regularly. I think there is a correlation there, yeah.

Jeff used the term "mindfulness" to describe a state that he believes is connected to intuition. He gave this advice to help other therapists access their intuition:

> Slow down, be in the moment, and don't worry or fret if you lose the narrative thread in favor of getting a—an intuition that might be helpful.

> It might even involve a little hint of mindfulness without completely detaching from the client to just be open to other things, other inputs.

Grace mentioned mindfulness in passing. Later in the interview, she discussed using guided imagery in her therapy. While she uses this as an intervention, she also finds herself in a state of tuning in. She explained, "I do a guided imagery body scan a lotta times with people, and so I am, again, just opening up to tune in as we're doing it, . . . tuning in to wherever I'm taking that. . . " She has found that another intervention she uses opens both herself and her clients to intuition: "I also do tapping, which is emotional freedom technique, and I find that incredibly intuit[ive]."

Lena has engaged in prayer for most of her life: "I remember talking to God from a young age, just in my head. Then what I learned what it was called, prayer, it was like, 'Oh, that's what I'm doing.'" When the interviewer asked Lena directly if she did anything to encourage intuition, she responded,

> Well, I pray. If I start to worry about a client too much, I just give it to [the] ether. . . . I just [say], "God, watch over this child of this family. God, keep them in your loving care. God, give them peace in their mind." I'm definitely not the be and end all.

Later in the interview she elaborated on her spiritual practices:

> I go to a. . . [redacted: Christian denominational] woman's retreat every year in the mountains. I go to . . . a center for prayer and pilgrimage. . . . . . we talked—we were talking about the third eye. . . . It was so interesting, because it was described by a mystic as the third eye being the eye through which I experience God, God is looking at me.

Deborah also engages in overtly spiritual practices:

> I'll ask the spirit to guide my work because I feel at sea. I don't know what's going on and being so lambasted with some negative feelings that I can't grab hold of anything that's happening. I just ask for help and guidance in the process, and I get it. . . . I pray to the Holy Spirit . . . St. Anthony sometimes . . . I've been on so many good retreats . . . I learned . . . how to really explore the depths of my spiritual feelings. . . .

Dinah thinks and prays, combining the two. When asked if she engages in any specific practices to enhance her intuition, she responded,

> Oh, I think all the time. I'm always thinking about living, dying, the clouds. I think I *live* on intuition. I mean, I think I take in a lot of data, but I think I'm sensing and feeling. What do I do? Well, here's what I do! I don't know if this enhances my intuition, but I know that it opens up and gives me space. Whenever I wake up in the morning, I say the "Shema," which is the Hebrew prayer. Whenever I get in the shower, and I think of the people who don't have water, I thank God for water. I do a lot of that kind of talking. I talk with God, and I think that enhances my intuition. . . . But I'm not sure I even believe in God, but I have this "practice" of just being in the clouds and thinking about things, having "intuition."

It is perhaps noteworthy that while Dinah identifies as Jewish and prays, she states she is not religious: "I do not have a religious gene."

Our research suggests that therapists who rely on intuition in their clinical practice engage in a number of practices that are difficult to separate or differentiate. They engage in meditation, mindfulness, and presence. They pray and engage in other religious experiences. Several of the therapists suggested that these practices support their intuition, with Sarah and Ellen noting that these practices support strong intuitive abilities they were already aware of.

Reflection/Thinking

As the quotes above indicate, drawing a line between prayer, meditation, and reflection can be almost impossible. While some of the therapists framed their reflection as a more meditative/mindful/spiritual practice, some discussed reflecting or thinking about clients and cases as a more distinct experience. Several of the clinicians discussed thinking about a client/case as a precursor to an intuitive insight. For example, Lailla engages regularly in reflection regarding her work with her clients:

> . . . my habit that I reflect upon the session, to see what went on, what I might have missed. Or, sometimes, just driving to work, and something from the session two weeks ago might just come to my mind. I pay attention. Why now? Why while I'm driving to work? I'm not even seeing the patient today, so what's going on? . . . sometimes during session, after session, before session. . . .

Other therapists engaged in intersession reflection on their clients. Felicia provides an example of this experience: "When I am driving to work, and I'm thinking about a client that I'm going to meet today, and a thought comes." Likewise, Ann engages in intersession thinking about a client as a precursor to her intuition.

> It's just when I'm thinking—if I'm thinking about them [a client] or after they leave the room. Just if something comes up. I'll note it. Before they're coming or if I'm driving to work for a session with the next person, sometimes I'll get some—a sense.

Several of the therapists who were not quoted here also indicated that thinking may initiate an intuitive insight. Many of those clinicians indicated that they engage in intersession reflection as part of the treatment process and that this practice helps them to access their clinical intuition.

As noted in Chapter 1, some of the current research and theory on intuition suggests that thinking is a separate cognitive process from intuition and may be cast as an opposite phenomenon. Among the professionals we interviewed, thinking was experienced as conducive to intuition. Perhaps a further distinction should be made. Perhaps the term "thinking" is used to describe two different processes. There is a form of thinking that is highly directive. Problem solving is an example of this process. There is another form of thinking that is more expansive and creative. In this form of thought, seemingly random factors arrive, combining and synthesizing into intuitive insights.

Openness as a Practice

In Chapter 7, openness is discussed as a personal characteristic shared by participants. We note that the term was used in two slightly different but highly related ways: a feeling of receptivity as well as the willingness to consider new possibilities. The therapists we spoke to also used the term "open" to describe a practice. For example, Ann discussed being open as a personal attribute as well as a practice. She describes this as a practice of opening to the influence of a higher power. To accomplish this, she asks for guidance:

> Well, I'm sure clients that I—that I feel pretty clear about what we're doing—that I feel freer to open up the channels, but then, that's not always true because sometimes, when I'm struggling with someone,

> and I'll just ask for help, and sometimes it comes through . . . if I'm particularly stuck with someone, I will ask for help from—in my belief system—I'll say, "You gotta help me with this because I'm really stuck." . . . It's just an opening up. . .

Janet experienced opening as a result of psychedelic drug use, which she views as a spiritual experience. "If I could be really honest, it would probably be some of the psychedelic drugs that I might have used in the '70s that helped me to touch into that. . . " She described her psychedelic experience as "the sense of the senses opening up so widely. . . "

Openness reflects receptivity and a willingness to consider new possibilities and capacities critical to effective psychotherapy practice. Each person who enters treatment has a unique personal history and current circumstances that merit the therapist's full attention and respect. The practice of opening may or may not be associated with specific spiritual/religious practices and beliefs.

Being in Nature

Nature is a common theme for those who use intuition in their practice. They felt it was important to their ability to access and use intuition. Elizabeth attributed her grandfather's intuition to his life as a farmer: "My grandfather had a farm. . . . There was more of a contact with nature and the constant death and life. . . " Felicia elaborated on the same theme. She closely identified her father's intuition as a result of his work on the farm:

> The other [intuitive] would be my dad, who farmed. He read the weather report and followed it carefully, but he would say sometimes, things like this. "It's not in the weather, but I know it's gonna rain." Part of that might be intuition, or part of that might just be because how the clouds look, and the air feels, you know? . . . "I know it's gonna rain today," or "Next week I think it's gonna be a sunny week. We'll have a good week with the crops." . . . I think he was very in tune with what was, very in tune with nature. Nature is spirit. One year when I was in fifth grade, I hated the music teacher at the church and I had to be in the choir, so I refused to go to Sunday school. My mother said, "Okay, you can go out with your father, fishing every Sunday if you wanna do that." I did, and that was wonderful because if that's where spirit is, then that's where the beauty of nature was, and Dad and I had such a wonderful time together.

In a similar vein, Sarah noted in passing that along with other practices, long walks in the woods help to expand her mind and support her intuition. This was reiterated by other therapists who cited attunement to the physical environment and/or being in touch with the cycles of life as being related to intuition.

Exercise

Several of the therapists indicated that exercise is important to intuition. There were two forms of exercise that received particular attention: yoga and those that are rhythmic or repetitive like walking, running, or swimming.

Then Lena was asked, "what personal study or practices helped you with your intuition?" She responded, "Well, my first yoga class that I took, I remember that was the first time I really integrated the mind–body thing. I had studied the mind body thing. I hadn't felt it until that training." Likewise, Brenda stated, "I exercise . . . when I swim, for me that's meditative. When I walk, and I think that refuels me. . . . " Dinah, too, exercises. "I do a lot of exercise, and that's very opening." She indicated that she practiced yoga and also discussed using a treadmill: "often on a treadmill— . . . when I'm like, *[simulates treadmill with hands]*, you know, it's very calming, rhythmic."

Sarah discussed exercise in the same context as meditation. She referenced Transcendental Meditation and remarked that it made her more creative. Then she added, "Right now I'm doing a lot of swimming, and I can get into a zone. All these things help me be more creative, I think, and that fosters intuition. . . " She continued to relate meditation and exercise when she added, "When I expand my mind, whether it's through meditation or something else, even a long walk, sometimes, in the woods, I feel that it translates into my work."

Grace, like Brenda and Dinah, finds that walking is helpful. "Walking and again, practicing openness in the world in my walking."

Brenda finds that exercise, along with other forms of self-care, is important to intuition.

> I do try to practice self-care. Essentially try to eat a decent diet. I exercise. I really, really like solitude. . . . I don't necessarily do anything deliberately. I don't meditate, but when I swim, for me that is meditative. When I walk, I think that refuels me. . . .

It is interesting to note that in the two accounts cited, exercise was related to expanding or opening one's mind. In another example, exercise was associated with creativity, which, in turn, enhances the person's intuition. In all cases, several of the therapists noted that either rhythmic exercise and/or yoga enhance their intuitive capacities.

Reading

A few of the participants indicated that reading is important. In some cases, the reading is related specifically to intuition. In other cases, the subject matter is unspecified. Dinah indicated, "I just do a lot of reading." Katherine appears to be an avid reader across domains. "I read a lot. I read a lot of Buddhist books and Buddhist philosophy. A lot of poetry. I read a lot of literature." For Ellen, the reading is targeted: "I used to—I haven't read any recently. I used to read a lot about it [intuition]."

Reading about worldview or philosophy, whether affiliated with a religion or not, is important to some of the therapists. Likewise, reading about intuition validated and supported their development of their intuitive process. Some books offer specific exercises to access intuition, including books written by psychotherapists who discuss its application in clinical practice. Intuition in the service of psychotherapy has important distinctions from intuition in private life; however, enhancing intuition in the therapist's private life supports mastering its use professionally.

Summary and Discussion

Therapists identified several experiences and practices that they felt were important to the development of their intuition. A recurring theme was the importance of validation. Clinicians found that acceptance of their intuition was very beneficial, whether it was on a cultural level, within their families, in their education and training, and/or among colleagues. This observation suggests that bringing the topic of clinical intuition out of the shadows and into acceptable discourse may have a profound effect on therapists' willingness and ability to use and share their wisdom about intuition in therapy.

Along with the overarching theme of validation, there was a leitmotif centered on the development and maintenance of a strong, positive sense of self, including a professional self. This theme was developed as clinicians discussed the benefits of their personal therapy and their self-care regimes.

Therapists shared several other experiences that they believe were helpful in developing their intuition. Some of these experiences were challenging.

For example, one therapist discussed how living in a social environment that was crowded and dangerous helped her develop her intuition. In some cases, participants felt that growing up in a family in which they had to be discerning, either because the family was volatile or because of having to meet others' needs, nurtured their intuition.

While some participants in the study credited difficult experiences with helping them develop their intuition, others found that difficulty is not the only route. Two of the intuitive therapists identified very supportive parents, and others painted pictures of generally happy childhoods. Perhaps this helped them to identify and be comfortable with their experiences and thus override negative messages they may have gotten about intuition elsewhere. Perhaps this is related to the strong positive sense of self that arose as a theme throughout the category.

This sense of self may be related to a research finding by Jeffrey and Fish (2011) indicating that "keen self-awareness based in self-of-the-therapist was . . . critical to this process" (p. 354). The personal therapy of the participants may have also served to validate their intuition and enhance their self-awareness and sense of self.

Therapists also suggested that professional training, and especially theory, can be a mixed blessing. Some found that certain theories or their associated practices were helpful in the development of intuition, while others found that formal training undermined their natural intuition. Therapists found that focusing on internal states and feelings, as well as attending to transference and countertransference, were helpful to their developing clinical intuition. Jeffrey and Fish (2011) similarly found that training and supervision can be important. One of their participants discussed a supervisor who taught that feelings that arise in treatment are important and must be attended to.

Besides having had a number of different experiences, the participants engaged in practices that they believe enhance their intuition. Perhaps the most endorsed response is meditation. Meditation, mindfulness, and presence, along with prayer and contemplation, are difficult practices to differentiate, however, taken as a whole the practices have had a great impact on the respondents. This finding supports that by Charles (2004). In her research on clinical intuition, participants mentioned meditation and mindfulness specifically in developing intuition and indicated that spirituality and spiritual practices in general were important.

Some of the therapists indicated that thinking or reflecting on their clients and practice, often between sessions, was an important element in the intuitive process. This finding contradicts the cognitive psychology tenet that system one thinking and system two thinking may be separate phenomena. It must be noted that while some of the participants suggested that thinking helps their intuition, others suggested that they need to curb analytic thought in order to access intuition. Perhaps this apparent contradiction may be explained by noting the difference between directed thinking and expansive thinking. It may be that the latter is more closely associated with intuition.

The intuitive therapists identified being open as an important personal characteristic. They also suggested that opening as a practice contributes to their intuitive abilities. To be sure, many different specific practices can be used to accomplish opening. For one participant, it was the use of hallucinogenic drugs. Others opened themselves to intervention by a higher power. While being in nature was important, perhaps this is in part because of the way it opens the therapist to the larger world. This finding supports a similar conclusion in the Petitmengin-Peugeot (1999) study. While her participants discussed opening as a sensation (perhaps related to "form" in the present study), it is possible that engendering the sensation may be, for some, a practice.

In all cases, our therapists serve as examples of how intuitive processes are used in clinical practice. To the degree that you find their experiences useful, you may find greater ease and comfort in working with your own intuition in the service of your clients' needs.

Implications of Experiences and Practices Associated With Clinical Intuition

1. Cultural Acceptance
   Implication: Awareness that many cultures value intuition and include it as central to their way of life supports its inclusion in psychotherapy.
2. Experiencing Different Cultures/Changes in Community
   Implication: Exposure to other cultures and systems of thought increases awareness, understanding, and respect among people. Cultivate curiosity and appreciation of differences.
3. Danger in the Social Environment
   Implication: Our environments have a profound effect on our sense of safety and security and our subsequent development of coping skills. Dangerous situations teach us discernment, a key aspect of intuitive development.

4. The Necessity to Discern Within the Family
   Implication: Our families provide our foundational experiences in relationships. What we learn about ourselves is forged navigating the waters of family life.
5. Intuition/paranormal Experiences Were Normalized, Validated, or Modeled in Family of Origin
   Implication: Validation of intuition and paranormal experiences in our family of origin supports our developing sense of who we are and how we are connected to the larger world.
6. Supportive Parent(s)
   Implication: Whether therapists have experienced supportive parents or not, support is fundamental in the development of self-awareness, self-esteem, and the ability to trust one's intuition.
7. Validated by Colleagues
   Implication: Professional validation supports development of a strong, positive personal and professional sense of self that enhances developing intuition.
8. Formal Training and Theory
   Implication: Awareness of understanding about clinical intuition varies by individual, educational, and theoretical setting. Use discernment in making choices about where and with whom you choose to train.
9. Developing Sense of Self
   Implication: The development of strong self-awareness and self-acceptance is fundamental to connecting with clients intuitively.
10. Meditation, Mindfulness, Presence, and/or Prayer and Other Spiritual Practices
    Implications: Incorporation of practices to support quieting the mind, connecting to spirituality/the transpersonal, and developing the ability to be fully present are fundamental to intuitive development.
11. Reflection/Thinking
    Implication: Intuitive insight comes during sessions, as part of intersession reviews, and spontaneously between sessions.
12. Openness as a Practice
    Implication: Intuition is facilitated by consciously choosing to open empathically to clients, including opening to spiritual sources for help, however they are personally defined.
13. Being in Nature
    Implication: Nature is healing, grounding us in our environment and connecting us more deeply within ourselves and to the larger world.

14. Exercise
    Implication: Exercise is good self-care, clears the mind, and supports the mind–body connection. In addition to its physical and mental health benefits, it supports creativity and expansive thinking, important elements of intuition.
15. Reading
    Implication: Intuition is supported by exposure to a wide range of ideas: those that are academic, inspirational—any material that the therapist is drawn to.

Application of Experiences and Practices Associated With Clinical Intuition in the Therapeutic Setting

1. Seek people who are comfortable with their own intuition and can validate yours.
2. Find a peer group, colleague, or consultant who understands intuition with whom you can process your experiences and begin to refine your intuitive capacities.
3. Develop your self-knowledge through personal therapy and other activities that enhance your personal growth. A good understanding of yourself supports your ability to trust your intuitive experiences.
4. Engage beliefs and practices that are compatible with clinical intuition and that fit your worldview: for example, the clinician who was raised in a Jewish family said Jewish prayers; the Christian engaged in Christian spiritual practices; there are also many forms of meditation that cross traditions. Likewise, the concept of presence, especially therapeutic presence, has gained increasing interest in the last couple of decades. Whatever your spiritual or nonspiritual orientation may be, some form of being in the moment and/or accessing a transpersonal phenomenon may help you access your intuition.
5. Build time into your clinical practice for intersession reflection, as thinking about clients primes the intuitive process.
6. Engage in "opening" as a practice: The exercise of opening can take any number of forms. It may have the feel of allowing the influx of transpersonal inspiration or help, it may be an act of imagination or visualization, or it may be somatic, feeling your body differently. For example, it may feel like an opening of your heart area or the opening of your senses.

7. Engage with nature: If you currently do not spend time in nature or live in an environment where there is not ready access to it, find ways to attune to the natural environment and the cycles of life.
8. Acknowledge the role culture has played in your willingness to use intuition. This extends to the culture of psychotherapy, where intuition is devalued in education, training, and practice programs, thereby mirroring the worldview that values the scientific method over direct experience.
9. Learn from difficult experiences, especially those from childhood, as they can serve as a springboard in developing your intuitive capacities. You may come to appreciate that intuition has been a strength you have drawn on. Early development of intuition, whatever the reason, translates to a valuable skill in professional practice.
10. Seek out life experiences and practices that are compatible with intuition, and draw wisdom from your experiences while developing empathy and compassion.

Works Cited

Charles, R. (2004). *Intuition in psychotherapy and counselling*. London: Whurr.

Jeffrey, A. J., & Fish, L. S. (2011). Clinical intuition: A qualitative study of its use and experience among marriage and family therapists. *Contemporary Family Therapy, 33*, 348–363.

Shinn, F. (1925). *The game of life and how to play it*. New York, NY: Simon & Schuster.

Petitmengin-Peugeot, C. (1999). The intuitive experience. *Journal of Consciousness Studies, 6*(2–3), 43–77.

Pierce, P. (2009). *The intuitive way: A guide to living from inner wisdom*. Hillsboro, OR: Atria Books/Beyond Words.

7

Characteristics and Values of Intuitive Therapists

In our interviews with therapists, we found some common characteristics that we believe support the use of intuition. Some of these are obvious: openness, for instance, enables a clear mind to take in the subtle messages that make up intuitive insights. Others, like being logical, may seem contradictory to the use of intuition. Most of these traits, one may argue, are characteristics of good therapists in general. While this is true, we've asserted from the beginning that most therapists use intuition and either are unaware of it or avoid using it because they lack training or understanding of it. Therefore it's not surprising that the qualities that constitute a good therapist also support the use of intuition.

Therapists discussed the importance of developing certain personal virtues, qualities, and/or values. The picture that emerges is that therapists who rely on clinical intuition tend to see themselves as logical/skeptical, open/receptive and curious, and observant/attuned. They care about others and express themselves by being helpful, nonjudgmental, understanding, and respectful and by drawing others out. They value religion and spirituality, transparency, and self-reflection. They appreciate aesthetics and associate the ability to be abstract with intuitive capacity.

The clinicians reflected on how clinical intuition rests on the inner life of the therapist: how self-aware they are; how they communicate with and treat others; their values and worldview; and their self-expression. Each of these characteristics and values shapes their inner world and is communicated to the patient whether verbalized or not; this lays the groundwork for what is possible in the application of intuitive processes.

Logical/Skeptical

In the popular stereotype, intuitive people are often considered "ungrounded." Even in the cognitive research outlined in Chapter 1, some researchers suggest that logic and intuition may involve different mental processes and might even be viewed as the opposite of each other. But the therapists with whom we spoke did not endorse this view. While they were comfortable with their intuition, they equally viewed themselves as being logical and skeptical. This is most likely because those traits offer a *check* to their intuitive thoughts; so while logic may not appear at first glance to be an inherent trait of intuition, the ability to confirm intuitive insights with reason is crucial to its effective use. Using logic in this way not only helps practitioners have more confidence in their intuition, it also legitimizes its professional use.

Elizabeth, Alejandro, and Jeff demonstrate this seeming paradox between being logical and skeptical and yet intuitive as well. Elizabeth emphasized her comfort with engaging in discursive thinking: "I'm just incredibly logical and practical and reasonable and realistic. That's my *modus operandi.*" It's important to note that Elizabeth is also confident using intuition in her practice. It is perhaps her trust in both forms of thinking that balances and enhances both.

Alejandro also identified as logical: "There is something in me that is very rational." He is equally skeptical of people who claim to have special abilities. In his case, this is because certain kinds of psi abilities bring enhanced power. "I'm kind of a bit of a doubter . . . because I see what people can do with [occult] knowledge and the power that can come with knowledge." It's important to note the cultural context of Alejandro's comment. He references, here, his negative experiences with new age spiritual groups in South America.

Jeff demonstrated a high degree of ambivalence regarding his growing awareness of and curiosity about his use of clinical intuition. He described his parents as people who "like to deal with factual matters." He described himself as "a little Socratic. I'm a little bit like a detective, occasionally, on certain subjects. Trying to follow leads. . . " Although he recognized that "it doesn't mean I'm only an intellectual and cognitive therapist." He described why he volunteered for the study: "I wanna be open to it, rather than say, 'well, it has no norms. Not a lot of statistics. It's BS until proven scientifically.' " Yet he admits that in the past he was

> . . . on the somewhat closed-off end to some of this paranormal whatever. It's winning me over a little bit, and I think, "Well, okay.

> You're a dyed-in-the-wool cynic. Why would this be making progress in you?" . . . I think more openness would help, but what's so interesting to me is that this has insinuated itself ever so delicately around any defenses or intellectual doubts I have.

Then he reflected, "It doesn't have to be scientifically proven and normed and replicated in 2,000 studies for me to be open." He described his ability to switch between logic/discursive thinking (which he identifies as "left brain"), and more creative/intuitive abilities ("right brain") and ultimately integrate the two modes of thought.

> My right brain is extremely active. I'm curious, I'm creative, but I wouldn't say I have lots of creative output. I think I'm creative verbally . . . I quest to understand things that feel murky in my right brain. I use my left brain to go into my right brain and say, "What's going on in there?" . . . I think there's a big interplay with each of them [right brain and left brain] running back and forth, feeding each other back and forth . . . I think my left brain got me through some difficult times.

Jeff's use of the word "interplay" is enlightening here. What others see as a conflict between two types of thinking Jeff sees as an opportunity for creativity and self-examination. Jeff's point of view is also useful because he points out the error of constructing a binary between reason and intuition.

Open/Receptive

Several participants suggested that openness is a vital part of their intuitive ability. "Openness" is defined by the participants as the ability to receive as well as the ability to allow for possibilities.

Lena related a narrative in which there was a breach in the therapeutic alliance. In the process of determining how to repair the alliance, she stated, "I was open, I kept myself open to intuiting." Later she stated, intuition relies on "Being able to open yourself up to how it may be for a person, any person. . . . it's a willingness. It's being open. . . . being open to receive. . . "

Lailla also referenced openness. She stated that intuition requires being fully present. She elaborated a bit later that "Present means openness, being in a receiving mode." But openness also can mean allowing for possibilities. Lailla used the term in this sense when she explained, "I think that there's still a lot of things about intuition that we don't know . . . I'm open to finding out."

Janet identified the site of her openness to be her heart. She also noted that openness is associated with curiosity:

> Curiosity keeps you open to the possibility . . . if I don't have an open heart, for whatever reason, because of what's happening between me and the client, or because of something has happened to me in my life, then it's hard. My heart has to be open.

Alejandro also valued his curiosity: "In my professional life and my outside life as a person that likes to grow and improve and know and learn and search for things. . . "

While in some instances clinicians stressed their logical and sometimes skeptical nature, they nonetheless noted their openness and curiosity. Of note, Alejandro sees himself as both.

Observant/Attuned

Our therapists offered an interesting observation about the role of attunement in therapy: it is an *active* form of observation driven by curiosity and a desire to figure out another's inner workings. The linking of attunement and observation—and even curiosity—is confirmed by the therapists framing the quality as present since a very early age. Deborah understood herself to be an observer of human nature.

> My mother used to say to me that I was an astute observer of human nature. She did tell me that once when I was a little girl. I was looking out the window of a car . . . I was pointing out some things that I was seeing or thinking. She goes. . . "you are one of the most astute people on what you see in the world. How observant." "Observant" was the word she used. "You're so observant."

Dinah's understanding of her observing nature was centered more on behaviors, or what was happening around her.

> . . . I think I learned hypervigilance and watching people. You know how a dog just sometimes watches everything? I think I just learned to study people . . . I. . . [would be] just sitting there watching and taking

> in. I developed a strong sense of intuition . . . they used to call me "Rubber Neck," because I used to take in everything that was happening. . . . I take in a lot of data. . .

Being observant may be linked to the ability to attune to others. Of note, the kind of examination that may be associated with attunement is an active endeavor rather than a passive taking in. Brenda explicitly collapsed observation and attunement. She identified herself as having "always been, I think, very attuned, just able to observe." She stressed that being an observer required a level of activity: "I'm sensitive. I'm attuned. I'm a Cancerian. We're watchers, but we're also active . . . I'm an observer, but I'm not a passive observer."

Dinah gave a counterexample of attunement and intuition. She stated that her mother would "not have wasted her time" with intuition. For Dinah, one of the things that stood out about her nonintuitive mother was that "she wasn't tuned in to people."

In these examples, clinicians reflect that being observant has been part of their self-definition from early childhood, enabling them to translate their natural observational skills to their work as therapists. This in turn serves as a foundation for adapting their skills to attuning to their patients and to integrating intuition.

Transparent/Authentic

The qualities of transparency and/or authenticity may be associated with comfort or ease in the use of clinical intuition as well. Several of the clinicians reported being transparent and/or authentic. Brenda stated, "I'm also very transparent as a therapist. Just as a person, I'm not telling them [my clients] my business, but I'm transparent. They can see me." Natalie said, "I had to be so authentic [with a client] . . . which wasn't hard, because I am, naturally that way."

Besides the terms "authenticity" and "transparency," the therapists tended to describe themselves as comfortable being and using their "self" in the therapeutic process. Jennifer expressed this concept in these terms: "I can be real. I can be me at this point in my life with all I've experienced and all I know and offer that." Jeff echoed his desire to be himself: "I want more of me to inform my work, and I think I have that confidence this far into my career." David referenced his understanding of being himself and accessing his intuition. He stated, "Being disconnected from one's self makes it very difficult to be aware of intuitive . . . sense or feelings."

The therapists who value intuition referenced being transparent and authentic, "being me," and using the self. The participants used these terms to express being in touch with and using their sense of self in therapy. Jeff was specific that he saw this capacity to be necessary to access his intuition.

Self-Reflective and Self-Aware

Being able to be oneself authentically and use the self therapeutically is predicated upon knowing yourself. Indeed, the therapists who discussed their intuition were, on the whole, highly self-aware and reflective. Jeff indicated that self-awareness is important to him. He noted,

> I've always been interested in what makes me tick, what makes me who I am, what makes other people who they are. I was fascinated by my own family dynamics once I got old enough and objective enough to not just be absorbed into them. . . . It's always been one step short of an obsession, maybe. Just what makes me tick? What makes people tick? I've had therapy, but I feel like I've had endless therapy with myself. . .

Knowing yourself on a deep level is an important quality for those who wish to develop their skill of using clinical intuition. There are several practices and experiences to help in this endeavor. Some of these were explored in Chapter 6.

Abstract

Being an abstract thinker may be associated with clinical intuition. Two of the participants identified being overly concrete as antithetical to intuitiveness. Dinah discussed her mother as a negative example of an intuitive person. She identified her mother as "very concrete . . . orderly, . . . task-oriented. . . " Likewise, Ellen stated, "I think there are people that are very concrete and wouldn't want to [use intuition]. . I mean it would just be so out there."

This may not be a characteristic that is easily changed or adopted. Certainly, it would be interesting to study the ability to become more abstract and whether or how this might change one's use of clinical intuition. It may very well be that, as Ellen suggested, more concrete thinkers are simply not interested in intuition.

Neurotic

A few of the participants indicated attributes that reflect their own anxieties. David was quite pointed: "I can be really neurotic. I'm a little crazy as a human." Ann disclosed that she suffered from depression and anxiety.

> I got depressed, rather than anxious. I mean, I do have anxiety but not—the depression's been more manifest, I think . . . I just learned to keep it inside, and I turned some of it inside. . . . It didn't come out in a lot of anxiety. It was more depression and feeling sad.

Katherine also noted her anxiety. "I think part of that is anxiety because I did learn that when we have an anxious period . . . we can see that. A lot of my life is like that." She noted somewhat later in her interview, "I do have a lot of insecurity around performance issues. Am I a good enough therapist? Am I doing this right? . . . my insecurity and competitiveness or judging myself with other—against someone else."

Guilt, depression, and anxiety were noted as personal experiences by a few of the therapists in this study. These are experiences that are common to most people during periods of their lives. Their openness to discussing their personal struggles with depression and anxiety may signal characteristics listed above that are compatible with intuition: openness, authenticity, and self-awareness. Further, one may wonder if they experience higher levels of these feelings than others or whether their high level of self-awareness makes these feelings more apparent to the therapists. They also demonstrate the importance of more "human" characteristics that relate to intuition; these characteristics, as noted before, allow for a less dehumanized or mechanical form of therapy. Their honesty about their anxieties is also refreshing because they affirm that perfection is neither possible nor desirable, even in clinical practice.

Helpful/Giving

The therapists also stressed the personal quality of being giving, helpful people. They discussed their desire to be helpful to others who are in need. Lena grew up with a mother who had a disability.

> I was always wanting to be helpful [to disabled mother] . . . I think it has to do with how I move in the world—is I'm willing to—for example,

> when I [went] so much out of the victim's assistant network, I felt compelled when I was in a better place to give of my time, to give back to that work. It's just how my parents were. It's how I am.

She believes that this experience helped her to resonate with the lessons of one of her professors during her social work education. She told the interviewers that her teacher repeated,

> "It's not about you." . . . I understood it, because I already believed that. I have to be able to step back and without my ego being involved or my feelings being hurt. It's not my process. My responsibility is to not get in the way of somebody's therapeutic process. . . . I don't wanna seem like I'm driving this [the therapy process]. . . . I try to fade into the wallpaper and allow them to shine on their own.

Brenda also discussed her desire to help others. She stated, "It seems like every time I turn around, somebody's asking me for help. I try to give it. I feel like I can do a good job of that. . . . I'm very much concerned, especially about children."

Jeff was clear that being a therapist and the desire to be helpful to others are very closely related to each other. His observation raises an important point regarding characteristics and values of intuitive therapists. Those characteristics and values that contribute to the decision to become a therapist are consistent with those that are associated with the willingness or ability to use intuition in that process: He observed, "[deciding on a career] was a process of elimination. Really, the only thing that I felt I could do in this life was be helpful in this way [as a therapist]."

Nonjudgmental

Likewise, being nonjudgmental arose as an important personal quality among the participants. Lena was explicit about the damage inherent in a judgmental stance toward others and the fact that it undermines intuition. She stated,

> I get in the way [of intuition] if I try to judge or come to any conclusions too quickly . . . I grew up in a very judgmental family. I knew I wanted to be the opposite of that, because I just knew how it felt to be judged. I didn't ever want to make anybody feel that way.

Jennifer revealed that she struggles against being judgmental. "For me, there is a little bit of a struggle between observing and judging. I have to keep that in check." Later she reiterated her struggle:

> I guess as I see it, it can get in the way, being too judgmental. I just feel like personally I have to be on watch for that. Like, "Is this an observation or is this a judgment?" And step back.

Closely associated with being nonjudgmental is the clinicians' ability to exercise patience rather than foreclose on conclusions. Jennifer was reflecting on how she has changed both as a result of having practiced for a long time and due to the human maturation process. She observed,

> I think as I've gotten older, and when I say older, I mean practiced more years as well, I think I probably don't jump to the conclusion. . . . I think I probably don't go to ten as quickly, I'm like, 'Well, wait a minute. Let's hold off on this. Let's see what else is going on.'

These participants explained that being judgmental can undermine intuition. Related to a nonjudgmental stance is patience, or holding back from foreclosing on conclusions. One participant explained that being judgmental blocks openness, which, as described above, may be related to intuitive capacity.

Understanding and Patience

Patience is another virtue clinicians associated with intuition and as antithetical to being judgmental. Likewise, being understanding and patient is valued rather than being reactive in the face of frustration. For example, Elizabeth described herself as being understanding of others' difficulties, as opposed to getting angry. She observed that not all clinicians have this quality.

> I remember when I was a young therapist that there was people—I worked in a clinic, and there were young therapists who would get really furious with their clients. They're coming to us because they have problems. Why are you getting angry with them for their problems? They had these terrible feelings, and the only reason I knew about it cuz I would draw them out and talk with them and help them with it because I never felt that. I never felt angry with people for having experiences and all the *mishegas* that they do.

In this way, the patience it takes to understand clients who can be frustrating is an important character trait for Elizabeth.

The qualities of patience and understanding with difficult clients is shared as a general pattern among therapists in the study: these individuals value other people and take care in interactions to demonstrate that care.

Respectful/Grateful

The code of ethics for therapists demands a respect for all patients; it's not surprising, then, that our therapists identified with this quality and that respect would play a large part in building the trust needed to build a therapeutic partnership. The value our therapists put on respect was exemplified in Lailla, who finds it central to her practice:

> To me, when you meet somebody, that moment of meeting—like this morning, you and I said hello. That's the moment of arrival, arrival in a space that requires respect, regard, and true belief in this objectivity of the other person. I don't know much about you, at this moment, but I do have a responsibility to the face that I said hello to.

Lailla emphasized respect as not just a therapeutic ethic but as a life imperative as well: "I think life without it [respect for others] . . . is not worth living."

Closely related to Lailla's use of the term "respect," two other therapists expressed a profound appreciation or gratitude for the opportunity to engage with others on a deep level. Lena put it in these terms: "I am constantly aware that it is a privilege. It's an honor and a privilege to be a part of somebody's process." David also noted his reverence for the treatment process: "If I'm sitting down here with someone it's a sacred undertaking."

Respect and gratitude for the opportunity to interact on a deep level with others is a trait shared among some of the therapists in this study. These qualities are consistent with their general patient-centered orientation, a theme that surfaced repeatedly.

Draws Out Others

A couple of the therapists noted that they value the fact that they tend to draw out others who are less socially engaged. Samantha related,

> I always felt something for the underdog or I felt very drawn towards the kids that weren't picked for the teams or for somebody that was being laughed at or left out. That kind of began my—I just wondered about them and would talk to them and then would find that they weren't all that different. It was easy for me to engage them and bring them into the group. . . . if you offer that olive branch or just hand of kindness, then they open up more.

Lena also noted that she values the ability to draw out less socially engaged individuals. She stated,

> I'm even that person who—okay. Give me ten colleagues, The one I'm drawn to is the one that's standoffish. I just wanna figure out a way to communicate with this person, because it's not easy. I don't know why I find that interesting, but I do.

Some of the therapists observed that they tend to engage those who may not be comfortable in social situations. This may simply reflect the therapist's desire to help others and also represent a deeper value for inclusion and a sense of community.

Spiritual

Most (but not all) of the participants identified themselves as having a spiritual orientation. While they represent a number of different religious orientations—Jewish, Christian, Muslim, and Buddhist—as well as being non-religiously spiritual, many of them share the general interest in spirituality. This was as explored in greater detail in Chapter 6 on experiences and practices. The point here is that many of the therapists identify as having an interest in or valuing spirituality and/or religion.

Illustrative quotes of this point come from a number of participants. For example, Lena stated, "I'm very interested in the study of spiritual experience across the human experience. One of my favorite classes in college was an overview of world religions." Lailla related, "I'm really not one of those people who walks around, wear my spirituality on my sleeve, so to speak. It's a very personal, private part of me. Not religious based. I respect all religions." Dinah put it this way: "I do not have a religious gene. . . [but I'm] very spiritually oriented. . . " Grace stated,

> I grew up with these parents that were agnostic and atheist, and proud of it, . . . I was never comfortable with [religion] . . . [that experience] has made it hard for me really to jump into a form [of religion]. . . . I feel like I could fit into any one . . . but I don't feel like I'm grounded in one particular [religion or religious form].

Our participants' reliance on spirituality brings up an important question: to what extent does their spiritual worldview inform their intuition? One connection we found was that religion and spirituality supplied many of them with a model for how intuition works.

Concerned About Social Justice

Two of the participants noted that they place high value on social justice. Brenda stated, "I do feel like just everybody has certain rights. I think that everybody has a right to have food and shelter." Likewise, Lailla observed, "I've always been concerned about social justice issues and inequality and whatnot." This supports previous findings that link empathy to the use of intuition.

Appreciates Aesthetics

Two of the participants demonstrated an appreciation of the arts. Brenda said, "I think people need art. They need music. They need to be in nature . . . I think it's tremendously healing to be in beautiful surroundings." Grace placed very high value on music. "I always grew up with music, so that was always a very important part of me and some part of our family growing up."

Extroversion and Introversion

Some of the participants identified the characteristic of extroversion, while others identified themselves as being more introverted. Lena represents the former.

> Well, I tend to be somebody who—I just put myself out there. I think it's because the first half of my life, I didn't really talk at all . . . I just talk to anybody who's willing to participate in conversation.

While some participants endorsed extroversion, far more suggested that they enjoy privacy and solitude. Brenda offered an example of this characteristic.

> I really, really like solitude. I really need a certain amount of solitude. I also like to be social, too, but I found more and more as I do this work, I feel like I really need less structured time when I'm not working. . . . I'm never gonna be a party animal. I like to be with people. I'm not shy, but I'm not wanting to be in front of the camera or something like that. That's, I think, a natural—that's part of who I am. That's integral to who I am. That doesn't mean I wanna be a hermit.

Katherine is also an example of an introvert: "I'm not somebody who would jump in. I'm pretty introverted."

The therapists in this study tended to skew toward the introverted side of the scale. This characteristic, however, was not universal.

Miscellaneous

There were a number of instances in which a single therapist noted personal characteristics in passing. Elizabeth identified herself as expressive: "I'm probably one of the world's most expressive people." Dinah observed, "I hate numbers! But I've always been fascinated with letters and words." Lailla stated, "I don't like dogma." Ellen noted, "I'm quite superstitious." Jeff described himself thus: "I can't take overstimulus. . . . I love good music. . . [but] I drive to and from work in silence." Katherine described her capacity to adopt multiple perspectives. "I think I can just see or feel things from different angles and different ways." Lauren noted her rebellious nature:

> I have a rebellious nature in the sense of not believing so many of—I didn't take things in. I think I would have been rebellious against a very narrow and rigid kind of a program. . . . It wasn't that I wanted to rebel but I just couldn't believe some of the stuff [being taught in her parochial school].

Sarah mentioned her creativity as important to her intuition. She stated, "All these things make me more creative. I think . . . that fosters intuition. . . " Dinah identified herself as an optimist:

> I think, also, it has to do with whether you're basically an optimist or a pessimist. I think if you're an optimist, you see the best in a person. . . . if you're optimistic, you see the possibilities, and then you open them. . .

David gave a series of attributes. He enumerated: "I'm a good guy. I'm a good human. I work hard in my work. I like to have fun with people." For Ann, sensitivity is an important personal characteristic. She related,

> I was always very sensitive . . . it was really probably through the process of my very first therapy, where I began to learn to value my sensitivity and my insights. . . [my mother would say], "You're too sensitive." Until I finally said to her as an adult, "You're not sensitive enough". . . . I could easily get my feelings hurt. . . . I am too sensitive. . .

Lena stated that she placed a high premium on being compassionate, then elaborated, "I think that that's probably why I do what I do. . . "

Two therapists gave negative examples of characteristics that may interfere with intuition. David stated, "I think being an unhappy human struggling in life in whatever way . . . makes it very difficult to be aware of intuitive . . . senses or feelings." Janet also gave a negative example of qualities that she associated with intuition. She suggested that being overly busy and logical may be inversely associated with intuition.

> My mother, I think, would be 180 degrees polarized with intuition because she stayed busy, she avoided. She, I would say, was anything but intuitive, and my father was an engineer, so he was very right-brained engineer, so there was not a lot of intuition in my household.

It must be noted that Janet may have meant "left-brain" here, as the left-brain is typically associated with linear-discursive thinking.

> This laundry list of personal qualities is broad and composed of offhanded observations by some of the participants. We cannot say with great certitude that cultivating these qualities will make you more intuitive, but the qualities taken together begin to paint a picture of a people who have a specific orientation toward others and toward life in general: sensitive, creative, kind, earnest.

Combined Attributes

There are several instances in which the therapists we talked to combined attributes in their descriptions of themselves. For example, Janet noted curiosity, being nonjudgmental, and openness in a single quote:

> . . . curiosity keeps you open to the possibility. It's almost the opposite of judgmental, if you will. When I'm able to stay curious about either what's happening, or what my client is saying, and help them to access their curiosity, then we're in a state of nonjudgmental awareness. I think that's then when I'm most able to access my intuition.

Later in the interview, Janet discussed helping her clients access their intuition. In doing so, she highlighted some characteristics she felt were associated with intuition. She observed that clients are

> . . . able to be more intuitive. . . [when] they're accessing more of their self-energy. There's less judgment there. They're . . . out of their thinking head, and they're more into their feeling and sensing parts of themselves. . .

David noted that kindness, patience, and a general desire to make the world better are important aspirational qualities.

> . . . it is really about trying to make the world a better place. All of us do our own part. Be kind. Be gracious. Be patient. . . . It's our job as humans to make life easier for each other along the way. We struggle mightily trying to do that, at least I do.

Dinah identified the personal characteristic of "being in her head." She stated,

> I think all the time. I'm always thinking about living, dying, the clouds . . . I used to stand by the window—this is probably wasting a lot of time—but I would say to myself, "If I remembered to remember to remember to remember, to remember, to remember"—and I was a kid who thought about things like that. Or making up a language, and I kept saying, "I figured out infinity, that I could say, 'What if I remembered to remember, to remember, to remember, to remember, to remember, to remember' "—I would do that for a long time! . . . Sort of like verbal

> mind games! . . . I think I was like a female Woody Allen, or something, you know? . . . A lot of in my head, a lot of in my head . . . A lot of trying to find truths. . .

This quote paints a portrait of a person who is reflective and self-reflective and who is also curious and fairly abstract.

Brenda demonstrated the value she places on the environment: "The environment, to me, is the most important, but also I care about humans. It's not either/or."

Individual therapists noted combinations of characteristics and values important to them in developing their clinical intuition. As stated above, we may eventually find that having an orientation toward others and the world in general may be more important than the presence or absence of any single quality. This would reflect the key role intuition plays in connection in all of its forms.

Summary and Discussion

This chapter presented material on what makes a more intuitive therapist, perhaps even a "how to." The overriding message is that who you are as a person—your values and virtues, even your shortcomings—may be central to the use of clinical intuition to enhance the quality of your work. There are ways to enhance one's intuitive process; committing to a plan of self-development is a good place to start. You probably already have many of these characteristics and values. The desire and intention to grow toward self-improvement in the service of others is a good place to start.

The therapists who shared their views may be classified generally as alterocentric people, that is, they are motivated and able to take another person's perspective and meet their needs. This is illustrated by their descriptions of themselves as observant and attuned to others, helpful and giving, nonjudgmental and understanding—both of which are associated with patience. They have a high degree of respect for others and value social justice. Certainly not all of the participants have all of these qualities, but it is noteworthy that a collection of alterocentric characteristics figures prominently in the attributes the therapists prize.

Some of the therapists indicated an appreciation for more humanistic concerns. Among those noted in the data are an interest in religion and/or spirituality and a love of music, art, and nature.

These therapists also placed a high value on self-development. Many discussed the value they place on transparency and authenticity. They discussed the importance of self-awareness and self-reflection.

The clinicians also listed a number of other characteristics or traits that they see in themselves or other intuitive people. Among them is neuroticism. Given the value they place on self-awareness, one may wonder if in fact these participants indeed would score high on this trait, or if their apparent neuroticism is a function of their high degree of self-awareness.

Another interesting question that the reflections of these therapists raise is the relationship between logic, skepticism, and intuition. As noted in Chapter 1 (Current Knowledge and Perspectives), some Cognitive Psychologists have suggested that intuition and discursive thought are different processes, while others feel that they are not distinct. At the very least, the data in this study suggest that they are not antithetical. Likewise, when logic induces skepticism, this does not appear to completely undermine the ability to engage in intuitive processes. Perhaps one need not "believe" in order to have the experience. This is yet again a question for further research.

Charles (2004), in her research on intuition in psychotherapy and counseling, uncovered several characteristics of "the intuitive type of therapist" (p. 39). These characteristics include being divergent thinkers, being able to see patterns or relationships or connections, and the "big picture." They tend to be future oriented, abstract, imaginative, introspective, moody, curious, and empathetic and to have a high awareness of self and the environment. Finally, the participants in the Charles study noted that the intuitive therapists must be able to put their egos aside. Many of the qualities were ratified by the participants in the present study, and yet there were significant differences in findings as well. Overlapping qualities include being abstract (or at least not concrete), curious, and empathetic, with a high level of self-awareness. Interestingly, the participants in the present study did not tilt demonstrably toward introversion. But it must be immediately noted that it was not a quantitative study, and thus no inferences regarding "the average" intuitive therapist can be drawn.

An important consideration is that some of the characteristics and values are consistent with being a social worker and/or therapist in general. Thus, one cannot say that these characteristics differentiate intuitive therapists from nonintuitive therapists. They nonetheless are a starting point for self-development.

The willingness and ability to develop one's character in the directions of alterocentrism, self-awareness and authenticity, and an appreciation of the world beyond people, along with other characteristics or combinations of characteristics, are important elements that influence the appropriateness of using one's intuition in their professional capacity.

Implications of Characteristics and Values of Intuitive Therapists

1. Logical/Skeptical
   Implication: These characteristics counter stereotypes/fears about practicing intuitively; logic and skepticism coexist with intuition.
2. Open/Receptive
   Implication: Openness to the experiences of others, including openheartedness and curiosity, are deeply held values in intuitive practice.
3. Observant/Attuned
   Implication: The ability to observe is a foundational aspect of clinical work supporting the ability to attune intuitively to the inner world of patients.
4. Transparent/Authentic
   Implication: Transparency and authenticity reflect a healthy sense of the self of the therapist and mastery of therapeutic skill.
5. Self-Reflective/Self-Aware
   Implication: Self-reflection and self-awareness are basic to all psychotherapy and essential to the nuances of working intuitively.
6. Abstract
   Implication: The ability to see the larger picture in addition to the smallest details is key to intuitive capacity.
7. Anxious
   Implication: Therapists are human beings who experience emotions; there is no need to expect otherwise. Self-awareness is key to understanding and managing emotional states.
8. Helpful/giving
   Implication: Therapists value their desire to be helpful and giving, considering them basic values in their work.
9. Nonjudgmental
   Implication: Being judgmental undermines the openness required in intuitive practice.
10. Understanding/Patient
    Implication: Understanding and patience are valued by clinicians in general and are essential to intuitive development.

11. Respectful/Grateful
    Implication: Clinicians respect all people and experience gratitude for the privilege to engage with their patients on a deep level.
12. Draws Out Others
    Implication: In social situations, awareness and empathy for those who are less socially engaged leads to acts of inclusion.
13. Spiritual
    Implication: Worldview, especially spiritual, supports a willingness to use intuition, sometimes providing a model.
14. Concerned About Social Justice
    Implication: A concern for social justice and intuition share a link to empathy.
15. Appreciates Aesthetics
    Implication: Sensory awareness developed through intuitive processes extends to the appreciation of aesthetics: to what is seen; heard, and experienced.
16. Extroversion and Introversion
    Implication: Both introversion and extroversion are represented as characteristics of intuitive practitioners.
17. Miscellaneous
    Implication: Sensitivity, creativity, kindness, and earnestness are reflected as characteristics of therapists who value intuition.
18. Combined attributes
    Implication: More important than any single characteristic in intuitive practice may be an orientation towards others and the world that values the role of connection.

Application of Characteristics

1. Integrate logic with intuition. Allowing interplay between the two. It isn't necessary or desirable to give up the use of logic nor to suspend healthy skepticism. Being comfortable using both logic and intuition combines the best of both worlds. Likewise, openness and receptivity reflect curiosity and discernment and are not antithetical to logic and skepticism.
2. Develop transparency and authenticity. These traits are supported in intuition literature as primary to effective practice. They reflect self-awareness and the capacity for self-reflection, modeling healthy behavior.

Being authentically present reflects a healthy sense of oneself and one's role as a psychotherapist.

3. Be helpful/giving. While these characteristics may seem obvious to many, they may not to others. As theory and practice have evolved over time, there has been a debate between the conducting of therapy as an analysis of defenses and the usefulness of supportive therapy. Being helpful does not exclude the goal of understanding defenses, and giving support does not exclude the hard work of introspection and developing self-awareness.
4. Be nonjudgmental. Like other personal characteristics explored in this section, it is a quality that is critical in the application of intuition. The capacity to see beyond one's own worldview, biases, and opinions is paramount to effective psychotherapy and essential to the application of intuitive knowledge. Judgment blocks the capacities of empathy and compassion that, along with understanding and patience, lay the groundwork for intuitive capacity.
5. Appreciate art. An appreciation for and interpretation of aesthetics can help sharpen the senses and intuitive thinking.
6. Practice empathy. Our therapists found a close resemblance between empathy and intuitive thinking. The ability to feel into the experience of our patients supports intuitive insights.
7. Consider your more social side. Characteristics tied to our social lives such as intro- and extraversion are characteristics therapists see as important to their intuitive skills. The interplay between being social and time alone to recharge are important personal decisions.
8. Reflect on your spiritual life or worldview. This can help you develop a model for intuition that works for you, and it may help you understand and use it more comfortably.
9. Examine the qualities in yourself you find compatible with intuition. Just as individualization is important for patients, so too therapists must work with their strengths and individual needs.
10. Be comfortable with imperfection. Our therapists emphasized that intuition is an iterative process of trial and error. It's important to know this and not let it discourage you. With time, as more experienced therapists have noted, your impressions will come with greater clarity and accuracy.

Works Cited

Charles, R. (2004). *Intuition in psychotherapy and counselling*. London: Wiley.

8 Concerns Regarding Clinical Intuition

Therapists who shared their experiences with clinical intuition identified some concerns in using it in the clinical encounter. Interestingly, several pointed out that the larger concern is associated with failing to use their clinical intuition. Considerations that arise in the use of intuition include the concern that intuition is fallible; that it may not be in the client's best interest to share such knowledge; and that intuitive information received may be so unexpected as to cause discomfort in the therapist. In addition, therapists were concerned that using clinical intuition when one is not properly trained—in terms of both formal theory and knowledge base as well as in personal development—can be problematic. Specifically, a therapist may mistake projection or countertransference for intuition. Finally, discernment must be used in discussing intuition: therapists in this study believe that because it has not been widely recognized as a valid form of knowledge in the psychotherapy literature and formal training, they must be careful with whom they share their use of this tool.

There are also concerns associated with failure to use intuition, including missing important information on how best to engage patients and to proceed in the most effective direction; ruptures in the therapeutic alliance; failure to take appropriate action in emergency and crisis situations; and treatment that is rigid or rote and thus dehumanizing and disembodied.

By dismissing or ignoring information that comes intuitively, therapists miss the discernment and clarity that intuition can provide. Thus, while the therapists express caution in promoting the use of intuition in the professional encounter, they are equally clear that not using it is problematic.

Accuracy

Several therapists discussed their concerns about accuracy when working with intuitive information. For example, Elizabeth, who shared some of the most remarkable examples of intuitive acumen in our research, also noted, "It's not 100 percent. Not even close."

Lena, Samantha, and Natalie address the issue of accuracy by verifying their impressions with their clients. Samantha stated, "I think listening to your gut first and then verifying somehow" is important. Natalie put it this way:

> I trust it, but I sort-of qualify it. Sometimes I'll say "yeah, I just had this really odd thought." You know, I'll sort-of qualify it so that the other person can have a lot of room to say, "no, that's not right."

These therapists understand that intuitive impressions are not always accurate and have learned how to work effectively with them. At times they hit the mark with specific information that transforms the treatment process, and at other times intuition provides clues that are not as well formed. Learning how to engage the patient in discerning the accuracy of impressions received is as important as the therapist's initial awareness of them. Skill in working intuitively is an art that develops with experience.

It should also be noted that one hundred percent accuracy is neither the point nor possible in treatment; if we are off-base or choose to not follow an intuitive thought right away, there will be other opportunities to do so. Therapists have experience with issues coming up in slightly different form until they are resolved. Except in emergency situations, there are always opportunities to address issues again. Much of psychotherapy is working through identified problems in all of their nuanced forms. Intuition is a human capacity that enriches and enlivens clinical process.

Deciding When to Share Intuitive Impressions With the Client

A few of the therapists noted that discernment is important in making the decision to share an intuitive insight. They cited the importance of considering several aspects of how it may impact the client, including how painful it might be to hear, how it might be unduly burdensome, and how language can be off-putting.

Brenda indicated that sometimes sharing an intuition can evoke a negative response from the client because it is too accurate. She stated, "Sometimes there's some consternation [with clients]. 'Oh, you hit it too much on the head.' It's painful sometimes." Brenda also implies here that tact and timing are important when sharing an intuitive insight that a patient may find painful to hear.

Lailla also felt that sometimes sharing the information one receives intuitively may not serve the client's interest or meet the client's needs. She said, "There is no reason for me to burden the client with some of this [intuitively acquired] stuff. It depends."

Natalie felt that the concept of intuition may in and of itself be off-putting to some clients. For example, "[s]ome people who come in are so concrete, and just what I call sort-of an engineer mind-set that the idea of using that word [intuition] would just freak 'em out." Natalie's strategy for dealing with such patients is to use vocabulary that they accept and understand.

Other therapists agreed that sharing one's intuitions is not always prudent, although they did not specify the reason for this. Jessica stated,

> I don't always necessarily share it [intuition], and I really can't think of that many examples. I wouldn't share this with—there's only been a few—I've been working with for months. It's a leap of faith to share it. . .

Not all clients in all situations are ready to hear—or may not be able to productively use—the information a clinician may gain from intuition.

Unsettling to the Clinician

Intuition may cause discomfort in clinicians as well. Ellen and David express important aspects of this concern. Ellen suggests that therapists themselves may not be ready for certain strong intuitive insights, while David expresses concern that they may not have a complete understanding of the message. David states:

> I'm really reluctant to say this because I don't know clinically yet—although this whole thing is weird to me, frankly. . . . It feels private. I don't know how to talk about it. I don't know what it is. I don't know that it matters to anybody else. . . . You don't read a whole lot about it. . . . I think more traditional training programs don't talk about things like this [intuition] in this way.

David's candor underscores the importance of education and training in the use of intuition. He points out that for him, intuition has been a private and unarticulated aspect of his practice. Because of this, he is unsure of its importance in his clinical processing and work with his patients. David further implies that he lacks confidence using intuition because "traditional training" fails to address it as a useful skill.

The Importance of Formal Training and Self-Development

The ability to use clinical intuition appropriately surfaced as an issue with several therapists; they noted the importance of training and self-development in relation to their ability to appropriately use intuition.

Lailla addresses this concern with a solution. She was clear that using intuition must be paired with proper theoretical training: "You can't sit there and say 'I practice,' without having some theoretical understanding. In other words, have some knowledge. Just coming off the street and saying 'I'm an intuitive,' I don't buy that. I'm very firm about that."

Alejandro echoed the importance of formal training as a foundation for intuitive work. He suggests,

> . . . you need an environment and certain people that need to be somewhat predisposed and willing, and someone serious and mature I think spiritually and emotionally, or psychically to take that and to learn with it. Or with someone, in terms of learning how to use that [intuition] to do the work we do. . . . I think we need to teach responsibility and good guidance. . . . it's something that is new that is not as measurable, and that's hard science. . . .
>
> I'm helping someone. They're paying me for that, and there's all this stuff. I need to have this profession before the rest [intuition]. That, I think, is a good guide to have.

Felicia put it more simply: "It's very important that the word 'responsible' is very important when we're talking about marrying intuition and theory."

Therapists noted the importance of training in distinguishing intuition from transference and countertransference. Justin put it in simple terms: "Is this coming from the client, or is this coming from me? . . . In the old countertransference, it would be, is this client-induced countertransference, or is it therapist-induced countertransference?"

Lailla elaborated a bit more, noting an ethical demand of using intuition with professional discernment:

> . . . I think sometimes, with things that are going on in our lives, the personal issues, et cetera, requires my prudence because is this my stuff, or is it something from outside? What I'm listening to, what I'm seeing, what I'm not understanding—which part of me is picking that up? . . . To me, that's a very important part of the complexity of intuition, of not just falling for the immediate meaning, but also be mindful of where the roots might be, and what other things connect. . . . Gut feeling sometimes is connected to things that might not be appropriate, might not be good for everybody. Again, I think [it] requires really professional discipline, and ethics of being with the other person.

Deborah addresses Lailla's concern of proper training by noting that self-development and self-awareness are integral to using intuition in practice:

> You can never assume anything. . . . I think it's such a nebulous area and such a scary area of loose associations we can get into . . . shooting from the lip if you allow. . . . Just saying whatever comes to mind . . . you have a therapist, you're giving them permission to just say, "oh, use your associations." Unless you're an experienced clinician who's had enough therapy to understand yourself and know yourself from the other and can differentiate and have enough separation, boundaries there, then I think you're in tricky territory with people. . . . It's sort of like one of these things that I have more of the fear of putting it in the hands of people that don't have the practice skill of understanding and being differentiated. . . . it's gotta be in the hands of good, experienced clinicians to do it.

The therapists who reflected on their concerns regarding using intuition in the clinical context observed that along with their knowledge base, it is important to continue self-development, to work on self-awareness including understanding of boundaries, and to practice self-discipline.

Charlatans

Alejandro expressed concern that intuition may open the field to charlatans. While not referring to clinicians specifically, he related knowledge of a

New Age group in South America in which intuition and other paranormal experiences were taught. He expressed his concern:

> This foundation began getting all these guys with long hair and weird stuff, cuz they thought it was important. Of course, when you're young and you go to that and you do all kinds of exercises and things with older people, or elders, or people that try to have some type of [power] over you and they teach you things.
>
> Then sometimes they do some things that are not kosher, that are not okay. As time went by, because that foundation . . . the people in them, I realized, that were as human as anybody else, but they portrayed themselves as not—they did nasty stuff . . . not ethical, sleeping with people when they're sleeping, taking advantage of someone. Then, as I was getting to this profession, I feel a lot of the folks that tend to go to this search could probably use a couple of years of good therapy. . .

In this way, Alejandro stresses the importance of ethical behavior and practicing according to a professional code of ethics. Personal psychotherapy, consultation, continued training, and personal development all contribute to the goals of clinical practice that serves the needs of clients who seek our help.

Professional Concerns

Another concern related to the use of intuition is the degree to which it is devalued by one's colleagues and clients. Because not all colleagues are receptive to using intuition as a clinical practice, it is assumed that one is not using theory appropriately or is being unprofessional. This can impact one's professional reputation. Though this problem is caused by a lack of understanding about what intuition is, our clinicians still suggest taking care when discussing it with skeptical colleagues and clients. This includes decisions about whom to engage in discussions on intuition and being mindful of the language used.

For example, Elizabeth described the care she takes when discussing an intuitive impression with a client. Her strategy is to gently lead her client by asking if he had any unusual experiences on vacation; she also eases him into the memory by choosing a neutral vocabulary. She stated, "I didn't want to say I had this picture in my head of you're almost drowning." When asked why not, she replied, "I didn't feel comfortable saying I had a vision. I used to use that word, but now, actually, I changed it and I say, 'I get this impression,' or, 'I sense something.'" The care she takes in describing her intuitions was confirmed a bit later when talking on the subject of the paranormal. Describing her experience of working in a hospice setting, she related repeated experience of "a door that kept continually flying open" and seeing spirits. She concluded, "This is the kind of thing I'd never tell anybody." She held this position regarding a near-death experience as well:

> I've told some people . . . little bits and pieces of it, but it's not the kind of thing that you can just rush right into. You have to really develop a relationship. . . . for the most part, I don't say too much; I can just see their wheels going. It's like, Oh, yeah. Yeah. Mm-hmmm. Sure.' If you don't have the experience, it sounds like voodoo or something, but it's really not.

She reiterated this theme later in the interview.

> I don't want to be thought of as being kooky. That's very important to me cuz I have studied so hard . . . I think what other people think of me is really important cuz when you're an educator or a therapist, you're going on your reputation, to a certain extent, and people can—if they come to you, then they can create their own judgments, but until that time—

Natalie related that she herself had consulted with a therapist who was also a psychic. She then stated that,

> I will talk with some colleagues about it [intuition], but I have to know that they're safe, and that they're not sort-of theoretical. I wouldn't even share with that many people about this [psychic] therapist I saw, because a lot of people would think it's totally crazy. . . . sort-of a little "woo-woo," or a little crazy, or not really wedded to theoretical concepts.

Natalie quickly followed her understanding of the uneasiness with intuition that some individuals have with a reflection of the cultural devaluation of the concept. "It's [intuition] been around forever, and it's so important, yet it's got a really bad rap in our society. I think other societies are much more open to the use of intuition. . . " She summarized both assertions with the observation, "There's something about that word [intuition] that I think isn't very well accepted for whatever reason."

Deborah expressed the concern that bringing up intuition may lead to conflict with people who are not open to the possibility.

> I don't wanna go into a conversation that's gonna be exploring something from their point of view that's gonna be argumentative about it [intuition]. I mean, I don't wanna get into a debate over this so much as if I open that door up I know I'm going down a road with someone who's got such a block towards this kinda thing.

Ellen discussed some uneasiness with telling people about her intuition as well. She said,

> I think people would think I was joking. I would think people would be—it would be kind of pressure. They might put me under pressure to show that I really was psychic. . . . I think it would put me . . . under pressure to perform.

The therapists in this study shared the experience of feeling protective concerning with whom they discuss intuition. They found ways to protect their professional reputations.

Responding Appropriately in a Dangerous Situation

In spite of the cautions regarding introducing intuition, the therapists who shared their experiences cautioned that failing to use intuition is equally problematic. The therapists in the study identified several potential pitfalls that one might face if they fail to use their intuition. Elizabeth described such a risk: one may not take the proper safety precautions in a dangerous situation.

> What happens when you do deny this gift that we're given? . . . when I taught sex abuse prevention to little children, the whole issue was, what do you feel in your gut? How does that person make you feel? Pay attention to that. That's intuition in a really concrete fashion.
>
> There's all these social customs that we have that prohibit that kind of experience, so much so that people don't even share it or even acknowledge that it's happening. Cuz this woman said, "I didn't really think about it until now," which I thought was really sad. The experience that she had was because she didn't pay attention to her gut. There was a fire in her house cuz her son was really angry, and he pushed some

> plastic toys next to the stove. It inadvertently turned on the stove, and the wires ignited the plastic. It was very serious.
>
> It was the kind of thing where it was a direct result of not paying attention to her intuition. A lot of people—people love to avoid the negative. Avoidance is a really highly valued part of our lives. We do things out of wanting to avoid. We don't have conflicts. We want to avoid. On and on and on and on. A lot of this is just even getting in tune with how much we avoid ourselves, our feelings, our intuitions. That's just as important as having the positive and you feel it, you acknowledge it, and work with it.

Lena also noted that intuition is often a reliable alarm that can help people avoid danger. She related the following instance:

> At age 14, I was sexually assaulted. The whole time when I was going into this area where I was sexually assaulted, I had this feeling that I shouldn't go. It was too scary. I didn't pay attention to it. In the way of negative learning, I learned to pay attention to my intuition.

The clinicians voiced the concern that intuition is a good harbinger of danger. Ignoring or failing to register vital information in emergency situations may lead to failure to respond appropriately.

Missing Vital Information

As discussed in Chapter 3, How Therapists Use Intuition in Therapy, intuition may give therapists missing information not verbally offered from clients. The corollary of this statement is that failing to use intuition may cause therapists to miss vital information. Lena addresses this concern by using intuition to know how to proceed with treatment. She stated,

> As we all know, people aren't just gonna give you something just because you've asked. They're not gonna—it's not like feelings on demand. You have to—at least I have to utilize intuition all the time to figure out how to engage them in a process that will work within their [worldview]—the way they operate in the world. It's different for every single person. I don't have a methodology that is a one size fits all. If I'm not intuitive about each person walking through my door from the time I have an intake with them, I would be lost.

Elizabeth echoed the concern that if intuition is not used in treatment, the clinician will not have access to information regarding treatment direction. She discussed graduate students in field placement whom she was supervising.

> It was really amazing, working with them. It never occurred to them to think, what might be the broader picture in this situation? They were learning in a very systematic, detailed, narrow way, and they were almost done with their program. I was like, these poor people don't have a clue in terms of looking at the [whole picture]—I'd say, "What do you think is going on here? What are some of the factors that led to this experience?" Cuz they were trained to look at an experience, and then you could do A, B, C, D, or E, or F with it. . . . What could be the broader issues, the factors that led someone to do this kind of an experience? They don't even look at the—I was teaching these people for years now. It's just shocking to me. . . . I found it really sad cuz, boy, did they learn a lot with me. At the end of the semester, they said, "Oh, my God. Thank you so much. We weren't even thinking like this before." Yeah. . . . They were under-taught. It's not just having that gunny sack full of tricks, even though that fits into those things that we have to fill out.

Janet related that when she does not use her intuition, she may lack clarity regarding treatment.

> If I'm more thinking and in my head, I can doubt myself more, so I struggle sometimes with polarizations, if you will. I'm thinking this, but there's this, there's this, there's this, so it gets muddied. Not always, but often, the thinking muddies things up. When I'm able to kinda access it from more intuition, there's a clarity. That's the word. There's a clarity.

Justin discussed a case is which he feels not using his intuition would have led to a rupture in the therapeutic alliance and would have prevented him from delivering what the client most needed.

> I think it was intuition that was telling me, "You don't wanna do what you would—you have been trained to do . . ." I said, "No. That's really not gonna work in this situation. I don't think it's best clinically," . . . I think that was the intuition. . . . the theories that I have been trained

> in and learned, they get at intuition, but I don't think—it's like they're just getting a piece of it. I don't think they're getting the full concept. . . . Again, I think it doesn't capture the whole essence of it. . . . I think the formal training would have . . . I think it could've led to more of a therapeutic rupture. I mean, I think it would've led to a negative outcome. . .
>
> Grace was explicit about an issue Lena alluded to, which is the concern that academic training was sometimes a barrier to understanding. She stated, "I do think a lot of academia is often disembodied, and I just think that that really—then we're not learning to use this instrument we have for picking it [information] up."

Ellen goes the furthest in her concern in not using intuition by emphasizing its importance in emergency and crisis situations. She related,

> I think, in emergency work, I think it's essential. I don't know how people do [it] unless you have intuition. I mean I used to do CPS work, used to supervise CPS work, and there's no way that, with all the training that you have, I know after, I guess like in the '80s, so it was a totally different field. I know that now they came out with these little charts. I don't know what they have now, but after that, they came out with these little charts, checklists that you do this and this and this, and that'll tell ya whether you need to remove the child.
>
> I looked at it, and I said, "Well, that wouldn't tell you." Yeah, so, there, I used it all the time. There is nothing that tells you what to do. I mean there's risk factors, and then they rank the risk factors, but still, that doesn't tell you. I don't know how people do crisis intervention without intuition. How are you gonna do therapy? . . . The people that get into really—I shouldn't say this, but people get into trouble in terms of crisis intervention, it probably is cuz they're not—I don't wanna say they're out of touch, but—

Ellen's experience in Child Protective Services brings up an important issue: using intuition in situations in which one must act quickly to protect vulnerable clients. She points out the stakes involved in not acting in potentially dangerous or life-threatening situations.

The psychotherapists expressed concern that failing to use intuition can be potentially harmful if not outright dangerous, leaving the clinician without information critical to decision making.

Treatment Becomes Dehumanizing or Unhelpful

Another concern therapists had with not using intuition is that treatment can become unhelpful and/or dehumanizing. Brenda discussed the use of intuition as an antidote to overly technical treatment. She stated that she believes "there is a desire . . . there's a longing. I think people have a longing to connect. They have a longing to be seen and understood. So often, they don't get that." She saw this problem as being related to technology but also to a larger trend to reduce treatment to numbers. "We're not adding up a row of figures." A bit further, she offered the suggestion that one way to mitigate this trend is

> . . . to model our own use of intuition. . . . supervisees are in a situation where their work supervisor told [them], "This is policy." . . . They're not feeling comfortable with that. I say, "Okay, tell me what do you feel when you sit with this person?" . . . I think that evidence-based has become fetishized . . . I think people can get too caught up in that and distracted by that. That is the measure. Then they're supervised at work by middle managers who have to please administrators—who are not even necessarily clinicians.

Jennifer also sees intuition as a corrective to overly structured treatment, which ultimately, she suggested, does not meet the needs of the client.

> . . . I think being too structured, being too—I mean, I've talked to some people who I'm sure they do some kind of work that is helpful, but when I listen to them talk I'm just like, "How in the world would anybody ever get anything from this?"
>
> I mean, I'm being very judgmental now, but that's how I—it's like, "How could this possibly be therapy or therapeutic?" I think that when people—this is my feeling—is when people get some sort of very structured training and it's like that's what they do and that is, by God, they're gonna do it no matter what. That, to me, gets in the way. Then there's not a person there. There's a theory there, but there's not a person there.

Felicia echoed the sentiment that intuition can countermand rigidity in treatment. She stated that intuition "frees people to not be quite so rigidly holding to the standards of the theory."

Samantha expressed the danger of not using clinical intuition in terms of the therapeutic alliance. Given that the therapists felt that one of the useful aspects of intuition is that it helps them create a therapeutic alliance, it may not be surprising that a danger of not using it is that there may be resultant difficulty in creating that alliance. This is what Samantha observed: "You can't not have some sense of intuition or feeling to be able to connect with a person, especially if they're having difficulty."

Samantha was concerned that in ignoring intuition, the therapist may depersonalize treatment. She said,

> . . . so I think to not listen to or to address the intuition that the therapist may feel or be receiving would be doing the client a disservice . . . it [using intuition] makes it more personal to that client . . . rather than having them be the form that you would fill out in your progress note or what you're gonna give them for their diagnosis code.

She gave a case example to demonstrate her point in which she did not use an intuitive insight and consequently did not connect with the client.

> I think that when I don't share [intuitive insights] . . . I just felt like I lost him because I was busy doing something else . . . I should've taken more time to sit with him and . . . not to hurry him along . . . I felt like I lost him. . . . There wasn't an alliance there.

Sharon also offered the following observation: "I don't think as a social worker how you cannot to some degree be intuitive." The interviewer probed, "What would happen if you had a clinical social worker who never used their intuition?" The therapist responded, "A robot. . . . Working with a robot. Don't we have a sense of something going on? Doesn't it make us good in our work?" A bit later, she expanded this perspective.

> I think if I didn't have that sense of something, "what's going on?" I don't think that—how would I be able to think through a process? Would I just be the person who checks off the boxes and says, "Okay, we'll add this up, and this is your problem. Let me get a syllabus out for you, and we're gonna write that treatment plan. Here it is." And that's it.

Sharon expanded the theme a bit later to express the view that failure to use intuition may undermine the ability to connect with the client and be helpful. "I think it's all about connecting with the patient, and the relationship, and helping them through their work."

The overwhelming concern our therapists express about avoiding therapy that is "dehumanizing" implies a crucial observation about the value of intuition itself: it is intuition that connects us to our most human qualities; its ability to humanize therefore necessitates its use in effective treatment.

Summary and Discussion

The therapists in our research were careful to stay mindful that intuition is fallible. Because of this, they have found ways to check their impressions with their clients. This finding confirms those of the Witteman, Spaanjaars, and Aarts (2012) study as well as the Jeffrey and Fish (2011) research. In the former study, participants addressed risks of intuition. They noted that it may lead to "tunnel vision, projection, and/or confirmation bias" (p. 24). The Marriage and Family Therapists who participated in the Jeffrey and Fish study also noted that intuition "is not infallible . . . they can be totally off base and based in things that are completely misleading. . . " (p. 355). Thus, one is well advised to be careful about the degree of confidence attached to any intuitively derived information and check these impressions fully and carefully before acting on them. It is also important to consider the timing of any intervention, including those that are informed by intuition.

The therapists also noted that sometimes intuition may provide information that the client is not ready to hear or in some way does not serve the client's best interest. Consistent with the observations above, intuitive psychotherapists must use discernment in sharing their intuitions with clients.

Other dangers associated with clinical intuition are in relation to the therapist: it may be unsettling to the professional, or the clinician may lack the necessary theoretical understanding or maturity to use intuition in the therapeutic context. The psychotherapist may not be able to differentiate between what is "theirs" and what is information about the client. These findings once again support those of Jeffrey and Fish (2011). Their participants indicated that supervision was the preferred training ground for the development of clinical intuition due to the nature of the type of learning needed to be adept at this ability. Specifically, they identified "self-of-the-therapist work and exercises" (p. 357), indicating what the interviews in our study suggest, which is that the use of clinical intuition requires a great deal of self-development.

Therapists also discussed their concerns about sharing their use of clinical intuition with their colleagues who may not understand its utility. The biases against the use of intuition keeps clinicians from openly discussing their experiences. It appears that Marriage and Family Therapists share this concern. Jeffrey and Fish (2011) found that the therapists they interviewed were sensitive to the negative valuation of intuition within their discipline as well.

While the therapists cautioned that there are concerns in using intuition to which the responsible clinician must be alert, they were equally concerned regarding failing to use intuition in the treatment process. There are two broad problems that they noted. One is that failing to use intuition will leave a gap in understanding the case and what a given individual may need for treatment to proceed successfully. The other is that without the use of intuition, treatment can become dehumanizing. It is through the use of intuitive insights that the therapist is able to treat the individual as a unique human.

The therapists who use intuition in their work are clearly thoughtful and cautious about its use. They believe that this powerful tool should rest in the hands of psychotherapists with a high level of clinical skill, self-development, and formal training. When these qualifications come together, the failure to use clinical intuition may deprive the client of the highest quality of treatment.

Implications for Concerns Regarding Clinical Intuition

1. Accuracy
   Implication: Care must always be taken to consider the meaning of intuitive impressions; skill in developing intuition, like a muscle, takes time.
2. Deciding When to Share Intuitive Impressions With the Client
   Implications: Connection with the client's worldview, using shared language, and taking care not to overburden with intuitive information is part of developing skill in the application of intuition.
3. Unsettling to the Clinician
   Implication: Intuitive experiences can be powerful; learning to accept them as possibilities and accepting unfolding events is part of the intuitive process.
4. The Importance of Formal Training and Self-Development
   Implication: accurate use of intuition is multiply determined; self-development that reflects ethical practice, personal maturity, self-awareness, and good boundaries are particularly important.
5. Professional Concerns
   Implication: intuition is not widely understood and appreciated; using your own judgment about how and when to speak openly about it is important.

6. Responding Appropriately in Dangerous Situations
   Implication: intuitive information often arrives in dangerous situations. Trust it.
7. Missing Vital information
   Implication: integrating intuitive impressions gives information that guides direction in the treatment. It is critical in emergency and crisis situations and prevents ruptures in the therapeutic alliance.
8. Treatment Becomes Dehumanizing or Unhelpful
   Implication: intuition enlivens treatment.

Application of Concerns Regarding Clinical Intuition

1. Pay attention to intuitive insights. Intuition is a human capacity that enriches and enlivens clinical process. There is no imperative to use it; it's a choice. Discernment about how and when to communicate an insight or not to express it at all is part of developing skill.
2. Trust then verify your intuitive impressions.
3. Let iteration clarify your intuition. There is plenty of time and opportunity to adjust our intuitive impressions. Be comfortable with intuition as a process.
4. Take care in the timing of when you share intuitive insights. Therapists noted a concern that patients may not be ready to hear them. Take into consideration, as an ethical imperative, that what you share must not harm your patient.
5. Check your intuition with your other capacities. For instance, rational thought isn't necessarily a barrier to intuition; it can be a check on your intuition.
6. Combine formal training with intuition. This is another check on intuitive thoughts. Look for theories and training points that are compatible with or complement the intuitive process.
7. Be gentle. Many of the therapists stress that being subtle with stronger intuitive insights is important.

Works Cited

Jeffrey, A., & Stone Fish, J. (2011). Clinical intuition: A qualitative study of its use and experience among marriage and family therapists. *Contemporary Family Therapy*, *33*(4), 348–363.

Witteman, C., Spaanjaars, N. L., & Aarts, A. A. (2012). Clinical intuition in mental health care: A discussion and focus groups, *Counselling Psychology Quarterly*, *25*(1), 19–29. doi:10.1080/09515070.2012.655419

9 Teaching Clients to Trust Their Intuition

The importance of clinical intuition in psychotherapy has been demonstrated throughout the book. We have focused on the clinician's inner awareness and development of intuitive processing, how the therapist applies intuition, and how it is relevant in working with each client. The therapist's ability to work intuitively, to communicate impressions accurately, and to work collaboratively serves as a working model for the patient. This chapter is about the collaborative process that aligns both therapist and patient with the goals set for the treatment and the role that teaching clients to trust their intuition plays in effective psychotherapy.

Intuition provides nuanced understanding of the complex factors operating at any given moment in clients' lives and the responses that will most effectively support their deepening sense of themselves in the world. The feeling of coherence that builds as clients experience their developing internal awareness supports their ability to effectively manage their lives, building a sense that things will work out even when they are very difficult.

More than half of the clinicians indicated that working with their clients' intuition is a treatment objective or an intervention. Because being open to and trusting intuition is related to overall improved well-being, validating clients' intuition and unusual experiences rather than pathologizing them is important to the therapists interviewed. They also discussed specific benefits they believe are associated with helping their clients' access and use intuition. Finally, a couple of the therapists indicated methods that they use to help clients connect to their intuition.

Validation

A few of the therapists discussed validating their clients' intuition and unusual experiences. Elizabeth disclosed that some clients seek her services because they know that she will take their intuition seriously. She gave one case example in which the client's concerns included paranormal activity other than intuition: "I've actually worked with clients that come to me because—for example, I had a woman come to me, and she said that she had heard this was something that I could tolerate." She described a client who wanted to discuss what the client understood to be visitation by the spirit of her deceased husband. The therapist related,

> She wanted to talk to me about that because she understood that I would validate that because a lot of people in hospice have very similar experiences with visitations from the dead. I assured her that she wasn't losing her mind.

Alejandro understands validating clients' intuition or other unusual experiences to be a matter of cultural competence. He discussed working with people from non-Western cultures, for whom intuition and paranormal experiences are common and acceptable.

> . . . they felt safe that they could talk about things, things that particularly were incredibly, incredible . . . and then in general were not very willing to use a little bit of an anthropological mind, a judgmental mind and call it "black voodoo" or whatever.

Natalie discussed a case example of working with one client whom she identified as "highly intuitive." She related,

> Well, mostly the challenge is helping her see that and accept that. You know, she hadn't seen that—I called it a "gift," she hadn't seen that gift and how it really helped her survive throughout her life, from the time she was a little girl, really.

Benefits to Clients

Several therapists identified specific benefits that clients may experience as a result of becoming more comfortable with their intuition. Improved self-awareness and a positive sense of self are important treatment goals in many forms of therapy. Symptom reduction is arguably a treatment goal for every form of psychotherapy. Some of the clinicians in this study suggested that these treatment goals can be profitably addressed by helping clients access and trust their intuition.

> For Elizabeth, being aware of and trusting intuition is a matter of client safety.
>
> What happens when you do deny this gift that we're given? That's something that would be worth [investigating] because when I taught sex abuse prevention to little children, the whole issue was, what do you feel in your gut? How does that person make you feel? Pay attention to that. That's intuition in a really concrete fashion.

In discussing client safety and intuition, Elizabeth gave a case example of a client who had denied her intuition, and as a result, there was a fire in her home. Not only does this narrative suggest that intuition is important to client safety, but it is also relevant to connecting to oneself and one's feelings.

> It was the kind of thing where it was a direct result of her not paying attention to her intuition. . . . A lot of this is just even getting in tune with how much we avoid ourselves, our feelings, our intuitions.
>
> Lena indicated that she talks to her clients "about their gut feelings." She gave an example of a woman who was in an unsatisfying relationship. This woman seemed to sense that the relationship "was not going anywhere." In pursuing this client's apparent intuitive experience of the relationship, the client opened to greater self-awareness. This seemed to reduce her anxiety.
>
> . . . [the conversation on trusting her intuition] opened up this whole thing, . . . we started talking about her gut feelings. . . . she has begun to have less—experienced less anxiety the more she pays attention to what she wants, . . . I think she has found that her interior life isn't as scary as she thought it was.

Sarah discussed awakening latent intuition. She related that validating is important, then discussed why this is so.

> I think that people will say things and then dismiss it. I encourage them not to dismiss what—they'll say, "Oh, that's so foolish," or that, "I don't know why I said that," but I encourage them to respect that data that

> they have. It works, and then people appreciate more whatever sense they have.

She tells her clients, "Honor what you just said, rather than dismiss what you just said. . . . Then people move forward, respecting their intuition." She elaborated, "I think it helps enormously. I think it enriches the therapy because then they are more in touch with their core self, in my view. Yes. I think it helps in recovery."

Ann also discussed the therapeutic value of helping clients open to their intuition. She stated, "It's really part, I think, of valuing yourself, knowing yourself, listening to your own voice, developing your own voice."

Janet relies primarily on Internal Family Systems Theory in her treatment. She discussed at length helping clients by identifying and accepting their parts. She related that when she does this work with clients,

> Then we're both able to be more intuitive, because they're then accessing more of their self-energy. There's less judgment there. They're less. . . [in] their thinking head, and they're more into their feeling and sensing parts of themselves. . . . when I'm helping them get into their zone of when they can heal their parts themselves and have a connection to their parts, then they're using their intuition.

Sharon also suggested that when a client accesses their intuition, they experience overall improved functioning. She stated:

> Well, I talk in terms of what, of course, what does that feel like, and when did that feeling start? Did something tell you, maybe, that something was wrong there? That, without using the word [intuition], I guess, might happen on occasion, but trying to probe with them what's going on. What they can, in themselves, pay attention to, and maybe, be more helpful in the future. . . . What did your gut tell you at that time? Okay. Did you pay attention to it? They say, "No, but I should have." Well, then do more of that as we move on in their problem solving, whatever it is. . . . I think they can make smarter decisions about themselves. . . . What their needs are.

For Natalie, clients' intuition is tied to their ability to trust themselves. She described how she interacts with clients around the issue of their intuition:

> Like sometimes a client will start talking about what I define as intuition. They may not call it that. . . . I will help them try to—well, what I call

> it in therapy is, "trusting themselves." You know, I see a lot of people that come in that really don't know how to trust themselves. . . . I think a part of being content and more capable and happy is learning to trust oneself. I think there's a bit of intuition in that. . . .

She continued to discuss the value of helping adolescent clients tune in to their intuition. She said, "I find these sort of issues [learning to recognize and trust feelings] really important for them. . . . They have so much going on, but they're also learning to be a person, and how to know themselves."

These clinicians feel that helping their clients access and trust intuition is related to improved safety, an enhanced sense of self, greater self-awareness, and more trust in themselves. This may help with reducing anxiety, as well as move clients toward the more general goal of increased happiness. These benefits of helping clients open to their intuition are at the core of client well-being.

Methods

A few of the therapists related the manner in which they go about helping their clients access and trust intuition. These include using guided imagery, helping clients look at their experiences with curiosity, or simply spending time analyzing intuitive feelings that a client may mention.

> Ann uses guided imagery to help her clients get in touch with their intuition.
>
> Sometimes I'll do that through just a guided imagery, where I don't set—I don't tell them the image. I have them tell me. What are you seeing or hearing if they're more audible? Just have them close their eyes and just open up to what it is they're seeing or hearing.

For Janet, helping clients approach their experiences with curiosity may lead them to notice and trust intuition more. She discussed what she sees as the relationship between curiosity and intuition. She said, "Curiosity keeps you open to the possibility." Thus, she works with clients' curiosity: "[I] help them to access their curiosity."

Natalie also encourages her clients to be more intuitive. She does so by shining a spotlight on any intuitive insights they may dismiss.

> How I go about [teaching clients to trust their intuition], . . . Sometimes people get feelings and they'll sort of minimize it. I say, "No, let's look

> at that more. Tell me more about that." There might be something valuable in that. You know, I try to help them learn to recognize and stick with those feelings.

These therapists focus on their clients' intuition. In one case, the therapist utilizes guided imagery specifically to help improve clients' access to intuition. Janet also encourages accessing intuition by supporting her clients' curiosity about any minor intuitive experiences they may reference. Natalie uses opportunities to keep the therapeutic focus on her clients' intuitions as a way to help them access and trust the experience more. Focusing on your clients' intuition may take any number of forms. Simply pulling forward any references to intuitive experiences and exploring them is perhaps the most basic way of encouraging clients to note and trust intuition. There are more structured methods, such as introducing guided imagery into your therapy, or guiding your client to tune into those experiences that represent forms that intuition takes.

Summary and Discussion

The therapists who shared their experiences concerning helping clients access and trust their own intuition did not expand on this topic to a high degree. And yet it was perhaps the most surprising finding of our research. No previous studies that we are aware of have attended to therapists' setting a treatment objective to help clients access or trust their intuition or intervening specifically for that purpose.

Therapists suggested that using client intuition as a treatment objective may bring specific improvements in the client's functioning. It may lead to greater personal safety, enhance self-awareness, increase their sense of personal worth, promote general happiness, and reduce anxiety. These observations are certainly deserving of further investigation.

Also of great interest in this category is the question of how a therapist may go about helping clients access and trust their intuition to a greater degree. Three therapists offered clues about how to orient a therapeutic conversation about the client's intuition. One can simply make the choice to engage in greater depth when the topic arises. One therapist suggested that this may be accomplished by helping the client turn their curiosity toward the topic. Another therapist uses a specific technique: guided meditation. Again, these observations suggest areas in which further research may provide the field of psychotherapy with highly important information on improving client well-being. Perhaps more importantly, they offer a rich field for growing the practice of intuitively informed psychotherapy.

Implications of Teaching Clients to Trust Their Intuition

1. Validation of Clients' Intuition Supports Its Use and Development
   Implication: validation of intuition is important in day-to-day experiences as well as unusual experiences such as visitations by deceased family members and other paranormal activity.
2. Benefits to Clients
   Implication: intuition improves self-awareness and is important in developing self-esteem. It provides information about safety in dangerous situations and helps patients to honor and trust their feelings in relationships.
3. Methods of Teaching Clients to Trust Their Intuition
   Implication: Make use of the components of your theoretical approach that support the identification and acceptance of senses and feelings.

Applications of Teaching Clients to Trust Their Intuition

1. Support clients in their development of inner awareness, teaching them to identify their intuitive processes, to trust and act upon them.
2. Use language that is based on the client's cultural background, experience, and worldview. Make mental notes of how the patient uses language and speak in that language.
3. Use metaphors as a bridge to deepen intuitive connections. Use imagery drawn from poetry, literature, music, and religion that resonates and attunes your client to their inner knowing.
4. Cultivate self-expression through the use of imagination, play, and creativity.
5. Model trust in intuition by honoring your own and your client's as a fundamental aspect of the treatment process.

10 Overarching Themes in Clinical Intuition

This chapter reflects the themes that emerged as important across our research interviews giving us a picture of how current practitioners understand and apply clinical intuition: inner awareness, alterocentrism, self-development, connectedness, energy, and the imperative to destigmatize.

Each of the chapters in this book represents a category of data from our study that illuminates the experiences of therapists who described their use of intuition. This descriptive material advances our understanding of how therapists conceptualize its development and use it as a psychotherapeutic tool. In turn, the observations they shared carry implications for ways to enhance your own clinical intuition.

Therapists described inner awareness as a key factor in obtaining intuitive information. By focusing on the patient and simultaneously being aware of their inner senses of what is seen, felt, heard, and known as described in Chapter 5, (Forms of Clinical Intuition), information arrives based on these intuitive forms. The ability to connect individual pieces of information—to connect the dots in popular parlance—is key to effective use of intuition. Returning to music as a metaphor for therapy, each instrument is important, but when combined with others, it produces music that takes the listening experience to an entirely new level. The parallel in psychotherapy is that the intuitive process combines individual pieces of information in to a whole that creates a new level of experiential awareness.

There were a number of experiences and practices therapists shared that support intuitive development. Prominent among the practices were meditation and/or spiritual practices centered on immediate presence or to a transpersonal source. In addition, communing with nature, engaging in repetitive exercise or yoga, selected reading, and personal therapy that is validating are helpful. Experiencing perspectives and ways of living that are different from your own are useful as well as being generally supported and validated for your intuition. Experiences and practices that interest you and that support physical, mental, and spiritual well-being will further support development of clinical intuition.

Characteristics that therapists believe support intuition include being open, observant, and authentic. Therapists also strongly identified with traits that include logic and skepticism.

There are likewise concerns regarding the use of intuition in clinical practice. Chief among them is the understanding that experiences that may feel like intuition do not always yield accurate information. Therapists also stressed the importance of developing discernment about how and when to share intuitive information. Therapists who are comfortable with their intuition have developed it over years of practice, always bearing in mind that the patient's well-being is central to any clinical interaction.

The therapists who shared information about their use of clinical intuition discussed their opinions and experiences. This information was analyzed by using a standard method of qualitative data analysis. This form of data analysis yields categories, or themes that emerge from the data. These categories were represented as chapters in this book. We observed several themes that were expressed in different ways across categories. This redundancy suggests that some themes bear particular importance to the therapists who contributed to the research and therefore to the phenomenon of clinical intuition.

One of the points that emerges from the data across categories is that clinical intuition may be a common factor across psychotherapy models. That is, it may contribute to therapeutic change regardless of theoretical orientation and be successfully integrated into most, if not all, schools of therapy. Given that there is a strong possibility that this is the case, the data are clear that clinical intuition should no longer be stigmatized.

Other issues that emerged from looking across categories are alterocentrism and personal development. By comparing the contents of the chapters on Characteristics and Values of Intuitive Therapists, Focus of Therapists' Attention, Concerns Regarding Clinical Intuition, Therapists' Understanding of their Intuition, and Teaching Clients to Trust Their Intuition, one may arrive at an awareness of specific areas of personal development that contribute to the ethical application of clinical intuition. This leads to a refined understanding of the role teachers, supervisors, and consultants can play in supporting the use of intuition in psychotherapy practice.

The role of connection is also prominent in the narratives of the participating therapists. They apprehend that connectedness within themselves, with their patients, and to a larger field of awareness, however it is personally defined, is the foundation of intuitive processes. Many of them also have an experience of energy. Their experiences suggest that while thinking in terms of energy is not common in Western psychotherapeutic traditions, they believe it to be an important aspect of the treatment process.

All of the data, all of the categories, all of the interviews we conducted with 23 therapists who rely on intuition in their professional capacity culminate to render an emerging definition of clinical intuition. While the capacity and mechanisms by which it works may be constant across contexts, there are clear implications for its professional use in practice. The therapists reiterated across categories that clinical intuition is real, is useful, and has a place in professional practice.

A Common Factor and the Imperative to Destigmatize

The ability to acquire and use information about the client and/or treatment process that has been gained through means other than overt communication may be more prevalent than is currently recognized in the literature. This study has demonstrated that regardless of theoretical orientation, religious or spiritual orientation, or practice setting, therapists in fact rely on intuition to navigate the complex terrain of psychotherapy. Thus, one of the implications of this study is that clinical intuition may in fact be a common factor across psychotherapy models.

The therapists in this study are clear and consistent that being able to access and apply intuitively acquired knowledge about their clients and the treatment process has been advantageous to their work. They identified the utility of intuition in every phase and aspect of treatment. And yet they tend not to share their knowledge and experiences relative to this advantage because of fear of stigma. One of the more profound implications of this study is that it is time to end the stigma against the use of clinical intuition. In this way the capacity can be subject to research, and clinicians can refine and purposefully utilize this tool.

Alterocentrism

An important cross-category issue related to clinical intuition is alterocentrism, that is, motivated and able to deeply perceive another person's subjective experience and act in accordance. By looking at the categories of Characteristics and Values of Intuitive Therapists, Focus of Therapists' Attention, Concerns Regarding Clinical Intuition, and Teaching Clients to Trust Their Intution, the data suggest that using intuition professionally requires that the therapist be genuinely alterocentered: in the category of Characteristics, the therapists reported being highly concerned with other people: they want to be helpful, they are observant and attuned, respectful, and understanding. In the category of Focus of Attention, the participants closely observe their clients. In Usefulness, the therapists reported using their intuition to understand their clients on a deep, intimate level and using this information to guide the treatment process in a way that honors the client's individuality. In Concerns, they report that they use intuition to avoid de-humanizing, mechanistic treatment approaches. Finally, in Intuition as a Treatment Objective, they suggest that in helping clients open to intuition, they are helping them achieve a higher quality of life. This picture is one of therapists who are deeply committed to their clients and their clients' well-being, who work empathically to bring about change by seeing through their clients' eyes; a stance that underlies clinical intuition. They indicated that in some cases, manualized treatment protocols undermine the ability to assume this stance and thus may impede the ability to acquire intuitively derived information. These are highly committed therapists whose clients' well-being is at the very heart of their practice. Their alterocentric stance is an important part of their use of intuition in the clinical context.

Self-Development

Across categories, participants express strong conviction that using intuition requires a good deal of self-development. They agreed that intuition is a natural capacity to which everyone has access (even if some people develop this capacity to a greater degree than others). But both the Charles (2004) research and the present study suggest that using intuition in the professional context of psychotherapy carries additional responsibilities. When considering the combined information the therapists in this study shared regarding focus of attention, characteristics, concerns, and understanding, it is clear that using intuition requires a high level of self-awareness, self-discipline, and personal resilience.

In the categories Characteristics and Values of Intuitive Therapists, Focus of Therapists' Attention, and Therapists' Understanding of Their Intuition, self-awareness is a theme that the participants repeatedly identified as important. As noted above, the various forms that intuitive insights take can render it relatively easy to overlook or to dismiss as a distraction. Thus, cultivating self-awareness supports the ability to note subtle, evanescent experiences. In education, supervision, and consultation, therapists from all theoretical orientations are urged to bring awareness to the meaning of passing experiences.

Self-awareness also means the degree to which therapists are able to identify and regulate their own issues, needs, and desires. The therapists in this study advocating for the use of clinical intuition noted the importance of not mistaking projections or their own needs and desires for intuition. This may be mitigated by both self-awareness and self-restraint relative to the client's best interest, which then recursively folds back on the alterocentrism noted above: the therapist must truly know oneself in order to manage their own needs and serve the best interests of the client. This degree of self-awareness is currently important in many but not all schools of therapy.

Another theme that emerged between categories was openness. Both as a characteristic and as in the practice of opening, both were highly valued by the participants in the study. Openness by definition implies the ability to tolerate vulnerability and is based on a healthy sense of self. Therapists who have developed their self-awareness have learned to trust themselves and serve as role models for their clients in developing their own intuition. The practice of opening is an invitation for support and connection.

Connectedness

Related to openness, the theme of connectedness also transcends categories. This may be implied by the stance therapists take toward their clients, as well as their concerns with dehumanizing treatments. It is apparent in their focus of attention, which they identify in some cases as a connection, as well as in their explanations of where intuition comes from: an ontological connectedness. This cosmic stance is consistent even though the therapists in this study hold a heterogeneous set of religious and/or spiritual orientations. Across belief systems, there is a widespread worldview that they share, which is that there is something that connects humans. They disagree on the nature of this "something": some feel it is "other," such as a divinity or external force, while others hold a more participatory worldview, in which the connection is the ultimate aim. This debate is well beyond the scope of this volume. Nonetheless, an important implication of the study is that intuitive therapists tend to apprehend and hold dear a connection between people or between "all" and understand the connection as an explanatory factor in their abilities to access information about their client and the treatment. Thus, an ability to sense connectedness enhances the ability to appropriately use intuition as a tool in therapy.

Energy

The concept of energy also spanned categories. Energy arose as both a form and an indicator that intuitive experiences take and as an understanding of what intuition is and where it comes from. Perhaps the concept of energy is related to that of openness. The participants suggested that energy flows between people as well as objects and within the environment. Being open to receive or process this energy may be part of the experience. The concept of the flow of energy is commonplace in Eastern philosophies but has not been a part of the Western scientific mechanistic worldview that underlies many of the currently accepted schools of psychotherapy. The concept has received a great deal of attention in the psi literature, appears in Transpersonal Psychology, and is fundamental to understanding in Energy Psychology but, again, does not tend to appear in the canonical psychotherapeutic methods. Given the fact that the therapists in this study viewed energy as both a form of intuition and an explanation for intuition, this is certainly a concept that deserves more attention in the psychotherapeutic literature.

An Emerging Definition of Clinical Intuition

We purposely declined to define the term "clinical intuition" at the outset of the study. As the review of the literature reveals, there are a number of sometimes contradictory and somewhat overlapping definitions of intuition (e.g., transpersonal, energy, knowing). These definitions are in some cases context dependent. This study is focused on the particular context of *clinical* intuition. The participants in this study indicated that they rely on intuition in the clinical context to varying degrees. We asked outright for their definitions and then asked for examples of how, when, and with whom the participants used the capacity. In this way, a definition of clinical intuition arose from the experiences of the therapists who use it.

After combining the experiences of 23 therapists and looking at their narratives across categories, we arrived at the following definition of clinical intuition: Clinical intuition is the acquisition of information about or relevant to the client and/or course of therapy, attained by means other than overt communication, and used to advance the goals of therapy and the client's well-being. As this definition suggests, clinical intuition has much in common with general intuition. It is also distinct in that it is used within a specific professional clinical context. Therapists are licensed professionals that require the acquisition of specific kinds of knowledge and capacities along with delineated codes of ethics. This means that clinicians who use intuition professionally must do so within the professional and ethical boundaries of their disciplines and licensure. They also have a fiduciary responsibility to their clients. Clinical intuition, like intuition in general, often arises spontaneously: a therapist may experience a sudden realization. The decision of if, how, or when to use this information therapeutically differentiates between intuition in general and clinical intuition. This, as the therapists in this study have discussed, requires self-development, combined with a deep concern for and knowledge of the client, along with an ability to work from a place of connection.

Application of Cross-Category Considerations

Suggestions that emerged from the research include tuning in to discrete, subtle subjective experiences that may arise both when you are with a client and when you are reflecting on a case between sessions. Set your intention to be aware of these experiences, considering them not as distractions but as carrying important information. Pay attention to images that arise either as snapshots or as unfolding events. Note affects and physical sensations that arise as well as words, songs, and phrases that come to mind. Be aware of feeling energy as it ebbs and flows.

Summary and Discussion

Questions about the interrelationships between discrete factors arose repeatedly in this study. The possible relationships between discursive thought and intuition are important. The data suggest that this relationship is complex. The effects of other factors on each other, such as different characteristics and values, different ways of apprehending intuition, various loci of attention, and different experiences and practices, are important. And yet there are so many factors that the participants identified that arriving at an understanding of what may work for one individual versus another regarding the ability to appropriately use intuition in therapy is exactly the kind of ill-structured problem that researchers have identified as amenable to intuitive judgment. This fact suggests that an intuitive mentor may be helpful to many who wish to import their intuitive capacities into the consulting room.

The cross-category data also suggest that the use of intuition in treatment requires a high level of self-development. Whether or not these areas of development are helpful in the use of intuition in one's personal life, using it in therapy brings added responsibility. Self-awareness, self-discipline, and a resilient sense of self that can process difficult experiences are important to the therapist who wishes to promote their client's best interest in therapy.

Developing concrete categories was an important part of reporting our research and deciding how to organize our book chapters. However, intuition is a much more complex phenomenon, as our cross-category considerations show. Intuition is dynamic; the qualities each therapist brings to their practice are diverse; the therapeutic process is nonlinear and iterative; and intuition itself, by resisting a single definition, is more about ways of connecting with patients than about a single method of analysis. This should be liberating to therapists, and so we therefore encourage you to see our research less rigidly and rather more imaginatively: what new possible ways of connecting and healing clients are possible when we use intuition as our starting point? Or even further, how can we interact with these categories to form new understandings of intuition as an approach to healing?

The categories in the present study all have implications for the nature and meaning of clinical intuition. The factors within each category may suggest ways one may introduce or enhance the use of their intuition into their clinical practice. Looking across categories, several points emerge as central. First, the study suggests a definition of clinical intuition, acknowledging that using intuition in the clinical context has implications that do not apply to the use of intuition in one's personal life. The data across categories also suggests that clinical intuition is a valuable tool in successful treatment and may well be a common factor among schools of therapy. As such, it must be destigmatized and better understood.

Finally, the therapists in this study suggested in two categories that they are able to sense energy and that the movement of energy is important to their clinical intuition. This is an area in which there is ample literature in non-Western and nontherapeutic arenas, such as the psi literature, to a growing extent the Transpersonal Psychology literature, and to the rapidly developing field of Energy Psychology. The current study suggests that the traditional schools of Western therapy are well advised to begin to understand this phenomenon.

The categories in this study represent the experiences and perspectives of therapists who utilize intuition in their professional lives, some to a high degree. By looking at data that arises in multiple categories, we can begin to better understand the nature of clinical intuition and begin to formulate how we can help individuals import their natural intuition into the clinical context.

Works Cited

Charles, R. (2004). *Intuition in psychotherapy and counselling*. London: Wiley.

Conclusion

The intuitive process was described more than seven decades ago by Theodore Reik (1948) in *Listening with the Third Ear: The Inner Experience of a Psychoanalyst*. The depth of Reik's comprehension of connection with all of its subtleties provides a roadmap for intuitive listening. He encourages therapists to

> rely on a series of most delicate communications when they collect their impressions; to extend their feelers, to seize the secret messages that go from one unconscious to another. To trust these messages, to be ready to participate in all flights and flings of one's imagination, not to be afraid of one's own sensitivities . . . The task of the analyst is to observe and to record in his memory thousands of little signs and to remain aware of their delicate effects on him.

Reik's metaphor for listening references one of the pillars of intuition, clairaudience—hearing, as an entry point for learning how "one mind speaks to another beyond words and in silence" (44). He was practicing psychotherapy with an attuned presence that reflects his deeply human understanding of clinical process.

The main narrative of psychoanalysis would follow the dominant Newtonian scientific theory of the time: the division of the body into reason and emotion, and the view that the therapist can be a neutral scientific observer. A second narrative based in quantum science has developed that provides a framework for understanding the direct experiences of clinicians that were once viewed as unverifiable and therefore unscientific. Decades of research have established the validity of these experiences that are based on the primary nature of connection in human experience. Quantum theory establishes the basis for this understanding. The implications for clinical practice continue to unfold as understanding of how focused attunement in the therapeutic relationship is itself healing. Scientific understanding and direct experience come together in the forward momentum of history.

We hope that in highlighting this parallel history, our work will give it more power, demystifying and destigmatizing it, giving intuition a proper place in clinical practice. It's in that spirit that we have done the research that forms the foundation of our book.

Looking back, we wrote from a desire to be a part of the legacy of impassioned listening. Thinking about Jeff's reference to "gentle thoughts," it's possible to also think of our writing as promoting a more gentle—a more *humane*—view of the therapeutic relationship. Our clinicians clearly share this desire: though they lacked the theoretical background to describe the intuitive process, they clearly rely on intuition to make decisions, to build trust with their clients, and to bring an aliveness to sessions that reflects the basic nature of the treatment process. This suggests that intuition is a deeply personal process, a foundational part of the human experience: a vital part of the acts of relationship, discernment, connection, and survival.

Works cited

Reik, T. (1948). *Listening with the third ear*. New York, NY: Grove.

Appendix A: Research Methodology

This book began as a research project aimed at helping to discern how therapists use intuition in their practice, with the clear purpose of helping other therapists who wish to incorporate or expand their own use of clinical intuition. The study on which the practice observations and suggestions are based was a basic qualitative design (Merriam, 2009). The study was designed to learn more about therapists who use intuition in their practice: what they do, how they explain it, and in general what clinical intuition means to them.

Because basic qualitative research does not have a predetermined process for carrying out a specific study, the researchers must identify methods that they believe are likely to capture the kind of information they wish to procure. They must determine how and from whom they will collect data, what kinds of data will be most helpful, how they will analyze the data, and how they will provide oversight to the process in order to deliver high-quality results from their research. These methods must fit the research problem but are also subject to the researcher's worldviews concerning what can be known about the world (ontology) and how one can come to know about that world (epistemology). These big questions have dogged research for decades, although not all research or researchers are explicit about where they stand on these issues. We believe that transparency about the worldview out of which this research emanated will help the reader make an informed decision regarding how likely it will be that the findings may be relevant to their practice.

We came to the study from very different perspectives and experiences regarding both clinical intuition and the research process. The primary researcher (MA-C) is an academic clinical social worker. She has conducted several research projects on clinical process. Her orientation toward intuition was formed by the peer-reviewed research generated by infant researchers, neuroscientists, and other research psychologists, as well as the theoretical formulations on clinical process. Her metatheoretical perspective at the beginning of this study was Constructivist (it has since changed as a result of the study). This basically means that she believes that the nature of a mind-independent reality, if such a thing exists, is beyond human comprehension. Therefore, the focus of research is on the subjective experiences of people rather than on an attempt at objective "truth."

From this perspective, the question of "truth" is bracketed. Truth is understood to be contextual and perspectival. In other words, the study was designed not to discover the truth about intuition or how intuition "is" developed or used in therapy but rather to offer the readers the opportunity to discover for themselves how they may develop and utilize clinical intuition. They may find the experiences of those who have developed this ability over time to be helpful in providing guidance for their own process.

The peer-debriefer/reviewer (MS) has knowledge of intuition from direct experience of intuitive processes for nearly 30 years. After postgraduate clinical training and her personal analysis, she returned to the positive experiences she had during graduate school and began to consciously incorporate intuition into her clinical practice. She has collaborated with intuitive consultants since 1993, learning how they structure and use this ability.

Her metatheoretical orientation most closely fits Transcendental Realism in that she believes that there is a mind-independent reality. Thus, she holds that there is an ultimate structure to clinical intuition and the development of this capacity.

The Research Design: Basic Qualitative Research

The researchers assumed the roles described by Rodwell's (1998) recommendations for Constructivist research: primary researcher (MA-C) and peer-debriefer/reviewer (MS). The primary researcher designed the basic research procedures and collected and analyzed the data. Rodwell has described the role of peer reviewer as such: a peer reviewer provides oversight. In this study, the reviewer made concrete suggestions that guided the design of the questionnaire and semistructured interview, attended the interviews and interacted with participants at the conclusion of the semistructured interview, and provided consultation on the interpretation of data. Given the significant differences in worldview between the peer-debriefer/reviewer and primary researcher, they were able to identify significant metatheoretical biases at both ends of the spectrum.

After obtaining approval from an Institutional Review Board for the Protection of Human Subjects, the investigators distributed a questionnaire to clinical social workers. We selected interviewees from among licensed practicing clinical social workers who were willing to engage in the interview process. The rational in recruiting based on these qualifications was that we wanted to learn from those who practice in order to pass along information to other therapists interested in engaging in intuitively informed therapy.

We encountered an unexpected issue in recruiting, which is that one therapist who related that she uses intuition during the clinical process did not want to engage in the research. When she was approached to participate, she responded that if she talked about what she has seen and heard to a general audience, it would be "explosive." She stated, "People aren't ready to hear it, I would rather stay invisible, my level of experience is so off the charts." This may indicate that some therapists who have had remarkable experiences regarding intuition may have chosen to decline the opportunity to share their experiences. It may be that more extreme or unusual instances of clinical intuition may be blinkered by the self-selecting nature of the sampling plan. While some of those who did participate had unusual experiences, these may represent only the tip of the proverbial iceberg regarding the nature of clinical intuition. Thus, the sample may be biased by the unwillingness of some intuitive therapists to discuss their experiences.

The Participants

We interviewed 24 clinical social workers. Interview 12 was lost due to a technical error. Therefore, the data analysis included 23 interviews. The participants all worked within a large Eastern U.S. metropolitan area. They were heterogenous in terms of practice setting, although most of the participants are in private practice. Most of them have also had professional experience in social work settings other than their current professional situation. They engage in diverse religious or spiritual beliefs, including no such orientation. It became clear as the interviews accrued that the practitioners overrepresented highly experienced clinicians, having engaged in the conduct of therapy for years and/or decades. While the therapists overwhelmingly identified as using an integrated approach to practice, the specific theoretical orientations that they integrated were diverse.

All of the names of participants are pseudonyms, and identifying information, when it appeared, was redacted. Elizabeth identified her religious orientation as a practicing Quaker. She utilizes an integrative approach to therapy, relying most on Psychodynamic and Behavioral theories and practices. Besides being in private practice, she has worked in hospice and has been teaching social work for more than 10 years.

Lena did not indicate a spiritual or religious orientation in her interview. She identified as utilizing an integrative orientation to her therapy, using Cognitive-Behavioral, Family Systems, and Solution Focused approaches. She indicated that she has been a clinical social worker since 2006, has worked in a victim's assistance network for domestic violence victims, and has worked with adjudicated minors.

Brenda referred to herself as "spiritual" but did not specify a religion or specific spiritual orientation. She referenced karma and astrology. She also indicated that her father was Muslim, and her mother was Methodist. Her theoretical orientation is a combination of Humanist, Existential, and Psychodynamic. She received her MSW in 1998 and referenced having conducted couples therapy.

Lailla was raised Muslim and later converted to Christianity. In spite of her conversion, she identified herself as "a follower of Rumi." Her therapeutic theoretical orientation is integrative, utilizing the bio-psycho-social perspective, Psychodynamic theory, Family Systems theory, and Feminist theory and incorporates findings from neuroscience into her work. She began her studies in social work more than 50 years ago and has taught in clinical social work programs.

Deborah identified Roman Catholicism as an important element in her life. She was raised in the faith and continues to practice, including attending Roman Catholic retreats. Her theoretical orientation is Psychodynamic, focused most heavily on the Relational-Intersubjective and Self-Psychology schools within this theoretical framework. She is primarily a group therapist.

Dinah identified as Jewish but also stated, "But I'm not sure I even believe in God." She branded her theoretical orientation as integrative, using energetic techniques and Family Systems theory as well as Humanist and Interpersonal theories. She stated she "grew up a psychotherapist," and indicated that "at 40 and 50, you really got it [psychotherapy]," suggesting that she has been a clinical social worker from early adulthood through middle age. She supervises field students in her private practice.

Sarah did not specify a religious or spiritual orientation and stated that she does not see intuition as being related to spirituality in any way. She identified her theoretical orientation as Psychodynamic. She has a private practice in a very affluent metropolitan neighborhood.

Ellen also did not specify a religious or spiritual orientation, but she did refer to praying to God and Jesus, suggesting that she has Christian leanings. Her theoretical orientation is a combination of Cognitive-Behavioral and Family Systems theories. She indicated that in the 80s, she was employed in child protective services. From this one may infer that she has been a social worker for about 30 years. She did not reference her current employment setting.

Jennifer indicated that she was raised Roman Catholic but does not currently practice. She did not specify a theoretical orientation. She did indicate that she is experienced in the field, stating, "I think as I've gotten older, and when I say older, I mean practiced more years as well. . . " She is currently in private practice.

David was raised Roman Catholic. He did not specify whether or not he still practices this faith. He is a psychoanalyst but did not specify the length of time he has been practicing in this arena.

Alejandro indicated that he is involved in a Christian church, although he did not specify a denomination. His theoretical approach, like those of most of the participants, is integrative. He was highly trained in Family Systems theory and indicated that he also uses Cognitive-Behavioral, Psychodynamic, Narrative, Feminist, and Solution-Focused theories, along with a recovery-addiction perspective. He indicated that "years ago" he worked with psychiatric in-patients, suggesting that he has significant experience in the field.

Felicia stated that she was raised in a "very strict" Methodist household. She did not indicate whether or how she practices religion or spirituality today. Her theoretical orientation is also integrative, utilizing Psychodynamic, Family Systems, Narrative, Cognitive-Behavioral, and Jungian approaches. She stated she has been in practice "many years." She currently engages in bereavement work. Clinical social work is her second career.

Jeff did not indicate a religious / spiritual affiliation. He identified his theoretical orientation as a combination of Cognitive-Behavioral, Psychodynamic, and Family Systems. In reference to his clinical experience, he referred repeatedly to the "length of his experience," and stated, "as I get older. . . " He further said, "I think I had to have a lot of years in the field to relax and center in. . . " and "When I was younger in the field. . . " He wondered, "what will be my last few years in this field?" These quotes suggest significant experience in the profession.

Ann was raised Roman Catholic and attended church as a child. She indicated that currently she prays to Jesus and believes that Jesus, Buddha, and

Muhammad are all prophets. Her theoretical orientation comprises Cognitive-Behavioral, Psychodynamic, Family Systems, and Feminist approaches. She appears to have substantial experience in the field, indicated by her statement, "I've done this work long enough to know. . . " She indicated that she has worked with a number of abuse survivors and women with personality disorders.

Janet identifies as a Buddhist. Her theoretical orientation is integrative, incorporating Psychodynamic and Internal Family Systems models. Conducting psychotherapy is her second career. In her interview, there is no indication regarding how long she has been a therapist.

Justin identified as practicing "Buddhist mindfulness." He was raised Roman Catholic but is currently not practicing this faith tradition. On his survey, he specified his theoretical orientation is integrative, based on combining Somatic Experiencing, Integrative Somatic Psychology, and Mindfulness. He also made reference in his interview to using psychodynamic concepts, such as transference-countertransference. There is no indication of the length of time he has practiced as a licensed clinical social worker.

Samantha was raised Roman Catholic. She stated, "I describe myself as a progressive Catholic, whatever that means, so I'm Christian." Her theoretical orientation is also integrative, including Cognitive-Behavioral and Psychodynamic approaches. Samantha had an internship at a women's center and currently conducts couples and individual therapy. In addition, she volunteers conducting therapy with veterans. She did not specify length of time as a therapist.

Katherine identified that she is a Reiki Master and that she "read[s] a lot of Buddhist books and Buddhist philosophy." She stated that she

> was raised in a variety of Protestant churches. I attended a Methodist church that my husband goes to. . . . I have a lot of problems with Christianity . . . the shorthand is I have one foot in Buddhism and one foot in Christianity.

Her theoretical orientation is integrative, in keeping with the majority of the participants. She specified utilizing Cognitive-Behavioral and Psychodynamic theories and practices. She is currently in private practice, although the length of time she has practiced was unspecified.

Jessica stated, "I'm not a spiritual person. I attend a Unitarian church, but it's not part of my life that's significant at all." She identified her theoretical orientation as integrative, comprised of Cognitive-Behavioral, Psychodynamic, Narrative, and Solution Focused approaches. In terms of clinical experience, she noted that she was in graduate school more than 30 years ago and obtained postgraduate clinical training.

In reference to her religious/spiritual affiliation, Grace stated,

> I grew up with these parents that were agnostic and atheist . . . I was never comfortable with it. . . . I had some connection to something that just felt left out of all of that, but it didn't really have a form . . . growing up in that—has made it hard for me really to jump into a form . . . mindfulness is something I use a lot and tap into. . .

She did not specify a theoretical orientation, nor did she relate any details regarding her clinical practice experience.

Natalie did not address her religious or spiritual orientation. On the questionnaire, she identified her therapeutic approach as integrated, blending Psychodynamic and Family Systems, although in the interview, she stated, "I'm not real wed to one particular theoretical orientation." Natalie implied that she has been a clinician for several years when she stated, "I had a client who I had worked with for years."

Sharon likewise did not specify a religious or spiritual orientation. On the questionnaire, she listed several theoretical approaches that she uses, including Solution-Focused and Cognitive-Behavioral. In her interview she referred to using transference-countertransference. Clinical social worker is her second career. She did not state how long she has practiced, but she did indicate that she provides clinical supervision for provisionally licensed therapists.

Lauren related that "I was raised in a fundamentalist family" and attended a Lutheran high school. While her mother was very religious, in the interview it was apparent that her grandmother did not hold the same belief system and was highly influential in Lauren pursuing spiritual and psi training. Therapeutically, she identified as integrative, incorporating Cognitive-Behavioral, Psychodynamic, Jungian, Family Systems, Humanist, Narrative, Solution-Focused, and the Satir model into her current practice. She did not elaborate on her clinical experience.

In summary, 6 of the 23 participants did not indicate a spiritual or religious orientation, leaving 17 who identified in some way as having some religious and/or spiritual beliefs. The overwhelming majority of the participants identified using an integrative approach to therapy or utilizing several different approaches. Of the 21 participants who indicated which theories they use, 14 of them utilize Psychodynamic or Psychoanalytic theory, 12 of them include Cognitive-Behavioral theory in their repertoire, and 10 use Family Systems theory. These are by far the most dominant models identified, although the participants also included other theoretical orientations in their work.

Data Analysis and Quality Assurance

As we were conducting the interviews, the primary researcher was simultaneously beginning the process of making sense of the material that the primary researcher and peer-reviewer/debriefer were collecting. The data was analyzed using a basic qualitative method for data analysis: "identifying recurrent patterns or themes supported by the data from which they were derived" (Merriam, 2009, p. 23) then placing chunks of the respondents' narratives into those categories to determine differences and similarities between participants in how they experienced each category. The primary researcher engaged in the process of identifying categories then placing the actual words of the participants into the categories. In this process, one typically sees that the hypothesized categories do not closely fit the raw data. The process of developing new categories and coding the data to place it in a category is repeated. The primary researcher engaged in this process five times, until the categories accounted for all of the data and were not redundant. The peer-debriefer/reviewer and the primary researcher were in ongoing communication during this process.

The question of what constitutes good or bad research has concerned qualitative and Constructivist researchers since they began promulgating methodologies. Based on a Constructivist perspective, "good" research is that in which the researcher's presentation of the data is a thorough and honest presentation of the results of the data analysis process. The report must give a plausible interpretation of the participant's narratives and provide information that is relevant to and usable by a specified community (Maxwell, 1992). Procedures undertaken to demonstrate the quality of the research are those that support the likelihood that the results are complete, representative, plausible, relevant, and usable. We undertook three such procedures in this study.

The first level of quality assurance was the researchers' roles in this study. As noted above, Rodwell (1998) recommended a peer-debriefer/reviewer for this purpose. Because the researcher who analyzed the data and peer reviewer held such differing perspectives prior to collecting data, the peer reviewer's role provided a form of perspectival triangulation. That is to say, all interpretations provided by the designing researcher were reviewed and endorsed by a person with a very different perspective.

The second method used to affirm the quality of the research was also highlighted by Rodwell (1998). This is the research audit. The researcher and peer-reviewer/debriefer created an audit trail over the course of the project that included emails, notes from telephone contact, journals, and the five sets of coded data. This material was reviewed by the auditor, who was unrelated to the research. This individual is a clinician whose practice includes the intentional use of intuition. She was able to review the procedures and findings and affirm that the results are plausible, consistent with the data, and provided new information that is usable by the community of therapists who may wish to incorporate intuition in their practice.

A third form of quality control for this study flowed from the intersubjective epistemology held by the primary researcher, who designed the study. Intersubjective epistemology is the view that meaning is co-created in interaction. If two or more individuals are engaged intersubjectively, they know the meaning a phenomenon has for another because to some degree they share that meaning (Arnd-Caddigan & Pozzuto, 2011). If, in fact, meaning is co-created in the interaction between researcher and participant, whatever meaning the researcher suggests for the data in the written report should be different from that which the researcher originally brought to the research. That is, if the interview is truly intersubjective, the researcher is changed by the new meaning that emerges in the exchange. From this perspective, high-quality research does not confirm what the researcher expects to find but rather surprises the researcher with a new understanding.

Indeed, the primary researcher experienced two changes in relation to her understanding of intuition as a result of her interactions with the participants. First, previous to this study, the primary researcher had published a case study on intuition in a clinical situation. She understood clinical intuition at that point to be the result of implicit processing of tacitly acquired metacommunication and paralinguistic behaviors. After interacting with the participants, she came to believe that this may explain some intuitive experiences but cannot explain all such events. In other words, her basic understanding about the source or cause of intuition opened up to include considerations she never would have previously entertained.

A second change is closely related to the first. As stated, this research was designed based on a Constructivist ontology. Slowly over the course of this study, in the process of expanding the literature review, interacting with the participants and peer-reviewer/debriefer, and in analyzing the data, the primary researcher experienced a slight shift in her worldview from Constructivist to Participatory. To be sure, these worldviews have a great deal of overlap. A full explanation of the nuanced differences between these orientations to the world is beyond the scope of this volume. The important point is that the primary researcher's orientation to the world changed as a result of engaging in this research rather than that orientation guiding the interpretation of the research experience. The participants' interactions with the therapist had a mutative impact on the research, as would be expected if the process was truly intersubjective.

Conclusion

We engaged in a basic qualitative study to determine how clinicians use intuition in their work, with the ultimate aim of using the information they collected to help other therapists who wish to engage in intuition-informed therapy. The specific steps in the research process were selected based on the likelihood that they would contribute to the discovery of useful information regarding therapists' use of intuition in their clinical work. Self-selected therapists who utilize clinical intuition submitted a questionnaire, then engaged in a semistructured interview in which both researchers participated. Data was analyzed by using a recursive process in which the primary researcher identified recurring patterns or themes in the data, in consultation with the peer reviewer/debriefer. The quality of the research is supported by the researchers' roles as data analyst and peer-reviewer/debriefer, as well as by an external audit. By using these methods, the researchers hope to provide information that is useful to psychotherapists who wish to initiate or enhance the use of clinical intuition.

Works Cited

Arnd-Caddigan, M., & Pozzuto, R. (2011). Toward a broader definition of evidence-informed practice: Intersubjective evidence. *Families in Society, 92*(4). doi:10.1606/1044-3894.4147

Maxwell, J. A. (1992). Understanding and validity in qualitative research. *Harvard Educational Review, 62*, 279–300.

Merriam, S. B. (2009). *Qualitative research: A guide to design and implementation* (3rd ed.). Hoboken: Wiley.

Rodwell, M. K. (1998). *Social work constructivist research*. New York, NY: Garland Publishing.

Clinical Intuition Appendix B: Participant Questionnaire

1. How do you define intuition?

2. How important is intuition to your practice? Please place an X on the continuum that best represents your experience: From not at all important, to important but not central, to the highest level, central.

   I____________I____________I____________I____________I

   not at all   important but not central   central

3. As you reflect on your intuitive experiences do they occur:

   ________ spontaneously

   ________ randomly

   ________ in response to specific practices you use to illicit this level of information

4. What kind(s) of information does your intuition supply regarding the client or treatment process, and/or in what process(es) does it provide clarity?

_______ diagnostic information

_______ clarity in emergency situations

_______ client intrapsychic processes

_______ client interpersonal dynamics

_______ identify important clinical issues

_______ create spontaneous interventions

_______ other (please describe)

5. What form does your intuition take? Please feel free to describe this process if you care to do so.

_______ pictures/images

_______ auditory stimuli (this may be sounds as well as language that may come in the form of "voices")

_______ smell

_______ feeling (clarity that comes from an integration of any/all physical senses in the primary form of an emotional state)

_______ knowing (clarity that comes from any/all of the above in the primary form of thought)

_______ other (please describe)

6. What has informed your understanding and development of intuitive experiences in your clinical work?

_______ academic training

_______ professional training

_______ personal study/practices

_______ life experiences (please describe)

_______ other

7. Do you feel that honoring your intuition in clinical practice enhances, takes away from, or confuses the mental models you use?
Enhances:

I____________I____________I____________I____________I

not at all somewhat very much

Takes away from:

I____________I____________I____________I____________I

not at all somewhat very much

Confuses:

I____________I____________I____________I____________I

not at all somewhat very much

8. Do you believe that your intuition is enhanced by your religious/spiritual/meditative orientation?

I____________I____________I____________I____________I

not at all important but not central central

9. Do you ascribe to a particular theoretical orientation in your clinical practice?

_______ Cognitive Behavioral Theory

_______ Psychodynamic/Psychoanalytic Theory

_______ Family Systems Theory

_______ Humanist Theory

_______ Narrative Theory

_______ Feminist Theory

________ Solution Focused

________ other (please identify)

________ Integrative Approach (please identify which theories you integrate)

10. Do you think clinicians can be taught to follow a model for working intuitively?

________ yes

________ no

11. Do you share with your colleagues that you use intuition in your clinical work?

________ yes

________ no

12. Do you share with your clients that you use clinical intuition?

________ yes

________ no

13. Do your intuitions tend to come before, during, or after a session?

________ before

________ during

________ after

14. Please supply any other information that you feel would be valuable for people to know about the use of clinical intuition.

Thank you for your participation. If you would like to be considered to participate in an interview about your use of clinical intuition, or if you are interested in more information about a possible interview, please attach your name and contact information **in a separate attachment or on a separate piece of paper** when you submit this form.

Appendix C: Chapter Tables of Research Findings

Participant Tables

I

Participants Religion/Spirituality

Not specified	Lena, Sarah, Ellen, Felicia, Jeff, Natalie, Sharon
Quaker	Elizabeth
Unidentified "spiritual"	Brenda, Grace
Muslim	Lailla, Brenda
Roman Catholic	Deborah, Jennifer, David, Ann, Justin, Samantha
Jewish	Dinah
Agnostic/atheist/nonpracticing	Dinah, Jennifer, Jessica
Nondenominational Christian beliefs or practices	Ellen, Alejandro, Ann, Grace
Methodist	Brenda, Felicia, Katherine
Buddhist	Janet, Justin, Katherine
Lutheran	Lauren

II

Participants Theoretical Approach

Integrative	Elizabeth, Lena, Brenda, Lailla, Dinah, Ellen, Alejandro, Felicia, Jeff, Ann, Janet, Justin, Samantha, Katherine, Jessica, Natalie, Sharon, Lauren
Psychodynamic/Psychoanalytic/Interpersonal	Elizabeth, Brenda, Lailla, Deborah, Dinah, Sarah, David, Felicia, Jeff, Ann, Janet, Samantha, Katherine, Jessica, Natalie, Lauren
Cognitive-Behavioral	Elizabeth, Lena, Ellen, Alejandro, Felicia, Jeff, Ann, Samantha, Katherine, Jessica, Sharon, Lauren
Family Systems	Lena, Lailla, Dinah, Ellen, Alejandro, Felicia, Jeff, Ann, Natalie, Lauren
Solution Focused	Lena, Alejandro, Jessica, Sharon, Lauren
Humanist	Brenda, Dinah, Lauren
Existential	Brenda
Feminist Theory	Lailla, Alejandro, Ann
Bio-psycho-social perspective	Lailla
Neuroscience	Lailla
Energy techniques	Dinah
Narrative	Alejandro, Felicia, Jessica, Lauren
Recovery-addiction perspective	Alejandro
Jungian	Felicia, Lauren
Internal Family Systems	Janet
Somatic Experiencing	Justin
Integrative Somatic Psychology	Justin
Mindfulness	Justin
Satir Model	Lauren

Chapter Tables

Chapter 2

UNDERSTANDING TABLE

Transcendent source	God, spirit, saints, and angels, spirit, from beyond, the universe
Universal connectedness	Everything that exists is connected, or one
Energy	Information carried in energy that flows
Accumulated knowledge/experience and wisdom	Learning and experience, can be applied unconsciously
Conscious processes	Can include application of overtly acquired information, e.g., from records or subtle differences in the client's presentation
A two-person phenomenon	Unconscious communication resonance, attunement: both client and therapist participate
A natural, normal human capacity	May be developed to greater or lesser degrees, but it is available to everyone
Neurological	Possibly mirror neurons
Bio-psycho-social-spiritual	The coming together of diverse factors
Unknown/complex	Current knowledge is rudimentary, and the phenomenon is so complex that we do not know what it is at this time

Chapter 3

FOCUS OF THERAPISTS' ATTENTION

Metacommunication and Paralinguistic Behavior	Client's facial expression, gestures, body language, tone of voice, prosody, etc.
Other Client-Generated Phenomena	Something that can be apprehended at a distance, energy

Therapist's Internal or Somatic Experience	Thoughts, feelings, internal processes, bodily sensations
Something Between the Therapist and Client	Connection, alignment, space between, parallel process
Environment	Physical environment (atmosphere, weather); interpersonal environment
Trance/Transpersonal	"Emptying out," focus on higher self, God, or collective unconscious

Chapter 4

Forms of Intuition

Commonplace	Therapist may not register an intuitive experience as such until s/he learns to identify them.
Unbidden	Sudden/effortless
Knowing	A sense of "just knowing." This may include knowledge that is exceptional.
Thoughts without Thinking	Intuition may be experienced as the arrival of a thought. In most cases the participants believed that thinking hampers the arrival of an intuitive thought. One clinician, however, uses contemplation to foster intuitive thoughts.
Affect	An emotion may arise that may or may not be particularly strong. It may be a shared emotion between the therapist and client.
Somatic	A physical sensation. Most often expressed as a gut feeling, but may also be a physical sensation in the chest/heart area, head, arms, throat, or an overwhelming feeling of fatigue/struggling to stay awake.

Somatic plus affective	The description of a combined sensate experience raises the question if synesthesia may be a form intuition can take.
Energy	"Chi," "vibes," "resonating," "in the flow." May be experienced as receiving energy from an external source.
Auditory/sound	Hearing things in the mind. Voice in the head, humming in the ears, songs, pieces of conversations seem emphasized or clear. May take the form of seemingly coming from "outside."
Visual/images	Seeing something in the mind. Imagined scenes, visual distortions of the environment or of people's bodies, auras, "seeing" the client as a child. May take the form of seeing something experienced as "outside."
Olfactory	Roses, grass
Unmediated action or speech	Taking action without having planed or decided to do so (seemingly without agency).
Association/symbolism	Something comes to mind that is meaningful, but the meaning is indirect: a song lyric may be symbolic of something important, or an "association" may arise.

Chapter 5

Usefulness Table

Understand the client	What the client may need, is experiencing or feeling; content that is unconscious or defended against
Dynamics and patterns	Patterns relevant to the client's functioning or issue
Client's past	Past experiences that may be influencing client's current functioning

Build rapport	Help client feel safe, understood, respond empathetically
Self-disclosure	If and when client may benefit from therapist self-disclosure
Diagnose	Determine differential diagnosis/ personality disorders
Individualize interventions	Avoid "cookie cutter" treatment; deliver what the client needs
Direction of treatment	In-session and intersession insights into where to direct treatment
On the right track	Know when treatment is appropriate
Possible future	What the client may experience in the future; potential growth or difficulty

Chapter 6

Characteristics and Values of Intuitive Therapists

Logical/skeptical	Rational, skeptical of psi phenomena
Open/receptive and curious	Open to intuition, open to others, receiving mode, open to the process, curious
Observant/attuned	Astute, watches, takes in data, in tune with others
Transparent/Authentic	Values being "real" with their clients, being connected to oneself, allow one's self to guide treatment
Self-reflective/Self-aware	Drive to understand "what makes me tick"
Abstract	Being too concrete was given as a negative example of qualities associated with intuition.
Neurotic	Prone to anxiety, depression, and/or guilt
Giving/Helpful	Giving, getting your ego out of the way, concerned, desire to be helpful
Nonjudgmental	Not judging too quickly, waiting
Understanding/Patient	Nonreactive in the face of others' pathology/difficulty

Respectful/Grateful	Owes all people respect. Sees engaging with clients as a privilege/sacred.
Draws out the less socially engaged	Cares about the under-dog, draws out the socially reticent
Spiritual	Values/is interested in religion and spirituality
Concerned about social justice	Interested in the rights of others/inequality
Appreciates Aesthetics	Interested in art, music, natural beauty
Extroversion/introversion	One participant defined herself as putting herself out there. Several participants value privacy, quiet, solitude.
Miscellaneous	Expressive, nondogmatic, rebellious, creative, optimistic, compassionate, superstitious, a good person, hardworking, sensitive, happy
Combined attributes	Attributes may mutually influence each other or work in combination

Chapter 7

Experiences and Practices Associated With Clinical Intuition

Cultural acceptance	Living in a culture that accepts, normalizes, or values intuition may make it easier for therapists to use it.
Experiencing different cultures or communities	The need to acculturate and/or exposure to the fact that different groups of people see things differently
Danger in the social environment	The necessity to be alert to potential danger in the social environment
Intuition normalized, valued, or modeled in family of origin	In childhood, intuition or psi/"paranormal" experiences are accepted
Necessity to discern	Growing up in a family in which one needs to read situations, either due to having responsibility for someone or because of potentially conflictual or dangerous situations

Birth order/family role	Growing up in a family in which one was constantly watched by older siblings and their friends, or in which one was expected to take others' perspectives
Supportive parents	Close relationships with supportive parents
Validated by colleagues	Being a member of a group practice or consultation group in which intuition is discussed and approved
Validated during training	Supervisors and/or training analysts support students' use of intuition
Formal training/theory	Theories and/or techniques may be helpful or limiting
Volunteer/professional experience	The exigencies of working with people in need
Personal therapy	Development of a strong positive sense of self
Illness	May be related to deepened spirituality
Meditation, mindfulness, presence, and/or prayer or other spiritual practices	Engaging in practices that include meditation, mindfulness, presence, prayer, or other spiritual practices
Reflection/thinking	Intersession review of cases
Opening as a practice	Opening to the client's experience or a higher power
Being in nature	Attuned to the physical environment and/or the cycles of life
Exercise	Rhythmic movement and/or yoga
Reading	Literature that concerns intuition, as well as a wider range of materials
Developing sense of self	In general and as a professional
Other experiences and practices	Reiki, focusing, writing by hand, maternity, attending to and trusting intuition, music
Negative examples	Things that may impede intuition: Negative feelings about the client; negative client states; fatigue, illness, emotional turmoil; being too analytical; invalidated and/or unvalidated personally or culturally

Chapter 8

Concerns Table

Not always accurate	Participants recommended that one verify intuitively acquired information before acting on it.
Not in client's best interest	May evoke a negative response from the client: may be too accurate, the concept may be off-putting to the client, may burden the client
Unsettling for the clinician	May cause discomfort in the therapist who is not prepared or does not understand intuition
Inadequate preparation: training and/or character	Requires proper knowledge base and maturity. Must be able to differentiate projection from intuition and identify countertransference, must understand the self thoroughly
Charlatans	People who claim to be intuitive may be taking advantage of clients
Negative reactions	Challenge professional reputation, may provoke conflict, challenged to perform
Failure to use intuition may lead to failure in responding appropriately in a dangerous situation	One may fail to take proper safety precautions.
Failure to use intuition may prevent one from gaining vital information	Miss information about how to successfully engage and work with clients, miss the broader contexts, poor decisions in emergency situations, lack clarity, induce therapeutic rupture
Failing to use intuition makes treatment dehumanizing/mechanical	Treatment can become overstructured and not meet clients' needs, becomes robotic

Chapter 9

Client Intuition as Treatment Objective and/or Intervention

Validation	Clients may seek therapists who can tolerate/not pathologize unusual experiences; is culturally competent practice.
Benefits to client	Improved client safety, enhanced sense of self, greater self-awareness, more trust in themselves, may reduce anxiety, increased happiness
Interventions	Guided imagery, explore with curiosity, challenge dismissal of intuitions

Appendix D: Additional Resources

Connection

Dossey, L. (1993). *Healing words: The power of prayer and the practice of medicine*. New York, NY: HarperCollins.

Dossey, L. (2009). *Premonitions: How knowing the future can shape our lives*. New York, NY: Penguin Group.

Dossey, L. (2013). *One mind: How our individual mind is part of a greater consciousness and why it matters*. Carlsbad, CA: Hayhouse.

Mayer, E. L. (2007). *Extraordinary knowing*. New York, NY: Random House.

McTaggart, L. (2007). *The intention experiment*. New York, NY: Simon and Schuster.

McTaggart, L. (2009). *The field: The quest for the secret force of the universe*. New York, NY: Harper Collins.

Rasha. (2003). *Oneness*. Santa Fe: Earthstar Press.

Stern, D. B. (2019). *The infinity of the unsaid: Unformulated experience, language, and the nonverbal*. New York, NY: Routledge.

Tanabe, M. K. (2015). *Quantum field theory and interconnectedness: Potential clinical implications for mental health professionals* (Doctoral dissertation), California School of Professional Psychology Alliant International University, Los Angeles, CA.

Medical Intuition

Orloff, J. (1996). *Second sight: A psychiatrist clairvoyant tells her extraordinary story . . . and shows you how to discover your psychic gifts*. New York, NY: Warner Books.

Orloff, J. (2005). *Positive energy*. New York, NY: Harmony Books.

Orloff, J. (2009). *Emotional freedom*. New York, NY: Three Rivers Press.

Schulz, M. L. (1998). *Awakening intuition*. New York, NY: Three Rivers Press.

Shealy, C. N. (2010). *Medical intuition: Your awakening to wholeness*. Virginia Beach: A. R. E. Press.
Shealy, C. N., & Caroline, M. M. (1993). *The creation of health: The emotional, psychological, and spiritual responses that promote health and healing*. Walpole, NH: Stillpoint Publishing.

Multidisciplinary Intuition and Psi

Atkinson, T., & Claxton, G. (Eds.). (2000). *The intuitive practitioner: On the value of not always knowing what one is doing*. New York, NY: Open University Press.
Benor, D. J., MD. (1993). *Healing research* (Vol. 1). Oxford: Helix Editions.
Benor, D. J., MD. (1994). *Healing research* (Vol. 2). Oxford, England: Helix Editions.
Braud, W. (2003). *Distant mental influence: Its contributions to science, healing, and human interactions*. Newbury, MA: Hampton Roads Publishing.
Brennan, B. A. (1987). *Hands of light: A guide to healing through the human energy field*. New York, NY: Bantam Books.
Brescia, T. (2007). A qualitative study of intuition as experienced and used by music therapists. *Qualitative Inquiries in Music Therapy, 2*, 62–110.
Bruyere, R. L. (1989). *Wheels of light: Chakras, auras, and the healing energy of the body* (Jeanne Farrens, Ed.). New York, NY: Simon & Schuster.
Castaneda, C. (1987). *The power of silence*. New York, NY: Washington Square Press.
Cavanna, R., & Ullman, M. (Eds.). (1969). Dreams and psi: Clinical dimension. *Psi and altered states of consciousness* (pp. 171–177). New York, NY: Garrett Press, Inc.
Ehrenwald, J. (1978). *The ESP experience: A psychiatric validation*. New York, NY: Basic Books Publishers.
Eisenbud, J. (1982). *Paranormal foreknowledge: Problems and perplexities*. New York, NY: Human Sciences Press.
Eisenbud, J. (1983). *Parapsychology and the unconscious*. Berkeley, CA: North Atlantic Books.
Emoto, M. (1999). *Messages from water*. Tokyo, Japan: Hado Publishing.
Feinstein, D., & Krippner, S. (1998). *Personal mythology: Using ritual, dreams, and imagination to discover your inner story*. New York, NY: G. P. Putnam's Sons.
Freud, S. (1955). *Dreams and telepathy* (Standard ed., Vol. 18, pp. 197–220). London: Hogarth Press.
Freud, S. (1955). *Psycho-analysis and telepathy* (Standard ed., Vol. 18, pp. 177–193). London: Hogarth Press.
Freud, S. (1964). Dreams and occultism. In *New introductory lectures on psychoanalysis* (Standard ed., Vol. 22, Chapter 30, pp. 31–56). London: Hogarth Press.
Grof, S. (1976). *Realms of the human unconscious*. New York, NY: E. P. Dutton.
Hall, M. P. (1990). *Invisible records of thought & action: A practical guide to subtle vibrations, their causes & effects*. Los Angeles, CA: The Philosophical Research Society, Inc.
Jahn, R. G., & Dunne, B. J. (1987). *Margins of reality: The role of consciousness in the physical world* (pp. 91–123). New York, NY: ICRL Press.
Jung, C. (1971). The concept of the collective unconscious. *The Portable Jung* (pp. 59–69). Ed. by Joseph Campbell. New York, NY: Penguin Classics.
Krippner, S. (Ed.). (1979). *Psychoenergetic systems: The interaction of consciousness, energy and matter*. New York, NY: Gordon and Breach, Science Publishers, Inc.

Krippner, S., & Villoldo, A. (1986). *The realms of healing*. Berkeley, CA: Celestial Arts.

Krippner, S., & Welsh, P. (1992). *Spiritual dimensions of healing: From native shamanism to contemporary health care*. New York, NY: Irvington Publishers & Co.

LeShan, L. (1966). *The medium, the mystic, and the physicist*. New York, NY: Ballantine Books.

Mitchell, E. (2008). *The way of the explorer: An Apollo astronaut's journey through the material and mystical worlds*. Franklin Lakes, NJ: New Page Books.

Mitchell, E. (2011). *Psychic exploration: A challenge for science understanding the nature and power of consciousness* (John White, Ed.). New York, NY: Cosimo Books.

Myss, C. (1996). *Anatomy of the spirit: The seven stages of power and healing*. New York, NY: Harmony Books.

Radin, D. (1997). *The conscious universe*. New York, NY: Harper Collins.

Radin, D. (2006). *Entangled minds: Extrasensory experiences in a quantum reality*. New York, NY: Paraview.

Radin, D. (2013). *Supernormal*. New York, NY: Deepak Chopra Books.

Sanders, P. A. Jr. (1989). *You are psychic!* New York, NY: Ballantine Books.

Talbot, M. (1991). *The holographic universe*. New York, NY: HarperCollins.

Targ, R. (2012). *The reality of ESP: A physicist's proof of psychic abilities*. Wheaton, IL: Quest Books.

Targ, R. & Putoff, H. (2005). *Mind reach*. London: Hampton Roads.

Tart, C. T. (1989). *Open mind, discriminating mind: Reflections on human possibilities*. New York, NY: Harper & Row.

Villoldo, A., & Krippner, S. (1987). *Healing states: A journey into the world of spiritual healing and shamanism*. New York, NY: Simon & Schuster.

Nonclinical Intuitive Practitioners

Day, L. (1996). *Practical intuition*. New York, NY: Villard Press.

Drenth, A. *Awakening your intuitive ability: Powerful practices to help you develop the 4 types of intuition*. Retrieved January, 2019 from www.consciouslifestylemag.com/awakening-intuition-ability-types-2/

K., Lisa. (2017). *Intuition on demand: A step-by-step guide to powerful intuition you can trust*. Scotland, UK: Findhorn Press. Retrieved from https://lmk88.com/intuition-book/

Myss, C. (1997). *Why people don't heal and how they can*. New York, NY: Three Rivers Press.

Peirce, P. (2009). *The intuitive way: The definitive guide to increasing your awareness*. New York, NY: Simon & Schuster.

Peirce, P. (2011). *Frequency: The power of personal vibration*. New York, NY: Simon & Schuster.

Peirce, P. (2013). *Leap of perception: The transforming power of your attention*. New York, NY: Simon & Schuster.

Peirce, P. (2017). *Transparency: Seeing through to our expanded human capacity*. New York, NY: Simon & Schuster.

Neuroscience

Applegate, J. S., & Shapiro, J. (2018). *Neurobiology for clinical social work: Theory and practice.* New York, NY: W. W. Norton.

Fernyhough, C. (2016). *The voices within: The history and science of how we talk to ourselves.* New York, NY: Basic Books.

Porges, S. W., & Dane, D. (Eds.). (2018). *Clinical applications of the polyvagal theory: The emergence of polyvagal-informed therapies.* New York, NY: W. W. Norton.

Siegel, D. (2010). *The mindful therapist.* New York, NY: W. W. Norton.

Stern, D. B. (2019). *The infinity of the unsaid: Unformulated experience, language, and the nonverbal.* New York, NY: Routledge.

Steven, L. C., & Woodruff, C. C. (2018). *The new science of empathy, compassion, and self-compassion.* San Diego: Academic Press.

Websites

Association for Comprehensive Energy Psychology: www.energypsych.org/
Hay House, Inc.: www.hayhouse.com
Institute of HeartMath: www.heartmath.org
Institute of Noetic Sciences (IONS): https://noetic.org/

Online Intuitive Tests

Search for intuitive tests online; there are many to choose from. They are informative, giving firsthand experience in the types of questions connected to the seeing, hearing, feeling, and knowing aspects of intuition.

Index

Note: **Boldfaced** page references indicate tables.